THE AFGHAN CAMPAIGNS OF 1878-1880.

THE AFGHAN CAMPAIGNS,
OF 1878—1880,

BY

SYDNEY H. SHADBOLT,

OF THE INNER TEMPLE, BARRISTER-AT-LAW;
Joint Author of "The South African Campaign of 1879."

Dedicated, by permission, to

LIEUT.-GENERAL SIR F. S. ROBERTS, BART., G.C.B., C.I.E., V.C., R.A.
COMMANDER-IN-CHIEF OF THE MADRAS ARMY.

COMPRISING HISTORICAL AND BIOGRAPHICAL DIVISIONS, AND CONTAINING A RAPID SKETCH OF THE WAR, MAPS ILLUSTRATING THE OPERATIONS AND THE MOVEMENTS OF THE FORCES, ONE HUNDRED AND FORTY PERMANENT PHOTOGRAPHS OF OFFICERS WHO LOST THEIR LIVES IN THE CAMPAIGNS AND OF RECIPIENTS OF THE VICTORIA CROSS, WITH MEMOIRS PREPARED FROM MATERIALS FURNISHED BY THEIR RELATIONS AND SURVIVING COMRADES, SUMMARIES OF THE MOVEMENTS IN THE FIELD OF THE VARIOUS REGIMENTS WHICH WERE ENGAGED, AND SEPARATE RECORDS OF THE SERVICES OF EVERY BRITISH OFFICER WHO WAS EMPLOYED IN THE WAR.

Biographical Division.

Τεθνάμεναι γὰρ καλὸν ἐπὶ προμάχοισι πεσόντα
ἄνδρ' ἀγαθόν, περὶ ᾗ πατρίδι μαρνάμενον.
TYRTÆUS, *Gnom. eleg.* iv., 1, 2.

LONDON:
SAMPSON LOW, MARSTON, SEARLE, AND RIVINGTON,
CROWN BUILDINGS, 188, FLEET STREET.
1882.

All rights reserved.

CONTENTS OF BIOGRAPHICAL DIVISION.

	PLATES.	PAGES.
Portraits and Biographical Notices of Officers who lost their Lives in the War	I.—XIX	1—255
Portraits and Records of Service of Recipients of the Victoria Cross	XX.	259—269

ERRATA.

Plate II. and p. 16, *for* "Beeke," *read* "Becke" throughout.

P. 108, l. 27 . . *for* "of his 44 men, 8 to 10 were wounded," *read* "of his 44 men, the survivors, from 8 to 10, were wounded."

P. 190 . . . . *for* "Edmund" Walker Samuells, *read* "Edward" Walker Samuells throughout.

Lieut. P. E. Anderson, Staff Corps,
25th (Punjab) Bengal N.I.

Major A. D. Anderson, Staff Corps,
23rd (Punjab) Bengal N.I. (Pioneers.)

Lieut. F. C. C. Angelo,
Probationer Staff Corps.

Surgeon-Major G. Atkinson, M.B.,
Army Medical Department.

Lieut. F. M. Barclay, Staff Corps,
45th Bengal N.I. (Rattray's Sikhs).

Lieut. H. J. O. Barr,
66th (Berkshire) Regt.

Captain W. B. Barker,
10th (P.W.O. Royal) Hussars.

Reproduced by permanent photo-process by the London Stereoscopic Company.

Major H. G. Becher, Staff Corps,
11th Bengal N.I.

Major Wigram Battye, Staff Corps,
Queen's Own Corps of Guides.

Captain John Beeke,
21st Bombay N.I. (Marine Battalion).

Major H. H. Birch, Staff Corps,
27th (Punjab) Bengal N.I.

Lieut. W. H. Bishop,
2nd Battn. 11th (North Devonshire) Regt.

Surgeon-Major R. H. Bolton,
Army Medical Department.

Major G. F. Blackwood,
Royal Horse Artillery.

Reproduced by permanent photo-process by the London Stereoscopic Company.

LIEUT.-COLONEL F. BROWNLOW, C.B.,
72nd (Duke of Albany's Own Highlanders).

BRIG.-GENERAL H. T. BROOKE,
Kandahar Field Force.

LT. A. BURLTON-BENNET, Staff Corps,
10th (Duke of Cambridge's Own)
Bengal Cavalry (Lancers).

CAPTAIN S. G. BUTSON,
9th (Queen's Royal) Lancers.

LIEUT. J. F. M. CAMPBELL, Staff Corps,
Attached 2nd Baluch Regt.

MAJOR SIR P. L. N. CAVAGNARI,
K.C.B., C.S.I.,
Minister and Plenipotentiary at Kabul.

CAPTAIN C. A. CARTHEW, Staff Corps,
Offg. D.A.Q.M.G., Khyber Brigade.

Reproduced by permanent photo-process by the London Stereoscopic Company.

Lieut. R. T. Chute,
66th (Berkshire) Regt.

Captain D. T. Chisholm,
59th (2nd Nottinghamshire) Regt.

Lieut.-Colonel R. S. Cleland,
9th (Queen's Royal) Lancers.

Bt. Lieut.-Colonel W. H. J. Clarke,
72nd (Duke of Albany's Own Highlanders).

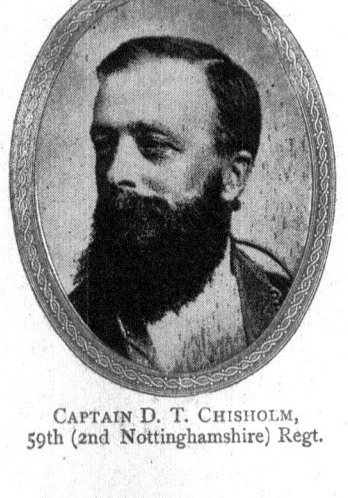

Lieut. Duncan Cole, Staff Corps,
Jacob's Rifles.

Bt. Major John Cook, V.C., Staff Corps,
5th Goorkha Regt.

Lieut.-Colonel J. J. Collins,
2nd Battn. 60th (King's Royal Rifle Corps).

Reproduced by permanent photo-process by the London Stereoscopic Company.

Lieut.-Col. G. B. Crispin, Staff Corps,
4th Bombay N.I. (Rifles).

Surgeon-Major H. Cornish, F.R.C.S.,
Army Medical Department.

Captain E. W. H. Crofton,
4th Batt. 60th (King's Royal Rifle Corps).

Captain G. M. Cruickshank,
Royal (late Bombay) Engineers.

Lieut.-Colonel A. G. Daubeny,
2nd Battn. 7th (Royal Fusiliers).

Captain F. J. Cullen,
66th (Berkshire) Regt.

Lieut. R. E. L. Dacres,
Royal Artillery.

Reproduced by permanent photo-process by the London Stereoscopic Company.

LIEUT. A. E. DOBSON,
Royal Engineers.

LIEUT. G. G. DAWES, Staff Corps,
1st Bengal Cavalry.

LIEUT.-COL. H. FELLOWES, Staff Corps,
32nd (Punjab) Bengal N.I. (Pioneers).

CAPTAIN J. DUNDAS, V.C.,
Royal Engineers.

LIEUT. T. O. FITZGERALD, Staff Corps,
27th (Punjab) Bengal N.I.

CAPTAIN ST. J. T. FROME,
72nd (Duke of Albany's Own Highlanders).

LIEUT. ST. J. W. FORBES,
92nd (Gordon Highlanders).

Reproduced by permanent photo-process by the London Stereoscopic Company.

Lieut.-Colonel James Galbraith,
66th (Berkshire) Regt.

Lieut. C. H. Gaisford,
72nd (Duke of Albany's Own Highlanders).

Captain E. S. Garratt,
66th (Berkshire) Regt.

Captain J. H. Gamble,
1st Battn. 17th (Leicestershire) Regt.

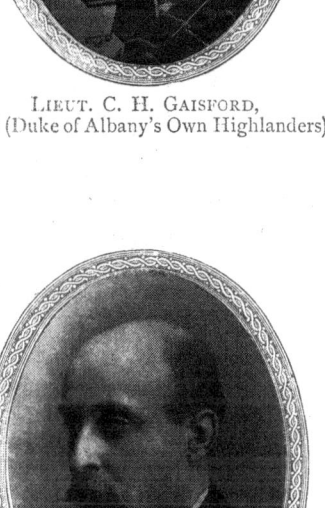
Captain F. T. Goad, Staff Corps,
5th Infty. Regt., Haidarabad Contingent.

The Rev. G. M. Gordon, M.A.,
Church Missionary Society.

Major J. Godson, Staff Corps,
4th Madras N.I.

Reproduced by permanent photo-process by the London Stereoscopic Company.

Lieut. W. R. P. Hamilton, V.C.,
Staff Corps, Queen's Own Corps of Guides.

Surgeon H. A. C. Gray, M.B., C.M.,
Bengal Medical Department.

Lieut. Edward Hardy,
Royal Horse Artillery.

Captain G. J. Hare, Staff Corps,
22nd (Punjab) Bengal N.I.

Sub-Lieut. F. H. Harford,
10th (P. W. O. Royal) Hussars.

Captain P. C. Heath, Staff Corps,
Brigade Major, Kandahar Field Force.

Lieut. C. J. R. Hearsey,
9th (Queen's Royal) Lancers.

Reproduced by permanent photo-process by the London Stereoscopic Company.

LIEUT. W. F. HENNELL, Staff Corps,
1st Punjab Cavalry.

LIEUT. T. RICE HENN,
Royal Engineers.

W. JENKYNS, M.A., C.S.I.,
Bengal Civil Service,
Secretary to the British Embassy at Kabul.

2nd LIEUT. A. HONYWOOD,
66th (Berkshire) Regt.

LIEUT. W. N. JUSTICE,
Probationer, Staff Corps.

SURGEON-MAJOR H. KELSALL,
Army Medical Department.

SURGEON A. H. KELLY,
Bengal Medical Department.

Lieut. F. G. Kinloch, Staff Corps,
5th Bengal Cavalry.

Captain J. A. Kelso,
Royal Artillery.

Lieut. S. E. L. Lendrum,
Royal Artillery.

2nd Lieut. E. D. Los,
1st Battn. 25th (King's Own Borderers).

Lieut. G. H. Lumsden,
Probationer, Staff Corps.

Captain W. H. McMath,
66th (Berkshire) Regt.

Lieut. H. Maclaine,
Royal Horse Artillery.

Reproduced by permanent photo-process by the London Stereoscopic Company.

LIEUT. C. A. MONTANARO,
Royal Artillery.

2nd LIEUT. E. S. MARSH,
2nd Battn. 7th (Royal Fusiliers).

CAPTAIN C. S. MORRISON,
14th Bengal Cavalry (Lancers).

LIEUT. A. R. MURRAY, Staff Corps,
11th (P.W.O.) Bengal Cavalry (Lancers).

BT. LIEUT.-COLONEL W. H. NEWPORT,
Staff Corps, 28th Bombay N.I.

LIEUT. C. NUGENT,
Royal Engineers.

LIEUT.-COL. NICHOLETTS, Staff Corps,
Commandant 2nd Baluch Regt.

Reproduced by permanent photo-process by the London Stereoscopic Company.

Major C. V. Oliver,
66th (Berkshire) Regt.

Colonel J. J. O'Bryen, Staff Corps,
Commandant 22nd (Punjab) Bengal N.I.

2nd Lieut. W. R. Olivey,
66th (Berkshire) Regt.

Lieut. E. G. Osborne,
Royal Horse Artillery.

Lieut. Lord Ossulton,
4th Battn. Rifle Brigade.

Captain E. W. Perry,
40th (2nd Somersetshire) Regt.

Lieut. W. C. Owen, Staff Corps,
3rd Bombay Cavalry (Queen's Own).

LIEUT. BROWNLOW POULTER,
Royal Engineers.

OFFG. DEP. SURG.-GENL. J. H. PORTER,
Army Medical Department.

CAPTAIN C. F. POWELL, Staff Corps,
5th Goorkha Regt.

BREVET-MAJOR L. A. POWYS,
59th (2nd Nottinghamshire) Regt.

CAPTAIN J. J. PRESTON,
4th Battn. Rifle Brigade.

CAPTAIN R. B. REED,
1st Battn. 12th (East Suffolk) Regt.

LIEUT. M. E. RAYNER,
66th (Berkshire) Regt.

Major W. Reynolds, Staff Corps,
3rd Regt. Sind Horse.

Lieut. T. J. O'D. Renny, Staff Corps,
Adjutant, 4th Punjab Infantry.

2nd Lieut. W. P. Ricardo,
9th (Queen's Royal) Lancers.

Lieut. J. T. Rice,
Royal Engineers.

Lieut. S. W. T. Roberts,
Probationer, Staff Corps.

Lieut. H. R. Ross,
Royal Artillery.

Captain W. Roberts,
66th (Berkshire) Regt.

CAPTAIN E. W. SAMUELLS,
Bengal Staff Corps,
Dep. Superintendent of Revenue Surveys.

CAPTAIN A. P. SAMUELLS,
32nd Bengal N.I. (Punjab Pioneers).

CAPTAIN E. D. SHAFTO,
Royal Artillery.

CAPTAIN T. A'B. SARGENT,
78th Highlanders (Ross-shire Buffs).

BT.-LIEUT.-COLONEL A. M. SHEWELL,
Staff Corps, Offg. Dep.-Com.-Gen. 1st Cl.

CAPTAIN H. F. SHOWERS, Staff Corps,
1st Punjab Infantry.

BT. MAJOR L. C. SINGLETON,
92nd (Gordon Highlanders).

Reproduced by permanent photo-process by the London Stereoscopic Company.

XV.

Major L. Smith, Staff Corps,
3rd Goorkha Regt.

Captain H. F. Smith, Staff Corps,
Jacob's Rifles.

Captain N. J. Spens,
72nd (Duke of Albany's Own Highlanders).

Surgeon W. B. Smyth,
A.B., M.B., L.R.C.S.I.,
Bengal Medical Department.

Lieut. H. H. S. Spoor,
1st Battn. 25th (King's Own Borderers).

Bt. Lieut.-Col. R. G. T. Stevenson,
Poona Horse.

Lieut. F. C. Stayner, Staff Corps,
19th Bombay N.I.

Reproduced by permanent photo-process by the London Stereoscopic Company.

Captain S. A. Swinley,
11th (P.W.O.) Bengal Cavalry (Lancers).

Captain E. Straton,
2nd Battn. 22nd Regt. (The Cheshire).

2nd Lieut. B. S. Thurlow,
51st (King's Own Light Infantry).

Major R. J. Le Poer Trench,
19th Bombay N.I.

Br.-General J. A. Tytler, C.B., V.C.,
Bengal Staff Corps.

Surgeon-Major J. Wallace,
M.A., M.D., M.R.C.S.,
Army Medical Department.

Lieut. E. P. Ventris,
3rd Regt. (The Buffs).

Reproduced by permanent photo-process by the London Stereoscopic Company.

2nd Lieut. E. H. Watson,
1st Battn. 17th (Leicestershire) Regt.

Surgeon J. E. Walsh, M.D.,
Bengal Medical Department.

Major S. J. Waudby, Staff Corps,
19th Bombay N.I.

Surgeon G. Watson, M.B.,
Bengal Medical Department.

Captain A. A. D. Weigall,
Army Pay Department.

Lieut. C. G. Whitby,
Probationer, Staff Corps.

Lieut. F. Whittuck, Staff Corps,
1st Bombay N.I. (Grenadiers).

Reproduced by permanent photo-process by the London Stereoscopic Company.

XVIII.

CAPTAIN F. H. WINTERBOTHAM,
Madras Infantry.

LIEUT. H. V. WILLIS,
Royal Artillery.

LIEUT. N. C. WISEMAN,
1st Battn. 17th (Leicestershire) Regt.

2ND LIEUT. F. P. F. WOOD,
7th (Royal Fusiliers).

LIEUT. I. D. WRIGHT,
Royal Artillery.

LIEUT. G. M. YALDWIN,
2nd Batt. 6th (Roy. 1st Warwicksh.) Regt.

SURGEON-MAJOR J. H. WRIGHT,
M.R.C.S., and L.S.A. Lond.,
Army Medical Department.

Reproduced by permanent photo-process by the London Stereoscopic Company.

RECIPIENTS OF THE VICTORIA CROSS FOR SERVICES IN THE CAMPAIGNS.

Bt. Maj. O'M. Creagh, V.C., Staff Corps,
Mhairwarra Battalion.

Lt. W. St. L. Chase, V.C., Staff Corps,
28th Bombay N.I.

Maj. A. G. Hammond, V.C., Staff Corps,
Queen's Own Corps of Guides.

Captain W. H. Dick Cunyngham, V.C.,
The Gordon Highlanders.

Capt. R. C. Hart, V.C.,
Royal Engineers.

Major E. H. Sartorius, V.C.,
The East Lancashire Regt.

Bt. Lieut.-Col. E. P. Leach, V.C.,
Royal Engineers.

Reproduced by permanent photo-process by the London Stereoscopic Company.

MAJOR A. D. ANDERSON, STAFF CORPS,

23RD (PUNJAB) BENGAL N.I. (PIONEERS).

WITH the news telegraphed to India of the assault and capture of the Peiwar Kotal on the morning of the 2nd December, 1878, came the melancholy tidings of the death of a distinguished officer of the 23rd Punjab Pioneers—Major A. D. Anderson—who had fallen whilst gallantly leading a handful of skirmishers against one of the advanced positions of the enemy.

Alexander Dunlop Anderson, the subject of this memoir, was the third son of Dr. A. Dunlop Anderson, some time Surgeon in H.M. 49th Regiment, and for forty years Physician in Glasgow. He was born on the 3rd February, 1841, in the city with which his father's name had already long been identified. Having received the rudiments of his education at a private school at Edinburgh, he was from thence transferred to Cheltenham College. In June, 1858, he passed his examination at Addiscombe. Entering the service as Ensign in September of the same year, he was temporarily attached to the 1st Battalion, 10th Regiment. In February, 1859, he was transferred to the 1st Battalion, 19th Regiment, then in India; and joining that corps shortly afterwards in Bengal, did duty with it for a period of three years and a half. In the meantime (July, 1859), he had been promoted Lieutenant. In June, 1862, he was appointed Interpreter to the regiment, and acted in that capacity, and subsequently as Station Interpreter at Mian Mir, till the following August. On the reorganization of the Indian army, he was posted, in September, 1862, to the 41st Bengal Infantry, to the adjutancy and quarter-mastership of which regiment he was, within a short period, successively promoted. In October, 1865, some little time after having passed the Interpreter's examination, he was transferred as Adjutant to the 23rd Punjab Pioneers, with which corps he served almost continuously till the day of his death.

Lieutenant Anderson accompanied the 23rd Pioneers to Abyssinia in 1868, and served with them in that country from the outbreak to the cessation of hostilities. For his conduct at the action of Arogee on the 10th April, 1868, he was singled out for special commendation in Sir R. Napier's despatch; and on the 13th April, 1869, he was present at the capture of Magdala.

Promoted Captain in September, 1870, and being at the time in Europe, on furlough, he vacated, in accordance with regulations, his appointment of Adjutant of the 23rd Pioneers. On his return to India in November, 1870, he was attached for duty to the 4th N.I., then at Allahabad, but at his own request was almost immediately retransferred to the 23rd Pioneers, of which regiment he was appointed, at the end of February, 1871, Officiating Adjutant. About the middle of March he was ordered to take over the duties of Wing Commander, *vice* Major Taylor, then on furlough, an appointment in which he was confirmed on its becoming permanently vacant in June, 1872. In the meantime (September, 1871), he had been offered the appointment of Commandant of the Bhutan Coolie Corps, but his services, unfortunately, could not be spared from his regiment, and he was reluctantly obliged to decline the post.

Having passed with high credit, in the first days of June, 1874, in Military Law, and obtained a certificate of proficiency in Fortification at the Garrison Course of Instruction held at Rawal Pindi, Captain Anderson again availed himself of eighteen months' furlough to Europe. While in England, he obtained an extra first-class certificate at Hythe, and completed a course of instruction in Reconnaissance and Field Works at the School of Military Engineering at Chatham. On the expiration of his furlough he rejoined the 23rd Pioneers at Jhelum. After taking part with the regiment in the Imperial Assemblage at Delhi at the latter end of 1876, he accompanied it, in the spring of the following year, to Simla. In September, 1878, he was promoted to the rank of Major, having already, from the month of March of that year, officiated as second in command, *vice* Major Collett, appointed to the Quarter-Master-General's Department.

On the massing of the troops on the frontier in the last days of September, 1878, preparatory to the invasion of Afghanistan, the 23rd Pioneers, which were detailed to General Roberts' Division, left Simla for the trans-Indus. Crossing the frontier at Thal with the regiment on the 21st November, Major Anderson accompanied it to Kuram, and was present with it at the reconnaissance in force at the foot of the Peiwar Kotal on the 28th November. It was on the morning of the 2nd December, 1878, while leading a party of skirmishers against one of the positions on the heights held by the enemy, that he lost his life, being struck with a shot whilst well in advance of his little band of followers. So hot was the fire of the enemy at the spot where he fell, that two of the four men who were with him at the moment of his death were also killed, and the remaining two were compelled, in retiring, to leave the bodies of their companions in the enemy's hands.

Major Anderson's remains, which were recovered on the following day, lie buried in the same grave with those of Captain Kelso, R.A., on a spur of the Peiwar range, overlooking the Hariab Valley. The love borne him by the men of the regiment was amply testified by the large concourse that assembled at his funeral to pay their last tribute of respect to his memory, as well as by the beautiful tablet which has been erected by his brother officers in the Cathedral of Glasgow.

LIEUT. P. E. ANDERSON, STAFF CORPS,

25TH (PUNJAB) BENGAL N.I.

THE subject of this memoir was the eldest son of the late Reverend Philip Anderson, a Chaplain in the Honourable East India Company's service, who for many years officiated at Kolaba in the Bombay Presidency, a memorial window erected to whose memory in his church records the estimation in which he was held by his congregation.

Philip Edward Anderson entered the service through Sandhurst; proceeded to India in 1867 at the age of nineteen years, and joined H.M. 96th Regiment, then in garrison at Barrackpur. From this corps he was transferred to H.M. 109th Regiment a few months later at Multan, from whence he subsequently proceeded to enter the Military College at Rurki. On the completion of his studies, after passing successfully in the native languages, he joined the Bengal Staff Corps, and was appointed to the regiment with which he served till the day of his death.

When war was declared against the Amir of Afghanistan in the autumn of 1878, Lieutenant Anderson's regiment was stationed at Umballa, in the Punjab. At extremely short notice it proceeded by rail to Multan, and joined a portion of the force under Sir Donald Stewart directed upon Kandahar. The 25th Punjab Infantry was one of the most advanced regiments of the force, and, in consequence, suffered to a considerable extent from the hardships inseparable from a long march over roadless deserts in a most trying climate. Almost immediately after arriving at Kandahar, the regiment proceeded towards Kalat-i-Ghilzai; and it was the fearful exposure and fatigue, combined with the intense cold endured during this expedition and the return march in the depths of winter, which laid the seeds of the disease (phthisis) to which the subject of this notice eventually succumbed at Kandahar, on the 6th August, 1879, after a most painful illness courageously borne.

Lieutenant Anderson was a talented and energetic young officer, and his loss is most deeply felt, not only by his regiment, but by the many friends he left behind both in India and England. He married in 1875; and owing to his untimely death his widow has been left dependent for her support on the small pension granted to the relict of a subaltern officer.

LIEUT. F. C. C. ANGELO,

PROBATIONER STAFF CORPS.

FREDERICK CANNING CORTLANDT ANGELO was the only son of Lieutenant Frederick Cortlandt Angelo, 16th Grenadiers, Bengal Army, and Superintendent Ganges Canal, Public Works Department, who was killed in the defence of the entrenchments at Cawnpore in June, 1857. He was born in Calcutta, three months after his father's death, on the 21st September 1857, and was educated at Dr. Thompson's Collegiate School, St. Heliers, Jersey. At the age of seventeen years he entered Sandhurst as Indian Cadet; and passing out from the College after the usual course, was gazetted, in February, 1874, to the 40th Foot. He joined that regiment in Calcutta, and remained with it until the autumn of 1879, when he applied for the Staff Corps, —having in the meantime (February 1877) obtained his lieutenancy.

Posted to the 31st P.N.I., then on service in Afghanistan, he joined the headquarters at Landi Kotal, and took part with the regiment in the Lughman Valley expedition, and the various operations in which it was subsequently engaged. In March, 1880, the 31st P.N.I. was moved to Safed Sang. Shortly after the headquarters left Jalalabad, Angelo, who had been left behind with various details, was ordered up to Fort Battye in charge of a detachment of 150 men. Reaching the Fort on the evening of the 25th March, the little force proved the means of saving it from falling into the hands of the vast numbers of the enemy who beset it during the ensuing night. In the ably conducted defence of the post, the subject of this notice met his death.

Though Lieutenant Angelo's life was too brief to admit of its including many brilliant achievements, this, at least, may be said of him: that in an hour of sore need he acquitted himself as was to be expected of one of his race and name. Descended from a family of soldiers in both the paternal and maternal lines, he found a soldier's grave amongst the same rugged hills where the remains of one of his uncles, thirty-six years previously, were carried to their last resting-place.

SURGEON-MAJOR GEORGE ATKINSON, M.B.,

ARMY MEDICAL DEPARTMENT.

THE subject of this notice, who died near Kabul on the 25th April, 1880, shortly after the battle of Ahmed Khel, was the second son of the late George Guy Atkinson, Esq., J.P., of Ashley Park, Nenagh, Co. Tipperary. He was born at Ashley Park on the 11th October, 1840, and received his education at Ranelah, Athlone, Mr. Weir's Collegiate School at Parsonstown, and Trinity College, Dublin, whither he proceeded in 1859. He graduated in 1863, and entered the Army a year later. After his Netley training, he was ordered to India, where he was posted to the 54th Regiment. He was subsequently transferred to the 1st Battalion 19th Regiment, with which he served in the Hazara campaign of 1868, including the expedition against the tribes in the Black Mountain, receiving the medal and clasp.

In 1873 he returned to Ireland on furlough, on the expiration of which he served at Portsmouth and Aldershot till 1876, when he was again sent out to India. In the meantime (April, 1876) he had been promoted to the rank of Surgeon-Major.

Dr. Atkinson was stationed in the Bengal Presidency when the Afghan war broke out in 1878. Immediately prior to the commencement of hostilities he proceeded in medical charge of G/4 R.A.—which had been detailed to General Stewart's Division—*via* Multan to Rurki; and crossing the Indus with the battery, accompanied it to Quetta. He then took part in the advance to Kandahar, and the subsequent operations in which the battery was engaged, sharing its perils and hardships, and coping successfully with the heavy work which the latter threw upon his hands. At the battle of Ahmed Khel on the 19th April, 1880, in which G/4 played an important part, Dr. Atkinson, according to the testimony of his commanding officer, "had hard work during the action." The nights were at this time excessively cold, and the exposure now began to tell upon him. In the course of the march to Ghazni he was seized with pleuromonia, to an attack of which he fell a victim at Hafazai, within a week from the day of the battle.

Dr. Atkinson was a devoted officer, distinguished for his strong sense of duty, and for an amiable disposition which endeared him to all with whom he came in contact. His memory is perpetuated by a marble tablet in Nenagh Church, erected by his bereaved mother and brother, who deeply mourn their irreparable loss.

LIEUT. F. M. BARCLAY, STAFF CORPS,

45TH BENGAL N.I. (RATTRAY'S SIKHS).

FRANK MILES BARCLAY, who lost his life in the first of the recent Afghan campaigns, was the sixth son of Surgeon-General Charles Barclay, Madras Army (retired). He was born in 1855, at Quilon, in Southern India. Although quite young in the service—having only entered the army in February, 1875—he had already, at the time of his death, given great promise of a bright future. He began his career in the 19th (Princess of Wales' Own) Regiment; and was present with the Corps when it received its colours from Her Royal Highness at Sheffield in 1875. Soon afterwards he was ordered out to India, and eventually passed into the Bengal Staff Corps.

Lieutenant Barclay was engaged in qualifying himself for the Political Department when the Afghan War broke out; and his regiment—Rattray's Sikhs—was amongst those ordered to the front. This famous corps did excellent service throughout the war, and Barclay was constantly engaged in unconspicuous, but none the less arduous and dangerous work in and about the Khyber Pass, including the second Bazar expedition.

On the 17th March, 1879, while he was in command of an escort attached to a surveying party under Captain Leach, R. E., a sudden attack was made upon them by a section of the Shinwari tribe. Captain Leach was slightly wounded, and Lieutenant Barclay received a gun-shot through the right shoulder, which penetrated to the lung. With the help of Captain Leach (who, for his gallantry in assisting his disabled comrade, afterwards received from Her Majesty the Victoria Cross), he was removed to Landi Kotal, where he died on the 31st March. In him the army lost a young soldier of high promise, and the Bengal Staff Corps a most accomplished officer.

CAPTAIN W. B. BARKER,

10TH (P.W.O. ROYAL) HUSSARS.

ILLIAM BROMBY BARKER was born at Mansfield on the 24th May, 1835, and received his education at the school in his native town. He entered the army as a trooper in the 16th Lancers at the age of seventeen years; and his genius for the service is attested by the fact that, after passing rapidly through the various non-commissioned grades, he obtained, in November, 1867, commissioned rank. In June, 1867, he was appointed Adjutant of the Regiment, in which capacity he served for a period of nearly ten years. He became Lieutenant in March, 1871; and in July, 1877, obtained his troop. In this interval, nine out of the twenty-five years of his service were passed in India.

Captain Barker now exchanged into the 10th Hussars; and in March, 1878, joined that regiment in India. On the concentration of the forces in view of the impending invasion of Afghanistan, he proceeded as second in command with the squadron of the regiment which, under Captain Bulkeley, was ordered to Kohat. Taking part in the advance into the enemy's country of General Roberts' division, to which the squadron had been detailed, he was present at the capture of the Peiwar Kotal; and for his conduct in the action at Matun on the 7th January, 1879, in the Khost Valley expedition, he was singled out for special commendation in Brigadier-General Hugh Gough's despatch to the A.Q.M.G. of the Force. In February, 1879, he was ordered to Rawal Pindi to take command of the Depôt. About the same date the detached squadron was directed to rejoin the head-quarters of the regiment, then at Jalalabad.

During the short time Captain Barker remained in charge of the Depôt, he suffered severely from the effects of recent exposure to the sun. He nevertheless proceeded by double marches on receiving orders, at the latter end of May, to rejoin the regiment. Just before reaching Daka Fort he was laid completely prostrate with sun-stroke, from the effects of which—according to his own testimony—he could not have recovered had it not been for the tender nursing he received at the hands of Lieut. Hearsey, of the 9th Lancers, a gallant young officer who subsequently fell in action at Kabul. His health continued fairly good from this time till the beginning of October, when he was ordered to Jhelum to fit saddles to the transport animals. The prolonged exposure to the sun which this duty entailed soon told upon him, and he began rapidly to lose strength; on the 4th November he was taken suddenly worse, and seven days afterwards, on the 11th, he died.

In a letter, covering a complimentary document from H.R.H. the Duke of Cambridge, penned after an inspection of the 16th Lancers, received by Captain Barker in the month of March, 1872, from General (then Colonel) Wilkinson, the latter writes :—" I cannot send you this without assuring you how thoroughly I appreciate your invaluable help; your untiring and unremitting exertions to support the credit and efficiency of the Regiment; and it is to this, in a very great measure, that I attribute the satisfactory state of things at the last autumn inspection, General Barton's report upon which has called forth the remarks of H.R.H." If evidence of the survival of this zeal to the last sad chapter of Captain Barker's life be needed, it is to be found in an eulogium bestowed upon him by Brigadier-General Sir Hugh Gough, written at Kabul, and bearing date 5th March, 1880, in which the able manner in which he performed his duties during the campaign is warmly dwelt upon.

Captain Barker married, in February, 1878, Bertha, third daughter of Mr. George Brothers, of Canterbury, who survives him.

2ᴺᴰ LIEUT. H. J. O. BARR.

66TH (BERKSHIRE) REGIMENT.

ARRY JAMES OUTRAM BARR, who, "At Maiwand about 4 p.m. on the 27th July, 1880, fell dead across the colour he was then carrying"—according to evidence adduced at the subsequently holden court-martial—was not the first of his family who forfeited his life in the Queen's service in Afghanistan—his maternal grandfather having been Colonel Keith, Deputy Adjutant-General of the Bombay Army, who died in that country whilst serving as Adjutant-General with the forces under Lord Keane in 1839.

The youngest son of Lieutenant-General Barr of the Bombay Staff Corps, he was born in Brighton on the 7th January, 1861. His education was begun under Dr. H. Barker, LL.D., at the Gymnasium School at Old Aberdeen, where he remained for a period of nearly seven years. From thence he was transferred to Weston-super-Mare, to read with Mr. Hoppel, M.A., for the Indian Civil Service; but showing a decided preference for the army, he was sent for one term to Captain Massie's to be prepared for the Sandhurst examination. In February, 1879, at the age of seventeen years, he was presented by Lord Cranbrook with an honorary East Indian cadetship, and entered Sandhurst; and in November of the same year he passed out eighteenth in order of merit, with honours, having obtained certificates in Fortification and Drill.

Gazetted to the 66th Regiment in January, 1880, he left England for India two months afterwards; and reaching Karachi by way of Bombay, immediately received orders to join the head-quarters of the Regiment, then at Kandahar. He proceeded thither with a detachment under Major Vandaleur of the 7th Fusiliers, arriving at his destination at the latter end of May.

To a mere lad, "fresh and blooming from England," as he described himself in a letter to his father, thrown suddenly into the whirl and excitement of actual campaigning at the very outset of his career, the life he had embarked upon presented many novel features. The physical features of the country, the customs of an alien race, even the necessity for taking precautions against danger on emerging from camp, were matter for perpetual wonder and reflection; whilst the ever-recurring rumours and counter rumours of the prospect of fighting kindled his hopes and fired his imagination. That he became popular with his brother-officers from the hour of his arrival amongst them, the numerous letters written by them to members of his family after his death amply testify.

On the 4th July, 1880, Barr accompanied the Regiment in the brigade which, under General Burrows, left Kandahar for Girishk with the object of encountering Ayub Khan. The march—which, in consequence of the excessive heat, had to be conducted at night—was a severe one: "stumbling, fumbling, slipping along; digging the Colour-shaft deep into the earth"—thus young Barr describes his own part in the performance.

Girishk was reached on the 11th; and three days afterwards—on the morning of the 14th—Barr received his baptism of fire in the successful encounter which took place with the Wali's mutinied troops. On this occasion he availed himself of an opportunity which presented itself for rendering valuable service. To the left of the second position taken up by the enemy was a garden, from behind the walls of which a harassing fire was being kept up upon his company. Captain Quarry, of the 66th, was ordered to advance with twenty men to take the garden; but on the way he was delayed by having to ford a stream with muddy bottom, in which his men floundered up to their armpits. Barr was now ordered to advance to his assistance, and succeeded, with Lieutenant Faunce, in reaching the further bank. Getting about twenty-five men together, they were enabled to take the wall with a rush, shooting down in their advance every individual of the band which held it.

After the action the Brigade returned to Khushk-i-Nakhud, en route for Kandahar. In the disastrous encounter with the enemy which ensued on the 27th, Barr lost his life, in the manner already recorded, with the three hundred officers and men of his regiment who fell, having been seen by the late Major C. V. Oliver, a few minutes before his death, "marching along as calmly and steadily as if on parade."

MAJOR WIGRAM BATTYE, STAFF CORPS,

QUEEN'S OWN CORPS OF GUIDES.

"THE Service has sustained the loss of one of its brightest ornaments, and the Government of India the services of a most distinguished and gallant soldier." Such were the words used by the Commander-in-Chief in his report on the action at Futtehabad in announcing the death of the subject of this memoir.

Wigram Battye was the eighth son of George Wynyard Battye, Esq., of the Bengal Civil Service, and brother of Lieutenant Quintin Battye, who, belonging to the same regiment as himself, was mortally wounded when leading his men against the mutineers at Delhi, on the 9th June, 1857. He was born in Kensington, London, on the 13th May, 1842, and was educated at Mount Radford House, Exeter, under the Rev. C. R. Roper; Corse Vicarage, Gloucestershire, under the Rev. C. H. Malpas; Clapham, under Mr. Long; Hampstead, under the Rev. W. H. Perkins; and Keir House, Wimbledon, under Mr. Murray. Passing the examination for an Indian cadetship in December, 1858, he was gazetted to an ensigncy in the 6th Europeans, and joined that regiment in March of the following year. Six months afterwards he obtained his lieutenancy. He was attached for duty to the 3rd Goorkhas from May, 1861, to May, 1863, when he was selected by the Viceroy to fill a vacancy in the Corps of Guides, then stationed at Mardan, one of the salient points of the north-west frontier of India. His subsequent career was passed with that corps, and in it he officiated successively as Wing-Officer, Adjutant, and Commandant of Cavalry.

Wigram Battye was with the Guides when, in 1863, the Umbeyla war broke out, and distinguished himself greatly in the subsequent operations in which the corps took part. Whilst leading his men to repulse one of the desperate night attacks made by the enemy, he was shot through the body. The wound was a most severe one, and for a long time a fatal result was feared. A good constitution, however, enabled him to pull through, but he was compelled to visit Europe to endeavour to complete the cure. Though, in course of time, the wound healed, he never shook off its effects. Whenever he took violent exercise, these made themselves painfully apparent.

Major Battye rejoined the Corps of Guides in 1865, and between that period, and his return to Europe on furlough in 1870, took part in the many expeditions, some of greater, some of less importance, undertaken against the wild tribes on the frontier. In all these he was to the front. In 1866 he accompanied the expedition to the Sundkhar Valley. In 1869 he acted as orderly officer to General Keyes in the Miranzar expedition, and for his services received the thanks of that officer. His daring, and his appreciation of their soldierly qualities, had gained for him the confidence of the stalwart frontier soldiers who served under him; and it is no exaggeration to say that he had become their hero, their Paladin, and that they would have followed him anywhere. Hence, whenever the expeditions, too numerous to detail, were despatched to the front, he was invariably selected to accompany them.

In 1870, Major Battye revisited Europe on furlough. On the breaking out of the Franco-German War in July of that year, he hastened to join the army led by the Crown Prince, and accompanied it as a non-combatant throughout, till the capitulation of Paris. For the services he rendered to the sick and wounded during the hostilities, he received the German war-medal in steel, with the non-combatant ribbon.

At the close of 1871 Wigram Battye returned to India, and once again rejoined his regiment. During the years that followed, until the breaking out of the Afghan War, he was constantly engaged on the frontier. He accompanied the detachment of Guide Infantry which formed part of a flying column despatched into Jowaki-Afridi territory in the last days of August, 1877. When, three months later, the Infantry of the corps were employed in another punitory expedition, he, being in command of the Cavalry, remained at Mardan commanding the station, and led a detachment in the surprise of the Utman Khel village of Sapiri, for his services on which occasion he received the thanks of the Secretary of State, and of the Government of India. He was present with the corps, under Major R. B. Campbell, in the surprise of the Ranizai village of Skhakat, on the 13th March, 1878, and of the Utman Khel villages, under Lieut.-Colonel F. H. Jenkins, on the 20th and 21st of the same month.

In October, 1878, Wigram Battye was selected to accompany Sir Neville Chamberlain in his mission to Kabul, and commanded the escort at the interview between the Master of the Amir's Horse and Sir Louis Cavagnari. He was present with the Infantry of the corps at the capture of Ali Musjid on the 21st November, and in the subsequent advance of Sir Sam Browne's force to Daka and Jalalabad; and he commanded a detachment of Guide Cavalry under Br.-General Tytler, C.B., V.C., in his operations in the Kama Valley, for his services on which occasion he was mentioned in the Brigadier's despatch.

On the 31st March, 1879, the Guide Cavalry, under Major Wigram Battye, marched with the Cavalry Brigade under Brigadier-General C. Gough, C.B., V.C., from Jalalabad to Futtehabad. It was at this place, on the 2nd April, that Battye was slain, leading his gallant men in an attack on the Kugiani Afghans, an attack which had virtually succeeded the moment he fell dead. The incident was thus described by an eye-witness:—

"Charging at the head of his men, Wigram Battye received a severe wound in the side from a rifle bullet. His men begged him to stop and have it attended to, but he refused, and continued to ride on, the blood pouring from his body. In traversing, a few seconds later, a deep *nullah* commanded by the enemy, and which it was necessary to cross to reach them, he was pierced in the heart by another bullet. His life at once passed away, but the Guides took a terrible vengeance."

In a despatch written by Sir Sam. Browne on the occasion of Major Wigram Battye's death, the following passage occurs:—

"Of Major Wigram Battye it is very bitter for me to speak. The Viceroy is aware of the noble end of this gallant officer, and it is some consolation to me in mourning over his loss to feel that he died, as he would have wished, at the head of his gallant Guides. Endowed both mentally and physically far beyond the average, it is no flattery to say that Wigram Battye united in his person all the best qualities which it should be the wish of every officer to emulate. Throughout his brief but distinguished career, he conducted himself in his private capacity as a high-minded English gentleman, and in his public, as an able and chivalrous soldier; and, it seems fitting, that to such a life the death of a hero should have been accorded."

The death of Major Wigram Battye called forth from the men he had so long commanded an unprecedented outburst of grief, which continued to find expression long after his body was carried to the grave.

"There is a very sacred spot at Jalalabad," wrote a correspondent to the "Pioneer," "where rest the remains of Wigram Battye, a hero whose praises fill every mouth. I lately overtook a Sepoy of the Guides proceeding to the grave to water the flowers with which the affection of his devoted comrades and soldiers has embellished it. 'The whole regiment,' said he, in his simple Punjab language, 'weep for Battye: the regiment would have died to a man rather than harm should befall Battye.'"

Subsequently, by the unanimous desire alike of officers and men of the Corps of Guides, the body of Wigram Battye was conveyed to Mardan, that it might rest in the place where he had been known and appreciated for so many years. A tablet to his memory and to that of his brother Quintin has been placed by the officers of his regiment in the crypt of St. Paul's.

MAJOR H. G. BECHER, STAFF CORPS,

11TH BENGAL N.I.

HE details of the services of the subject of this notice, which have been received up to the time of going to press, though somewhat meagre in character, are sufficient to denote that his career was a not undistinguished one.

As a volunteer civilian, Henry George Becher served in the Indian Mutiny, in 1857, and was decorated by Government with the medal.

After obtaining a commission, he took part, in 1860, in the Sikkim expedition, raising and commanding the Coolie Corps, and having sole charge of the transport.

His next term of active service was in the Bhutan campaign of 1864-1865, throughout which he served with the 11th Regiment Bengal Native Infantry, and for which he received the medal with clasp.

In 1868 he took part, as an officer attached to the transport train, in the Abyssinian expedition, for which he received a third medal.

His active career was brought to a close in the Afghan war. Taking part with his regiment, the 11th B. N. I., in its advance to Kohat, he performed garrison duty with it for a time at that station, and then accompanied it over the Peiwar Kotal to Bian Khel, subsequently returning with it down the Kuram Valley to the line of communications. On the renewal of hostilities in the autumn of 1879, he proceeded with the regiment to Ali Khel. A few days after that post was reached, however, his health so completely broke down as to necessitate his being invalided to England; but the change came too late, and he eventually died in this country on the 26th October, 1880.

The deceased officer's commissions bear date as follows:—

Ensign	6th January, 1859.
Lieutenant	12th December, 1859.
Captain	6th January, 1871.
Major	6th January, 1879.

CAPTAIN JOHN BEEKE,

21ST BOMBAY N.I. (MARINE BATTALION).

HE subject of this notice, who died of cholera at Jhelum, Punjab, on the 27th October, 1879, was the second son of John Beeke, Esquire, of Northampton. He was born on the 24th July, 1842; was educated at Addiscombe; and entered the army in 1860. In February, 1867, he was appointed to the Bombay Marine Battalion. He served through the Abyssinian War of 1867-'68, with especial credit, and received from Colonel Merewether, at its termination, both an official and a demi-official acknowledgment of his good services. In 1878 he accompanied the expedition to Malta and Cyprus, and distinguished himself by the zeal and energy with which he carried through the duties allotted to him. Shortly after the renewal of hostilities in Afghanistan, in the autumn of 1879, he was sent on special service to the Punjab. At the time of his death he was engaged at Jhelum in superintending the transport of ponies to the front; and it was when he had almost brought this duty to a successful conclusion that he was attacked with cholera, and died in a few hours.

In Colonel Carnegie's Battalion order of the 29th October, 1879, the following passage occurs:—" In Captain Beeke the battalion has lost one of its oldest and best tried officers, who, by his friendly disposition, untiring zeal, and devotion to his duties, endeared himself to all ranks, and proved himself a most valuable servant to Government." And on the 5th November, 1879, a copy of the following intimation was published:—" The Commander-in-Chief has received with much regret the intelligence of the sudden death, while engaged on special service, of Captain Beeke, Wing Commander 21st Regiment Native Infantry (Marines), who was an officer of marked ability and professional knowledge."

At the instance of the officers and men of the 21st, by whom the deceased was greatly beloved, a memorial fund was raised; and, in order to promote the efficiency of the Regiment, in which he took a heartfelt interest, and to perpetuate his name therein, the money was invested for the purpose of establishing two prizes to be shot for annually, to be called the " Beeke Prizes."

Captain Beeke married, in 1870, Rosina Elizabeth, only daughter of Archibald Low, Esquire, of Porchester, Hants.

MAJOR H. H. BIRCH, STAFF CORPS,

27TH (PUNJAB) BENGAL N.I.

HENRY HOLWELL BIRCH was the first of the long roll of British officers who rendered up their lives in their country's service in the war with which these volumes deal. He was the youngest son of Lieut.-Colonel F. W. Birch, who was himself killed in the Indian Mutiny of 1857 whilst in command of the 41st Royal Infantry at Sitapur, Oudh. Born in India on the 2nd September, 1837, he was sent at an early age to England for his education. After some thirteen years he returned to the country of his birth, serving as officer on board an India merchantman until 1857. In that year, while he was on leave and staying with his father at Sitapur, the Mutiny broke out, and he, with some relatives and friends, had to fly to Lucknow, where he formed one of the illustrious garrison throughout the defence of the Residency. He subsequently served with the field force at the Alum Bagh in 1857-58, and was present at the capture of Lucknow in 1858. For the services he rendered on these occasions he received a medal and two clasps, and obtained a direct commission in Her Majesty's army.

In 1860 Major Birch was posted to the 19th, now the 27th, Punjab Infantry, and in the following year served with that corps in China, obtaining the medal. He was present with his regiment in 1866 with the force in Eusofzai under Brigadier-General Doran, C.B., and again with the force sent out to Lushai under Brigadier-General C. Brownlow in 1871-72, and for his services on this occasion he received a third medal. He rose steadily in his regiment through the various grades, and in 1875 was appointed second in command.

During the Jowaki campaign of 1877-78, the 27th Punjab Native Infantry was again ordered out for service; and in consequence of the temporary appointment of the Commandant to the Brigade Staff, the command of the regiment devolved upon Major Birch.

It was as Acting Commandant of his corps that he took part, on the outbreak of hostilities with Afghanistan in the autumn of 1878, in the advance of Brigadier-General Appleyard's brigade into the Khyber Pass, and in the direct attack on

Ali Musjid on the 21st November. By the time that it was reluctantly decided, as darkness closed in on that day, to postpone the assault, and the order was given to cease firing, the 27th Punjab Native Infantry had pushed forward to the support of the 14th Sikhs on to the steep slope leading to the peak which formed the right flank of the Afghan position, and the leading companies were actively engaged with the enemy in their successive lines of entrenchment. Whilst a steady musketry fire was being poured upon them, and the enemy's artillery was simultaneously enfilading them, Captain Maclean, of the 14th Sikhs, who was badly wounded, finding his men in extreme peril, shouted for help. To this appeal Major Birch responded with eager alacrity, and it was while gallantly leading his companies forward that he fell shot through the heart. How his body was recovered by his gallant Adjutant, Lieut. Fitzgerald, who rendered up his life in defending it, is written elsewhere. On the morning after the attack it was found untouched by the enemy, and was conveyed to Peshawar, where it was buried, with full military honours, on the 24th November.

Major Birch's commissions bear date as follows:

Ensign	4th August, 1858.
Lieutenant	26th April, 1860.
Captain	4th August, 1870.
Major	4th August, 1878.

LIEUTENANT W. H. BISHOP,

2ND BATTALION, 11TH (NORTH DEVONSHIRE) REGIMENT.

HE subject of this notice, who died at Kandahar, of dysentery, on the 23rd November, 1880, was the elder son of William Louis Mosheim Bishop, Captain 46th Bengal Native Infantry, who was killed on the 9th July, 1857, by the mutineers of the 9th Bengal Cavalry and the 46th Bengal Native Infantry at Sialkot, Punjab, where he was officiating as Brigade Major to the troops—his wife (born Emma Rebecca Usborne), and his two children, who were with him at the time, making their escape into the fort at the station.

William Henry Bishop was born on the 28th June, 1855, and received his early education at a school at Blackheath. When about sixteen years of age, he went to study with a private tutor at Bonn, on the Rhine, and from thence proceeded to Queen Elizabeth's Grammar School, Cranbrook, Kent. Evincing some taste for farming, he entered, in January, 1873, the Agricultural College at Cirencester; but receiving, in the month of December of the same year, a Queen's Indian Cadetship in recognition of his father's services, he decided to embark on a military career. In January, 1874, he passed his examination, and on the 17th April, 1874, was gazetted to a Sub-Lieutenancy in the 1st Battalion, 11th Foot. Being desirous to see foreign service, he exchanged a few months afterwards into the 2nd Battalion of the regiment, then stationed in the Bombay Presidency, and sailed to join Head-quarters in October, 1874. He obtained his Lieutenancy in September, 1876, and in the course of his Indian service held the appointment of Interpreter to the regiment, and for two successive years was employed on the Famine Staff.

On the regiment being ordered into Afghanistan in July, 1880, Lieutenant Bishop took part with it in its advance into the enemy's country. His term of active service, eagerly looked forward to, was destined, alas! to be of short duration. The hardships he endured in the disastrous march through the Bolan Pass in the burning summer heat completely sapped his health, and within a month of his reaching Kandahar he succumbed—to the heartfelt regret of the regiment—to the fatal disease which had already claimed as victims so many of his gallant countrymen.

MAJOR G. F. BLACKWOOD,

ROYAL HORSE ARTILLERY.

ON the 27th of July, 1880, the memorable death of Major George Frederick Blackwood, on the field of Maiwand, added yet another honoured name to the already long roll of gallant Scotch officers who had fallen in the war with which these volumes deal.

The subject of this memoir was the second son of the late Major William Blackwood, of the Bengal Army, and a grandson of the founder of the eminent publishing house of that name. Born at Moradabad, India, in the year 1838, he was educated at the Edinburgh Academy, under Dr. Harvey, now its Rector, who speaks very warmly of his former pupil, and characterizes his translations from the Latin as having been marked by a spirit and fidelity beyond those of any of his class-fellows. He subsequently studied under the late Captain Orr, at the Military Academy in Lothian Road, Edinburgh, and from thence passed to Addiscombe, where, in due course, he made choice of the Artillery branch of the Bengal Service. Gazetted to a Lieutenancy in December, 1857—a time when a chapter of stirring events was being unfolded in the East—Blackwood was at once sent out to India, and had not long to wait before being engaged in the stern work of actual campaigning. Immediately after arriving at Bombay, he was hurried up to the seat of war, and served in the suppression of the Mutiny with the Rohilkhand Moveable Column, under the command of Lieutenant-Colonel Wilkinson, 42nd Royal Highlanders. In this force he was entrusted with the command of two guns. The services he rendered during the operations gained for him, at their conclusion, a Divisional Adjutancy of Artillery, the duties of which he discharged from 1859 to 1862 at Bareilly and Gwalior. From November, 1862, to December, 1863, he acted as Adjutant of the 22nd Brigade, R.A., and afterwards as Adjutant of the 19th Brigade, until September, 1864, when he was appointed to A/C, R.H.A.—now known as A/B, R.H.A.—one of the first troops of the old Bengal Horse Artillery which was ordered home after the amalgamation. In February, 1867, he received promotion.

In the autumn of 1871, Captain Blackwood had the honour of being specially selected by Lord Napier of Magdala, from a large number of officers whose claims were submitted, to command the Artillery in the Lushai expedition, under Brigadier-General Bourchier, C.B., and in the month of November he was again in the field. In the course of the operations which ensued, he was present at the attacks on Tipai Mukh, Kungnung, and Taikuni; and by the ability he displayed, not only in action, but on the march, amply justified Lord Napier's selection. In General Bourchier's despatch of the 29th March, 1872, the following passage occurs:—"Captain Blackwood and officers R.A. nobly sustained the reputation of the corps. The word 'difficulty' was unknown to them." A report drawn up by Blackwood on the Artillery in the campaign contained many valuable suggestions as to the nature of the gun most suitable for such service, and on the management of artillery and the equipment of elephants in mountain, jungle, and morass campaigning; and was printed and published by the Government of India. For his services in the expedition, the subject of this notice was rewarded, in September, 1872, with a Brevet-Majority.

During the absence of Lieutenant-Colonel Hills, C.B., in England, Major Blackwood temporarily commanded a battery of the Royal Horse Artillery. Promoted to a Regimental Majority in 1876, he exchanged into G/3, R.A., and subsequently brought this battery to such a state of efficiency as to call forth expressions of approbation from the highest military authorities in India. In February, 1878, the Duke of Cambridge was pleased to remark that the battery was "in a very high state of efficiency: Major Blackwood highly commended."

In the summer of 1878, failing health rendered it necessary for Major Blackwood to return to England on sick leave; and, to his deep regret, he was prevented, on the outbreak of hostilities with Afghanistan in the autumn of that year, from taking part in the first campaign. He had, however, the gratification of hearing that, notwithstanding the ranks of the horses of G/3, R.A., having been almost decimated with the frightful scourge known as the Ludiana disease, the battery had been selected for service with the fighting column under General Roberts in the Kuram Valley.

Returning to India, the subject of this memoir was appointed to the command of E/B, Royal Horse Artillery. In January, 1880, he proceeded with the battery on active service to Kandahar; and in the operations of General Burrows' brigade in the month of July, commanded it both in the encounter with the Wali's mutinous troops, and on the bloody field on which it won imperishable renown. In the action first alluded to, on the 14th of the month, E/B, R.H.A., performed distinguished service; and General Primrose reports that "the remarkable energy with which the battery was brought up to the front reflects the highest credit on Major G. F. Blackwood." Blackwood himself, in the last letter, alas! that he was destined ever to write, gives a graphic account of this smart little affair:—"I got into action four times, and did a fair amount of execution," he observes modestly with reference to his own share in the proceedings. A short quotation, too, from a letter written home by a corporal of the battery, will not, perhaps, be here out of place. "One shell," remarks the writer, "dropped close to the Major, but he stood his ground and gave his words of command the same as if we were on the field of drill, without shot or shell flying about;" and then adds—in simple language, but with an honest enthusiasm which Blackwood's nature was well calculated to inspire —"There is not a man in the whole Battery but what would go through fire and water for a Commander like the Major."

At the disastrous battle of Maiwand, on the 27th of the month, Major Blackwood was the senior Artillery officer present with General Burrows' force. While directing the movements of the battery in the centre of the fighting line, he was struck, some little time after he had been in action, with a bullet through the thigh; and giving over the command of his guns to Captain Slade, he retired for a few minutes from the front to have his wound dressed. It is characteristic of the man, and of a piece with other instances of his indomitable pluck, that, finding he could not receive, without leaving the field, the attention he urgently needed, he preferred to return to rejoin his battery; and he was actually with his guns when the order to limber up and retire was given. The evidence relating to the next stage of the disaster is conflicting and uncertain; but it is clear that, sore spent with his wound, and unable to mount, Blackwood managed to make his way on foot with the remnant of the 66th Regiment, the Bombay Sappers, and others, to the garden in the right rear of the line of battle, where the last desperate stand was made. Before reaching this garden his wound broke out afresh; and it is pleasant to relate that a young officer of the 66th (Lieutenant Pearce), affording one of the many instances of self-abnegation which were not wanting on that sad day, stopped to assist him in binding it up. The manner in which the devoted little band in the enclosure fought on till only eleven of them were left, is recorded, on evidence received from a Colonel of Artillery of Ayub Khan's Army, in the letter bearing date 1st October, 1880, written to the Adjutant-General in India by General Primrose, who goes on to tell how the eleven remaining charged out of the garden and died with their faces to the foe, fighting to the death. "Such was the nature of their charge and the grandeur of their bearing," adds the General, "that, although the whole of the Ghazis were assembled around them, not one dared approach to cut them down. Thus standing in the open, back to back, firing steadily and truly, every shot telling, surrounded by thousands, these eleven officers and men died." It was in this charge—as has been now clearly ascertained from the subsequent examination of the ground, from the positions in which the bodies were found, and from other corroborative evidence—that the gallant and lamented Major Blackwood fell, bringing to a close, not unworthily, a career of the finest promise and a life which he deemed it a high honour to render up in the service of his Queen and country, and in sustaining untarnished the honour of the British arms.

We may fitly close this brief notice with two extracts from private letters, which may be taken to represent the estimation in which the deceased officer was held throughout the service. "Blackwood's death," wrote General Sir James Hills, "weighs also most heavily on his brother officers and friends—not one of whom but deeply regrets his loss, not only as a personal one, but also as a public one to the regiment and the army, for no better officer ever entered the Service"—a tribute to the memory of Major Blackwood which is supplemented by one who enjoyed his friendship for upwards of twenty years—Major Anthony Murray, R.A.—in these words:—"We loved and admired him for his genuine and unselfish character. Whatever he undertook, he entered into with his whole heart; and whatever he did, he did well. In him the Service has lost a thorough soldier, and our regiment one of its brightest ornaments. Had he lived he must have risen to high distinction."

SURGEON-MAJOR R. H. BOLTON,

ARMY MEDICAL DEPARTMENT.

ROBERT HENRY BOLTON, who died at Kandahar on the 27th February, 1880, was the second son of Robert C. Bolton, Esq., of Doneraile, County Cork. He was born on the 1st October, 1839, and after receiving his education at the Royal College of Surgeons, and the King and Queen's College of Physicians, Ireland, served for a period in the Royal Elthorne (Middlesex) Militia. In September, 1863, he entered the Army Medical Department as Assistant Surgeon, and was shortly afterwards detailed for service in the Madras Presidency. After doing duty for two years at various stations in India, he was despatched to Burmah, and there completed three years more of his service. Returning to England at the beginning of 1869, he was posted for duty a few months later, to the 3rd Dragoon Guards. He served with that regiment for three years, at the expiration of which period, on rumours of the proposed unification system taking effect, he became anxious to return to India. With this object in view, he exchanged into the 2nd Battalion 23rd (Royal Welsh) Fusiliers. Almost immediately afterwards the Ashanti War broke out, and the regiment was ordered to the Gold Coast. Accompanying it in medical charge of the left wing, he served with it through the whole of the second phase of the war, and received the medal with clasp for Coomassie.

On the departure of the 23rd Fusiliers to Gibraltar, Surgeon-Major Bolton reverted to the Staff. In January, 1878, he was again ordered out to India, being detailed for duty to the Bombay Presidency. On the second outbreak of hostilities in Afghanistan in September, 1879, whilst in charge of the Station Hospital at Nimach, Rajputana, he was transferred, with nine other medical officers, to the Bengal Presidency, and received orders to proceed immediately to Kandahar. The great hardship and exposure which he underwent in the march through the Bolan Pass and on to his destination, pursued in the depth of winter and in the face of innumerable delays and difficulties which presented themselves, proved too much for a constitution which had been previously weakened by ague and dysentery; and shortly after his arrival—on the 27th February, 1880, at the age of forty years—he died from the effects of the rupture of an abscess in the liver.

BRIGADIER-GENERAL H. F. BROOKE,

COMMDG. 2ND INFANTRY BRIGADE, KANDAHAR FIELD FORCE.

ENRY FRANCIS BROOKE, who was killed in the sortie from Kandahar on the 16th August, 1880, while endeavouring to save the life of Captain Cruickshank, R.E., who was mortally wounded, was the eldest son of George and Lady Arabella Brooke, of Ashbrooke, Co. Fermanagh. He was born on the 3rd August, 1836. At the age of eighteen years he was gazetted, in June, 1854, to an ensigncy in the 48th Foot; and landing with that regiment in the Crimea on the 21st of April, 1855, served with it in the siege and fall of Sebastopol, earning the medal with clasp and the Turkish medal. Throughout the campaign of 1860 in China, he acted as Aide-de-Camp to Sir Robert Napier, being present in that capacity at the action of Tangku, the assault of the Taku Forts—in which he was severely wounded,—and the final advance on and surrender of Pekin. For his services on these occasions, for which he was several times mentioned in despatches, he received the brevet of Major and the medal with two clasps.

In addition to the post of Aide-de-Camp to Sir Robert Napier in China, General Brooke held, in the course of his distinguished career, the following staff appointments:—Bde.-Major, Bengal, from 14th April, 1863, to 3rd Jan., 1865; Assist. Adjt.-Gen., from 3rd Jan., 1865, to 23rd April, 1866, and again from 31st July, 1872, to 18th Jan., 1876; Deputy Adjt.-Gen., Bengal, 19th Jan., 1876, to 15th Nov., 1877; Adjt.-Gen. (local Br.-Gen.), Bombay, 23rd Nov., 1877, to 28th March, 1880; Br.-Gen., Commanding 2nd Infantry Brigade, Kandahar, 28th March, 1880, till the day of his death. It will thus be seen that, in order to assume command of a brigade on active service, he gave up temporarily the better paid and more comfortable, though responsible position, of Adjutant-General of the Bombay Army.

General Brooke arrived at Kandahar about the 23rd April, 1880, and at once assumed the command of the garrison, which, up to the date of his arrival, had been held—in addition to the chief command of the forces in Southern Aghanistan —by General Primrose. For the benefit of those who enjoyed his friendship or acquaintance it will be unnecessary to mention that his first thought was to make a thorough and complete inspection of the limits of his command, and of the troops placed at his disposal; but it is probably not generally known that he considered it his imperative duty to place on record his sense of the very imperfect condition of the fortifications, and to point out the obvious necessity for some defensive works being at once thrown up. These representations were re-submitted, on his arrival shortly afterwards, by General Burrows. Economy being, however, necessary, it was considered by the authorities inadvisable to incur the considerable charges which would be entailed by placing the defences of the city in a satisfactory state.

General Brooke's next care was to make himself acquainted with the surrounding country; and many were the excursions carried out by him over road, by-path, hill-pass, and river, to a distance of fifteen miles in every direction. Accompanied sometimes by a small party of officers, sometimes merely by an escort of a couple of sowars, one a qualified interpreter, the active Brigadier would start at daybreak, and after remaining for an hour or two in some village or orchard to converse with the natives, would return to barracks late in the day. In this manner he had made himself thoroughly acquainted with the environs of the city—a most necessary knowledge in a country so deficient in road-communication as Kandahar. It was due also to General Brooke's representations that a system of cavalry patrols and reconnaissances was initiated, which, though not furnished to the extent which he deemed advisable, was productive of good, and increased the general stock of knowledge.

Thus affairs went on till the approach of Ayub Khan's army began to arouse the turbulent spirits among the population, and disturbances began. General Brooke and Major Adam were fired upon on the 16th July in the Morcha Pass by a party among the rocks above them; and though the hill was surrounded by cavalry till nightfall, and a party of infantry was scrambling over it all the day, no trace of the would-be assassins was found. Fortunately their shots only killed one of the sowar's horses.

Thus far General Brooke in quiet times; but it was when the news of Maiwand was brought in, and dangers and difficulties arose, that his cool head, clear understanding, and soldierly insight made his influence more important. It was in compliance with his request, personally made and strongly urged, that the small detachment of all arms was sent out under his command to cover the last few miles of the retreat. Though the relief it was able to render was restricted by the orders it received not to proceed beyond the village of Kokaran, there can be little doubt that several lives were saved through its instrumentality, the large bodies of the country people, who had collected on either side of the route, dispersing rapidly on its approach.

On General Brooke's return to the city at about 2 p. m., after an absence of some seven hours, it was discovered that the orders for the withdrawal of the outlying corps, which it had been found necessary to issue, had been misunderstood. Instead of having packed up everything, and brought it into the central enclosure, preparatory to the retirement to the city, most of the troops in the cantonments had withdrawn at once, leaving their baggage and camp equipage in their quarters, where it had been looted by the villagers. Portions of it were subsequently recovered by detachments sent out for the purpose. By nightfall all the troops were withdrawn into the city, in an orderly manner, under General Brooke's directions.

In the train of important subsequent events—including the elaborate and now eagerly pushed forward defence of the city, the house-to-house visitation, and search for arms in the disaffected quarters, and the ultimate extra-mural ejection of the Pathans—the energy and perseverance of General Brooke were conspicuous. Always good-humoured, smiling, and cheerful, he was just the man to restore the drooping spirits of troops smarting under such a defeat as that of Maiwand; and his youth, and powerful frame, rendered him apparently impervious to fatigue.

Thus he continued to set a brilliant example until the fatal 16th of August. The sortie of that day, to the village of Deh Khwaja, was undertaken in opposition both to his own advice and to that of General Burrows; and had, indeed, been planned for the previous week, but abandoned in deference to their opinion. Other counsel, however, prevailed; and when, on being sent for on the evening of the 15th, General Brooke was told that the operation was to be carried out, and that he was to have the command, his mouth was, as he himself said, closed. He was so emphatic in expressing his disapproval of the project to some private friends, that the opinion gained ground with some of them that he felt a presentiment that the morrow would be fatal to him, and desired thus to place on record his opinion of the unwisdom of the movement. His phrase was: "It will either be a walk over, or a very serious business. In the former case, it will be useless as a demonstration; in the latter, it must entail heavy loss." Whether the idea as to his presentiment of his own fate be correct or not, there can be no question as to the soundness of his estimate of the value of the sortie.

After the two attacking columns had forced their way under a heavy fire through the southern portion of the village, General Brooke, in the face of remonstrances, returned almost alone to render assistance to Captain Cruickshank, R.E., and a party who were gallantly endeavouring to escort that officer, then dangerously wounded, to the walls. Running the gauntlet of the village, attended by his mounted trumpeter (Mr. Glynn, of Battery C/2, R.A., who remained with him till he fell, and miraculously reached Kandahar unwounded), and assisted by a sergeant of the 7th Fusiliers, he succeeded in reaching Captain Cruickshank, and began to carry him towards the Kabul gate. It was in this enterprise that he lost his life.

The night of the 16th of August was a sad one in Kandahar. Each regiment had its own loss—especially in officers—to deplore; but it is not too much to say that in no case was the regret more wide-spread and deep than that which was evinced for the death of the gallant Brigadier.

Sprung from a family of soldiers, the subject of this memoir was possessed, in a marked degree, of the qualifications for success in the profession whose interests he held so deeply at heart. Of sound and excellent judgment; of rare humanity; a devoted friend; contemptuous of his own personal safety, yet holding it a sacred charge never to risk the safety of the constituents of his command without due reason, he would surely, had he been spared, have fulfilled the high promise of his brief but distinguished career. It was otherwise ordered; but it is some consolation to his relations and friends to feel that his death was not unworthy of himself.

After skilfully conducting, in the face of overwhelming difficulty, the operation which had been entrusted to his hands, he deliberately sacrificed his life in the vain attempt to save that of his friend.

LIEUT.-COLONEL FRANCIS BROWNLOW, C.B.,

72ND (DUKE OF ALBANY'S OWN HIGHLANDERS).

HE subject of this memoir, whose name will long remain identified with that of the distinguished regiment whose fame, during a lifetime, he did much to sustain, and whose honour he held jealously at heart, was the eldest son of William Brownlow, Esq. (eldest son of the Rev. Francis and Lady Catherine Brownlow, daughter of the 8th Earl of Meath), by his marriage with Charlotte (daughter of William Browne, Esq. of Brownes Hill, Carlow, and Lady Charlotte, daughter of the Earl of Mayo). He was born on the 19th July, 1836, and was educated at Harrow. Entering the 72nd Highlanders as Ensign by purchase on the 8th September, 1854, he had not long to wait before undergoing the stern experience of active service. He embarked with the regiment, a month after joining head-quarters, for the Crimea; and serving with it throughout its various operations in the war, was present in the expedition to Kertch, at the siege and fall of Sebastopol, and at the attack of the 18th June. In the last days of July, 1856, he returned with the regiment to England; and had barely attained his twentieth year before he bore on his breast the Crimean and Turkish medals, with the clasp for Sebastopol.

His term of home-service was of short duration. In September, 1857, the 72nd was ordered out to India, and Brownlow proceeded with it to earn a second medal by participating in the serious work which was to fall to its lot. He was present in the Mutiny at the siege and capture of Kotah; was with the leading column of assault on the 30th March, 1858; and subsequently served throughout the operations in Central India, being present in the pursuit of the rebel forces under Tantia Topee and Rao Sahib in 1868-59. In August, 1862, he obtained his company.

After returning with the 72nd to England, and continuing with it during its tour of home service, he again accompanied it to India, embarking with it from Ireland in February, 1871. In the meantime (May, 1870) he had obtained his Majority; and in August, 1877, he succeeded to the command of the regiment.

Colonel Brownlow was still in command of the 72nd, when, in view of the impending invasion of Afghanistan, it received orders, in the autumn of 1878, to join the Kuram Valley Field Force. Taking part with it in the advance into the enemy's country, he commanded it throughout the operations which were brought to a close by the signing of the treaty of Gandamak. For the brilliant manner in which he led his men in the assault of the Peiwar Kotal on the 2nd December, 1878, he was mentioned in eulogistic terms in Sir Frederick Roberts' despatch, and subsequently received the Companionship of the Bath.

After the conclusion of peace, Colonel Brownlow proceeded, in July, 1879, on leave to England. He had scarcely arrived in this country, however, when he was recalled to the theatre of the recent operations by the renewal of hostilities. Hurrying out with all speed, he succeeded in reaching Kabul on the 3rd December, in time to command the 72nd throughout the critical series of events with which the year closed. In the storming of the Asmai Heights on the 14th December, he led the advance; and for the brilliant example he set his men was spoken of in terms of warm admiration by Colonel Jenkins, the officer in command of the advance. On the withdrawal within the Sherpur cantonments, one of the five sections into which the defences were divided was entrusted by the General to his charge.

Colonel Brownlow continued in command of the regiment for the remainder of the time it remained in Kabul, and during the memorable march to Kandahar. It was in the battle with Ayub Khan's army on the 1st September, 1880, whilst gallantly leading the regiment through the lanes and walled enclosures in the stubbornly contested advance of Baker's brigade, that he met his death.

It is not too much to say that the loss of their beloved Colonel was regarded in the light of a personal bereavement by every officer and man of the gallant regiment which he had so often led to victory.

"In his death," wrote Sir Frederick Roberts in his despatch of the 26th December, "the Army has experienced a great loss. He had on many occasions highly distinguished himself as a leader,—at the Peiwar Kotal, during the operations around Kabul at the latter end of 1879, and notably on the 14th December, when he won the admiration of the whole force by his brilliant conduct in the attack and capture of the Asmai heights,"—words which have been supplemented in an earnest tribute paid by the General to Colonel Brownlow's memory in a farewell address delivered by him to the 72nd and 92nd Highlanders on the occasion of his departure for India, and which found an echo in the hearts of all to whom the deceased officer was known.

Colonel Brownlow married, in 1878, Effie Constance, daughter of the late Colonel Robert Tytler, 38th Bengal Infantry, by whom he leaves issue a son.

LIEUT. A. BURLTON-BENNET, STAFF CORPS,

10TH (DUKE OF CAMBRIDGE'S OWN) BENGAL CAVALRY (LANCERS).

ARTHUR BURLTON-BENNET, who died at Norwood from illness contracted whilst on field service in Afghanistan, was the son of John Robert Burlton-Bennet, Esq., late Postmaster-General of Bengal. He was born on the 12th June, 1851, and was educated under the Rev. J. W. Tottenham, at St. Leonards, and the Rev. Drs. Brackenbury and Wynne, at Wimbledon College. He entered the army in September, 1869, being gazetted to the 37th Foot. Proving himself an efficient and accomplished young officer, he was offered, after a brief term of service, the Adjutancy of the regiment; but having decided to embark on an Indian career, was unwilling to accept the appointment. After applying himself diligently to a course of study, he passed the higher standard examination in native languages, and was posted to the 30th Native Infantry. He was shortly afterwards, however, transferred to the 10th Bengal Lancers, with which regiment he served till immediately prior to his death.

After being admitted to the Staff Corps, and passing successfully through a course of garrison instruction, Burlton Bennet held various Staff appointments. Shortly before his death, he was selected to fill the post of Adjutant of the regiment.

On the outbreak of hostilities with Afghanistan he proceeded with the regiment into the Khyber, and participated in the arduous duties which fell to its lot in the Pass. The hard work he performed, and the constant exposure he underwent, laid the seeds of the disease to which he eventually succumbed. Shortly after the signing of the treaty of Gandamak, it was found necessary to invalid him to England; but the change failed to restore his shattered health, and barely two months after he reached his destination, he died, on the 23rd October, 1879, at his father's house at Norwood.

Arthur Burlton-Bennet's loss is deeply regretted, not only by his brother officers but a wide circle of friends. His love of sport of every description was intense, and his presence will be more especially missed by his companions in the hunting-field. On the news of his death being received in India his commanding officer made feeling allusion to the fact that the regiment had lost a valued friend; and H.R.H. the Duke of Cambridge, who was pleased to say he had made his acquaintance while in Malta, wrote expressing the regret he felt at the sad occurrence which had deprived the service of so smart and promising an officer.

CAPTAIN S. G. BUTSON,

9TH (QUEEN'S ROYAL) LANCERS.

STRANGE GOULD BUTSON, who was killed at Siah Sang, in the neighbourhood of Kabul, on the 13th December, 1879, while charging the enemy at the head of a squadron of the 9th Lancers, was the elder son of the Very Rev. C. H. Gould Butson, M.A., J.P., Vicar of Clonfert, and Dean of Kilmacduagh, St. Brendon's, Clonfert, Eyre Court, Ireland, by his marriage with Helena Eyre, only daughter of the Rev. Edward Eyre Maunsell, M.A., Vicar of Galway; and was a grandson, in the paternal line, of the late Venerable J. Strange Butson, M.A., J.P., Archdeacon of Clonfert.

The subject of this notice was born in the year 1851, and was educated by Mr. Walter Wrenn, London, and by him prepared for the Royal Military College, Sandhurst. He was gazetted, in July, 1870, to a cornetcy in the 9th Lancers; and after a term of some three years of home service, embarked with that regiment for India. In October, 1871, he was promoted Lieutenant, and in February, 1878, obtained his troop.

Captain Butson was serving with the regiment at Sialkot, Punjab, in the autumn of 1878, when, in view of the impending hostilities with Afghanistan, it was ordered up into the neighbourhood of Peshawar. He accompanied the first expedition to the Bazar Valley, under Major-General Maude, as a volunteer, in December, 1878; and subsequently served with the detached squadron of the 9th Lancers under Captain Apperley in the Kuram Valley, from the 17th March to the 27th September, 1879. Shortly after the renewal of hostilities he was appointed Aide-de-Camp to Brigadier-General Massy, and took part in the advance on Kabul, the actions of Jaji Thana, Charasiab, Kabul (8th and 9th October), and the operations in the second week in December. For his services during the march he was most favourably mentioned in despatches. It was in the action of Siah Sang, on the 13th of December, while leading a squadron on the summit of a hill up which he had just charged against large numbers of the enemy, that he fell, pierced to the heart by an Afghan bullet.

In a letter written by Brigadier-General Dunham Massy, the following words occur:—" He (Captain Butson) has died a soldier's death, and is deeply lamented by his brother officers and by all who came in contact with him. By his death the Service has been deprived of a most gallant and promising officer, and one who, had he been spared, would have proved a brilliant ornament to his profession."

Captain Butson's remains were buried, with military honours, on the evening of the 13th December, in the little cemetery at Sherpur, where those of so many of his fellow countrymen have found a last resting-place.

LIEUT. J. F. M. CAMPBELL, STAFF CORPS,

ATTACHED 2ND BALUCH REGIMENT.

JOHN FREDERICK MELFORT CAMPBELL was the eldest son of the late Captain Patrick Campbell, R.N., of the family of Melfort, Argyleshire, by his marriage with Gertrude, only daughter of the late Captain Joseph Barnes, R.A. He was born on the 12th December, 1856, and was educated at the Royal Naval School, New Cross. From this establishment he passed, in the midsummer examination of 1875, tenth out of a hundred and thirty-five candidates for direct commission in the Line; and being shortly afterwards gazetted to the 70th Foot, joined that regiment at Peshawar.

While serving in the Punjab, young Campbell passed with distinction through the Garrison Class at Sialkot, the preliminary examination in Native Languages, and, in due course, the final examination for the Staff Corps. There is something touching, judged in the light of after events, in a passage penned by him in reference to this period of his career, in a letter written a few days before his death to his mother. "My mind," he writes, "is at rest, now that I have finished that examination. Hitherto my life has been one long preparation for these examinations, and I am becoming rather tired of them."

In October, 1878, he accompanied the 2nd Baluch Regiment, with which he was then serving as a probationer, from Dera Ghazi Khan to Quetta, where the regiment joined the force under General Biddulph, which, in view of the impending invasion of Afghanistan, was then in course of concentration. He proceeded with the regiment in its advance, two months afterwards, into the enemy's country, and was present with it, in Palliser's Brigade, at the action at Takht-i-pul, and with Sir Donald Stewart's force in the subsequent advance on and occupation of Kandahar.

In the last days of January, 1879, he took part in the advance of General Biddulph's Division to Girishk, and on its return performed garrison duty at Kokaran. It was while marching from this post to Chaman, in the month of August, that he began to feel the effects of the hardship and exposure which, in common with his brother officers, he had undergone. Immediately after arriving at Chaman he was seized with cholera, and a few hours afterwards, on the morning of the 19th August — exactly a month from the date on which his Colonel (Nicholetts), towards whom he entertained a strong attachment, had fallen a victim to the same disease—he died, deeply regretted by his brother officers, with whom the gentleness of his ways and the unassuming manliness of his character had made him a general favourite.

CAPTAIN C. A. CARTHEW, STAFF CORPS,

16TH BENGAL CAVALRY,

OFFG. DEPY. ASST. QR.-MR.-GENL., KHYBER BRIGADE.

HARLES ALFRED CARTHEW was the second son of General Morden Carthew, C.B., of H.M. Indian Army, Madras. He was born on the 3rd September, 1841, and was educated at a private school and at Cheltenham College. In April, 1861, he entered the army as Ensign in the 33rd Regiment, having obtained a direct commission by purchase; became Lieutenant, also by purchase, in April, 1865; and in February, 1866, entered the Bengal Staff Corps.

Posted to the 16th Bengal Cavalry, Carthew served as 1st squadron subaltern in that regiment during the campaign in the Black Mountain, Hazara, in 1868, and obtained the Frontier medal with clasp. In 1871, having suffered from repeated attacks of Indian fever, he was sent home on medical certificate; and although during the whole of his visit to England he continued in a low state of health, he was so anxious to improve his professional knowledge and fit himself for higher employment, that he obtained permission to attend a course of Military Surveying and Field Engineering, and took a Chatham 1st class certificate in those subjects. He also went through a course of instruction in Army Signalling and Telegraphy, for which he obtained a certificate as Instructor. In April, 1873, after completing his twelve years' service, he was promoted Captain.

After his return to India he officiated from time to time in the Quartermaster-General's Department. In May, 1876, he was appointed Officiating Quartermaster-General of the Allahabad Division for three months, on the expiration of which period he was sent to the Presidency till April, 1877. In October, 1878, he was appointed, again, in the same position, to the Umballa Division under General Hughes, and retained the post till September, 1879, when, at the beginning of the second Afghan campaign, he was appointed to the staff of Brigadier-General Arbuthnot as Deputy Assistant Quartermaster-General.

Captain Carthew was returned as slightly wounded when crossing troops over the Kabul River on the 9th June, 1880, under fire of the enemy, on the return from the Lughman Valley expedition. The zeal and energy and soldierlike qualities he displayed commended him to the favourable notice of those he served under. Brigadier-General Arbuthnot, on being relieved of the command of his Brigade, wrote on the 17th June, 1880, as follows:—" I wish to bring to the notice of the Lieutenant-General Commanding the Khyber Line Force, Captain C. A. Carthew, 16th Bengal Cavalry, the Deputy Assistant Quartermaster-General, as an officer of untiring zeal, with a good knowledge of the working of his department. I would also recommend him to the favourable consideration of the Lieutenant-General Commanding." And Major-General Bright, writing on the same date, heartily concurred in the terms of the Brigadier's favourable report.

On the return of the army from Kabul to India, Captain Carthew was directed to superintend the passage of the troops over the Indus at Attock; and the able way in which he organized and carried out all the arrangements, received the marked approval of the Commander-in-Chief in India, and of Brigadier-General Hankin, commanding the Peshawar District. Between the 20th of August and the 21st of September, 1880, he passed over the ferry at Attock no less than 20,496 soldiers and followers, 13,345 animals, 762 carts and 80 guns and waggons, without a single accident or mishap of any kind; and not a bale of goods was reported lost, although the Indus was in a state of heavy flood, the current running about seven miles an hour. But the constant exposure to the sun day after day during the most trying time of the year, acting on a constitution already enfeebled by the fatigues of the campaign, was more than he could bear; and when his heavy work of the passage of the troops was done—but not till then—he was once more and for the last time laid low with the deadly Peshawar fever, and died at Landi Kotal on the 12th October, 1880, in the thirty-ninth year of his age, within a few months of the time when he would have obtained his majority.

It is some poor consolation to his friends to know that Captain Carthew's exertions were appreciated by the Commander-in-Chief and the Government of India. On the 29th of October, 1880, the Quartermaster-General of the Army wrote to the Military Secretary to the Government, expressing his Excellency's satisfaction with the arrangements made in this work of the passage of the troops over the Indus; and his regret that by the death of Captain Carthew the Army and the Government of India were deprived of a most valuable public servant; and on the 9th November, 1880, the Military Secretary to the Government of India wrote to the Quartermaster-General of the Army concurring, on behalf of the Government, with Sir Frederick Haines' verdict. The practical result of this marked approbation of Captain Carthew's exertions and services was, that he was gazetted permanently to the Quartermaster-General's Department just one day before he died. Had he been spared he would, in all human probability, have risen to distinction. The fact of his having to retrace his steps and return to the pestilential climate of Landi Kotal to take up his appointment, gave the finishing blow, and extinguished the last spark of hope of his ever leaving Afghanistan.

Captain Carthew's remains were buried at Peshawar. His wife and three daughters survive him.

MAJOR SIR P. L. N. CAVAGNARI, K.C.B., C.S.I., B.S.C.,

MINISTER AND PLENIPOTENTIARY AT THE COURT OF KABUL.

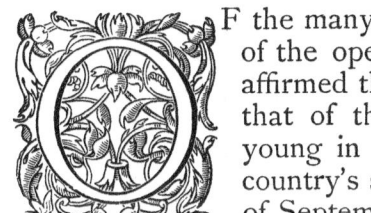F the many brilliant and promising careers cut short in the course of the operations with which these volumes deal, it may safely be affirmed that there was none more brilliant or full of promise than that of the widely-lamented subject of this memoir, who, still young in years but full of honours, rendered up his life in his country's service in the burning Residency at Kabul on the 3rd of September, 1879.

Pierre Louis Napoleon Cavagnari, the eldest son of Major the Count Adolphe Cavagnari, by his marriage with Caroline, third daughter of Hugh Lyons Montgomery, Esq., of Laurenstown House, Co. Down, Ireland, was born at Stenay, Department of the Meuse, on the 4th July, 1841. The Count Cavagnari, belonging to an ancient and noble family of Parma, served with the French forces under the first Empire, and subsequently became Private Secretary to Prince Lucien Buonaparte. His son, though born in France, was brought up from an early age in England, and received the whole of his education in the country of his adoption. After five years' study at Christ's Hospital, London, he passed into the East India Company's Service as a direct cadet, entering on a career which, from its outset, was an eventful one. No sooner had he set foot in India than he became engaged in the stern work of actual warfare. He joined the 1st Bengal Fusiliers (now the Royal Munster Fusiliers), in April, 1858, as Ensign; and serving with that regiment through the Oudh Campaign of 1858-59, was present at the capture of five guns from the Nasirabad Brigade at Shahelatganj, earning the mutiny medal. In March, 1860, he obtained his Lieutenancy. He was appointed, in 1861, to the Bengal Staff Corps, and the same year (the twentieth of his age) was gazetted Assistant-Commissioner in the Punjab, a post he continued to hold, and the duties of which he discharged with signal ability, for a period of five years. In 1866 he was given the political charge of the Kohat district, where he remained, incessantly active, until 1877, finding, in the tenure of the appointment, wide scope for his peculiar abilities, and steadily acquiring a reputation amongst his contemporaries for the skill and address with which he acquitted himself in dealing with the subtleties of frontier diplomacy. During this period of his career, besides being constantly employed in minor affairs, he acted as Chief Political Officer with the Kohat forces under General Keyes in the Bazoti expedition, and was present at the surprise and destruction of the village of Gara on the 27th February, 1869; again served, in the same capacity, in the Waziri expedition of April, 1869, and again in the blockade of the Kohat Pass Afridis in 1875-77. In the course of these operations his marked ability brought him prominently to the front, and his name was constantly on the public tongue. Up and down the frontier, from year to year, he added achievement to achievement, till his restless energy became a by-word amongst the turbulent hill-tribes, who were made by him to feel, in some instances for the first time, that their mountain fastnesses were powerless to shelter them from retribution due for their misdemeanours. For the services he rendered, he received, on several occasions, the thanks of the Secretary of State for India, the Governor-General and Council, and the Punjab Government; and on the 1st of January, 1877, on the Imperial title being proclaimed at Delhi, he was appointed a Companion of the Order of the Star of India.

In May, 1877, Major (then Captain) Cavagnari was transferred from Kohat to Peshawar; and in the Jowaki expedition of that year he was again to the fore. The Sapiri expedition of February, 1878, was, with the consent of Government, arranged and carried out by him, its object being the capture of the principal and leader of the band of robbers who, in December, 1875, had attacked and killed several native workmen near the English fort of Abazai, a raid known as the Swat Canal outrage. With this purpose in view, Cavagnari procured fifty men of the Corps of Guides, made a rapid night march, and surprised the object of his search in a mosque in Sapiri, capturing both him and his son. This feat, which was accomplished fifteen months after the perpetration of the crime which was its motive cause, has been spoken of as one of the most dashing little affairs on the frontier. Major Cavagnari immediately afterwards undertook, too, the Skhakat expedition of February, 1878, and the Utman Khel expedition of March of the same year, adding, in the conduct of them, fresh honours to the long roll already acquired by him.

Chosen to accompany Sir Neville Chamberlain on his mission to Shere Ali in September, 1878, Major Cavagnari was sent into the Khyber Pass with a small escort to ascertain the intention of the Amir relative to the reception of the embassy. The advance of the mission was stopped; and had it not been for the peculiar tact displayed by the avant courier at the interview which took place between him and the governor of Ali Musjid (Faiz Muhammad Khan), it is probable that the lives of himself and the escort who accompanied him would have been sacrificed, the governor of the fort remarking that, had the leader of the party been any other than Cavagnari, he would have fired on it.

It is an open secret that, after the rejection of the mission, a course of proceeding in reference to what had happened, fraught with great issue, originated with Major Cavagnari and was actually accepted by Government—a course which, had it been found possible to carry it into effect, might even have averted the war with which these volumes deal. The proposition was, that taking immediate action with regard to the insult offered to the Indian Government in the rejection of its ambassador, the little force at the time stationed at Jamrud should make a dash on Ali Musjid and surprise and capture it. On the eve of the attempt, however, intelligence that the garrison of the fort had been largely augmented, and that further reinforcements were then *en route* from Daka, was received. The proposed course was consequently abandoned.

On the outbreak of actual hostilities in November, 1878, Major Cavagnari accompanied the force under Sir Sam. Browne, as Chief Political Officer, into Afghanistan; and by his unrivalled knowledge of the character of the hill tribes who commanded the passes on the northern line, by the sagacity he displayed in the delicate and difficult dealings he had with them in his political capacity, and by the rapidity and dash with which he acted when the employment of force proved necessary, more than sustained his high reputation both as a soldier and a diplomatist. It was Cavagnari who, on the 22nd November, 1878, after the defeat and flight of the enemy at Ali Musjid, rode on, accompanied by a handful of Guide Cavalry, to Daka, a post beyond the northern débouchure of the Khyber Pass; and who, on the arrival of the advance guard of the column two days afterwards, had turned his time to such good account, that he was ready to tender to the General the submission of the powerful Khan of Lalpura, and to proffer the services of the head men of the villages in the Khurd Khyber: again, on the 1st December, availing himself of inter-tribal hostility as a means for inflicting punishment on the Zaka Khels, a section of the Afridi clan who had been harassing convoys and raiding on the line of communications, the unresting "Political" led a body of armed Kuki Khels, supported by mountain guns, against them, and, taking them by surprise, burned their villages, broke up their hostile combination, and was back at his post within twenty-four hours from the time of his quitting it; and when, after the death of Shere Ali, the recognition of Yakub Khan as his successor was ultimately decided on, it was Cavagnari who successfully conducted the negotiations which resulted in the treaty of Gandamak. "Although there are certain names not mentioned amongst those who are most conspicuous in the field and in council," observed the Secretary of State for India (Viscount Cranbrook) in motioning, in the House of Lords, a vote of thanks to the Army, "still I think your lordships would not feel justified in passing them over, and among them is the name of that distinguished person who negotiated the treaty with the Amir, Major Cavagnari. Before the affairs in Afghanistan, his name was not much known in England, but now it is well known for the intelligence and sagacity which enabled him to bring about the treaty of peace which in less skilful hands might have failed." In recognition of his eminent services, the subject of this allusion was subsequently created a Knight Commander of the Order of the Bath.

Selected at the close of the operations to proceed to Kabul as Envoy and Minister Plenipotentiary of the British Government to the Court of His Highness the Amir Yakub Khan, Major Cavagnari, accompanied by a small escort, made his way to the capital, reaching his destination on the 24th July, 1879. As is related elsewhere, the mission was received on its arrival with every outward manifestation of respect, although, as early as the 6th of August, signs of hostility towards it on the part of a section of the army and the people were not wanting. On that day, large bodies of turbulent soldiery, who had returned to Kabul on the previous evening from Herat, paraded the streets of the city, and manifested their dissatisfaction by beating drums to gather the people together, and abusing the Ambassador by name. A native officer of an Indian Cavalry Regiment, Ressaldar-Major Nakshband Khan, who happened at the time to be spending his furlough at one of the suburbs of Kabul, his native village, hastened to warn the Envoy of the coming storm. "Keep up your heart," the latter is reported to have responded: "dogs that bark don't bite." With earnest iteration the Ressaldar-Major urged that the danger was real and imminent. Cavagnari's reply was characteristic of the man, and of a piece with other instances of his notorious disregard of personal danger when the dignity of the Government he represented was to be upheld. "They can only kill the three or four of us here," he said quietly, "and our death will be avenged."

As time went on, the relations subsisting between the Embassy and the Amir appear to have become somewhat strained, and indications of the menacing attitude of the people to have multiplied. Notwithstanding this, no cause for immediate alarm seems to have been felt at the Residency; and even up to the last, the Viceroy of India was able to telegraph to the home Government: "All well at the Kabul Embassy." That this confidence was misplaced, the sequel disastrously proved. On the 3rd of September occurred the revolt which brought the labours of the mission, and with them the life of the subject of this memoir, to a sudden and tragical close—an episode which, from the stubborn character of the defence of the Residency against overwhelming numbers, and the heroic bravery displayed by the little band comprising the Embassy, has made a page in history which the British nation will be slow to forget. It was not until after repeated onslaughts had been made upon the building by the infuriated rabble of soldiery and townspeople that Sir Louis received his first wound, a contusion of the forehead from a half-spent rifle-ball. Concerning what immediately followed, such evidence as exists is vague and conflicting; but it would appear that, when the Residency was fired, the subject of this memoir was conveyed to another part of the building, and tended by Dr. Kelly. The last act of the drama is more clearly written. After a portion of the wall of the bath-room in which the last stand was made had been knocked away, and the assailants swarmed in hordes through the breach, Sir Louis was rendered senseless by a sword-cut from behind which clove his head, and was immediately afterwards crushed to death by portions of the burning wall and roof of the building falling in upon him. Thus was cut short the brilliant career of a soldier and diplomatist who, by his wisdom, his gallantry, his chivalry, and his humanity, had won not only the admiration but also the affection of his countrymen, and whose death has been aptly referred to as a distinct step backwards in the work of frontier progress and pacification. Endowed with an instinctive delicacy of apprehension; possessed, to an extraordinary degree, of the power of gauging relative magnitudes, and ever ready, in council, to forego a temporary advantage to secure a permanent gain; having the gift of tongues; profound in his knowledge of native character, and therefore readily able to deal with natives; holding his own life as naught where the interest or dignity of the country he represented was at stake, Sir Louis Cavagnari was a public servant who had made himself indispensable, at a critical juncture, to the Government of India, and it is not too much to say that his loss can be regarded as nothing less than a national calamity.

The news of the massacre at Kabul, which produced in England a thrill of consternation comparable only to that which followed the announcement of the disaster sustained by our arms at Isandhlwana, was telegraphed to Lady Cavagnari by the Viceroy, Lord Lytton, who, interpreting the emotion of the country, brought his message to a conclusion with the words: "Every British heart in India feels for you."

Her Majesty the Queen, telegraphing from Balmoral, expressed her sympathy with the bereaved lady in her great sorrow, referring to the death of Sir Louis as "a loss to the nation at large;" and again, in an autograph letter, condoled with her in her great affliction. In a paragraph in the "Gazette of India," the Government hastened to express its keen sense of the loss which the empire had sustained by the tragic and premature death of so able a public servant. The Chancellor of the Exchequer (Sir Stafford Northcote), the first member of the Ministry to publicly comment on the deplorable news, spoke of the Envoy in these terms: " It is impossible that England can fully appreciate the very serious loss we have sustained by the death of one so eminent, so worthy of our gratitude, as that distinguished man Sir Louis Cavagnari." Many more public utterances, denoting a feeling widespread as it was deep, were made on the same melancholy theme; and with a quotation from one of them—a speech of Lord Lytton's, delivered at Calcutta—as interpreting the feeling of all, we may fitly close this brief memoir. "The high abilities of Sir Louis Cavagnari," observed the Viceroy, " were known to all by the valuable results of their successful exertion in the service and for the interests of India; and by all, I believe, they were ungrudgingly acknowledged. For rarely has any man, in attaining so rapidly to public eminence, provoked so little private jealousy or personal animosity on the part of his less successful contemporaries. But to me, his immediate chief, throughout a period of much difficulty and anxiety, special opportunities were given to appreciate, not only the steadfast courage, the foresight and sagacity, the rare fertility of resource which marked his public service, but also the nobility, gentleness, and modesty, the manly unselfishness and endearing charm of his personal character. By the premature death of Sir Louis Cavagnari, India has suffered an irreparable national loss."

CAPTAIN D. T. CHISHOLM,

59TH (2ND NOTTINGHAMSHIRE) REGIMENT.

THE subject of this notice was the fourth son of the late Rev. Charles Chisholm, J.P., Rector of Southchurch, Essex, Rural Dean, Chaplain to the Duke of York; was grandson of the Rev. Cooke Tylden Pattenson, of Storden Park, Kent, Rector of Ulsted and Frinsted, in the same county; and was a cousin of the Chisholm of Erchless Castle, Inverness.

Duncan Tylden Chisholm was born on the 14th June, 1832. After serving for a time in the East Kent Militia, he was gazetted, in April, 1861, to an ensigncy by purchase in the 3rd West India Regiment, and did duty with that corps for a period of four years in the West Indies and on the West Coast of Africa, being promoted Lieutenant in October, 1864.

In January, 1865, he exchanged into the 59th Foot, in which regiment he remained till the day of his death. He served with it in the suppression of the Fenian riots of 1866-1867, and in Ceylon and the East Indies from 1867 to 1878. From February, 1870, to May, 1871, he acted as Paymaster to the Karachi Depôt.

Accompanying the regiment on active service into Afghanistan in the autumn of 1878 as Paymaster, he took part with it in the advance on Kandahar, and in the subsequent advance on and occupation of Kalat-i-Ghilzai. In July, 1879, while at Kandahar, he was stricken down with typhoid fever, to which disease he fell a victim, after a few days' illness, on the 30th of the month, sincerely regretted by all who knew him. He was buried in the old cemetery of the city, where a handsome tombstone erected to his memory by his brother officers, marks his grave.

Captain Chisholm was twice married. He leaves a widow (Mary, daughter of Mr. John Gordon Lillie, of Aberdeen) and two sons to mourn his loss.

LIEUTENANT R. T. CHUTE,

66TH (BERKSHIRE) REGIMENT.

RICHARD TREVOR CHUTE, who was killed in action at Maiwand on the 27th July, 1880, was the youngest son of the late Richard Chute, Esq., D.L., of Chute Hall, Co. Kerry, and the Honourable Mrs. Chute, daughter of the late Lord Ventry; and was a nephew of General Sir Trevor Chute, K.C.B. He was born in Kerry on the 17th September, 1856, was educated at Wimbledon School, and in 1875 joined the Cavan Militia, from which, in October, 1877, he received his commission as 2nd Lieutenant in the 66th Regiment. He embarked, shortly afterwards, for India to join the Headquarters, and after serving for a period at Kolaba, Haidarabad, and Karachi, he received, in June 1879, his lieutenancy. He was subsequently appointed Acting Quartermaster to the regiment, in which capacity he served till the day of his death.

On the 66th being ordered to the front, in February, 1880, Chute proceeded with it in its march through the Bolan, and shared with it at Kandahar the duties which fell to its lot. He took part, in the first week of July, in the advance of Burrows' Brigade to the Halmand, and during the action in the neighbourhood of Girishk on the 14th of the month his company was one of those detailed to guard the camp on the left bank of the river. In the disastrous battle of Maiwand on the 27th, he fell fighting gallantly against the overwhelming numbers of the enemy, being one of the little band who sold their lives so dearly in the garden where the last desperate stand was made.

BREV. LIEUT.-COLONEL W. H. J. CLARKE,

72ND (DUKE OF ALBANY'S OWN HIGHLANDERS).

WILLIAM HENRY JAMES CLARKE, who died at Allahabad on the 7th April, 1880, from illness contracted on service in the field, was the son of the late Colonel W. H. H. J. Clarke, 53rd Regiment. He was born on the 14th July, 1833. After preliminary education, he entered the Royal Military College, Sandhurst, and having completed the usual course of study in that institution, was gazetted, in August, 1851, to an ensigncy in the 53rd Foot, then stationed at Mhow. He served with that regiment until 1860, and was present with it in the Indian Mutiny at the actions of Chutra, Gopalganj, Khodaganj, and the entry into Fatehgarh; the storming and capture of Mianganj, the siege and capture of Lucknow, the affair of Kursi, the passage of the Gogra, at Faizabad, on the 25th November, 1858, the action of Tulsipur, and several minor affairs. For his services on these occasions he was mentioned in despatches and received the medal with clasp. In 1860 he obtained his company, and in the following year exchanged into the 72nd Highlanders, with which distinguished corps he served continuously till immediately prior to his death.

The regiment was ordered home in 1866, and was quartered at various stations in Great Britain and Ireland for some five years, at the expiration of which it again returned to India. Eighteen months afterwards (June, 1872) Captain Clarke succeeded to a Majority consequent on the promotion of Colonel Page to the Brigade Staff, and in 1877, in due course, became senior Major of the regiment, obtaining also the rank of Brevet Lieut.-Colonel in November, 1878.

In October, 1878, the 72nd Highlanders was one of the first regiments ordered to the front in view of the impending hostilities with Afghanistan. On arriving at Kohat from Sialkot, at which place the 72nd had been for some time quartered, the right wing of the regiment was detailed for the advance of General Roberts' Division into the enemy's country, while the left wing, under Colonel Clarke, remained temporarily at Kohat. In January, 1879, the subject of this notice proceeded in command of his half battalion to take part in the Khost Valley Expedition, and was present at the capture of Matun. For the soldierly qualities he displayed, and for his capability for command in the field, he gained for himself the respect of all ranks, as well as the approbation of the General Officer Commanding. The left wing rejoined the head-quarters at Peiwar about the end of March, and shortly afterwards the regiment proceeded to Ali Khel, where it remained until after the conclusion of the peace of Gandamak. On the renewal of hostilities in the autumn of 1879 in consequence of the massacre of the Embassy, Colonel Clarke, on whom the command of the regiment had devolved in the absence on furlough of Colonel Brownlow, advanced with Sir Frederick Roberts' force over the Shutargardan towards Kabul. At the battle of Charasiab, on the 6th October, during which his horse was shot under him, he displayed great coolness and personal gallantry. He was subsequently present with the regiment at the occupation of Kabul and the Bala Hissar, throughout the investment of Sherpur, and in the attack on the Asmai heights.

About the middle of December, 1879, Colonel Clarke's health, undermined by the vicissitudes and hardships of field service, began to fail, and later in the month he was seized with a sharp attack of pneumonia, followed by other severe and dangerous symptoms. It was therefore deemed absolutely necessary to invalid him to India with a view to his ultimately proceeding to England, as the only means of obtaining his restoration to health—a hope, unfortunately, never to be realized. Under great difficulties he reached Bengal, but while proceeding down country towards Bombay by easy stages, he fell into so precarious a condition at Allahabad that he was obliged to remain there, and shortly afterwards died at that place, on the 7th April, 1880.

By the death of Lieut.-Colonel Clarke the army lost a most distinguished and gallant soldier, and one who, had he been spared, would have doubtless added to the high reputation he had so justly earned throughout the service, especially among those with whom he was more intimately associated. His interest in his regiment was always of the greatest, and was only equalled by his anxiety and jealousy for its honour and good name, to uphold which none strove harder than he.

Lieut.-Colonel Clarke married, in 1868, Laura, daughter of the late Herbert Taylor Lewis, Esq., 40th Regiment, and granddaughter of the late Sir E. Lacon, Bart., M.P. for Great Yarmouth.

LIEUT.-COLONEL R. S. CLELAND,

9TH (QUEEN'S ROYAL) LANCERS.

ROBERT STEWART CLELAND was the third son of the late Samuel Cleland, Esq., of Stormont Castle, in the County of Down, and grandson of the Rev. John Cleland, Precentor in the Cathedral of Armagh and Rector of Killevey. He was born on the 24th June, 1840, and was educated at Eton and Harrow, subsequently being prepared for examination at Sandhurst by the Rev. A. Morrison, of Wotton Bassett. Gazetted in July, 1857, to a cornetcy in the 7th Dragoon Guards, he embarked, a few months later, for India. After the suppression of the Mutiny, he returned to England in charge of time-expired men; and exchanging into the 9th Lancers within a few months from the date of his arrival, remained in that regiment, serving in successive grades and in various parts of the world, till the day of his death.

Colonel Cleland was in command of the 9th Lancers at Sialkot in the autumn of 1878, when, in view of the impending outbreak of hostilities with Afghanistan the regiment was ordered to Taru, to form part of the 2nd (Reserve) Division of the Peshawar Valley Field Force. On the forward concentration of the northern force, the regiment was moved into the Khyber, and there shared the duties connected with guarding the communications which devolved upon the troops under General Maude's command. About the time of the signing of the treaty of peace at Gandamak Colonel Cleland fell ill, and was invalided to Murree, from whence, shortly afterwards, he proceeded to the Chini Hills.

On the renewel of hostilities in the autumn of 1879 the 9th Lancers, then at Sialkot, were ordered to the front, to form part of the Kabul Field Force under Sir Frederick Roberts. Colonel Cleland, though still suffering, hastened up with all speed to resume his command. From the effects of making two long marches daily, his pony fell lame. After proceeding twenty-eight miles on foot in one day, and fifteen the next morning, he reached Simla, and eventually rejoined the regiment at Jhelum.

The 9th Lancers arrived at Kabul in the first days of November, 1878, and a month afterwards took part in the critical events which marked the close of the year. At the action of Killa Kazi on the 11th December, while gallantly leading the cavalry charge against overwhelming numbers of the enemy during the retirement, Colonel Cleland was dangerously wounded. Becoming unconscious, he was placed in a dhoolie, which was subsequently abandoned by its bearers, with the guns, in a watercourse; he was, however, saved from the approaching enemy by the gallantry of Serjeant-Major Young of the regiment, who, finding that he did not reply when spoken to, dismounted, and dragged him out of the litter into the water, the contact with which revived him. The sergeant offered him his horse, which Colonel Cleland refused. A few moments afterwards he managed to seize the bridle of an animal galloping past with empty saddle, and was assisted to mount. Ordering Young to collect and lead the scattered men who were by this time coming up, and taking a sergeant (Finn) to accompany him, he started for Sherpur, eight miles distant. His elbow-joint had been shattered by a sword-cut, and a bullet with which he had been struck was still in his side. That he managed to reach the cantonments over such country as lay before him, speaks of itself for his heroic courage and endurance.

During the time Colonel Cleland remained at Kabul, he was most kindly and carefully tended. When he was able to be moved he was taken by easy stages in a dhoolie to Jamrud, accompanied by his devoted friend Captain Stewart Mackenzie, 9th Lancers, who asked and obtained the necessary permission from Sir F. Roberts. It was found necessary, however, to halt for some little time at Fort Battye and at Gandamak on the journey down, in consequence of alarming attacks of dysentery coming on. From Jamrud, where the road for wheel traffic commences, he was driven to Rawal Pindi, in Sir F. Maude's carriage, reaching that officer's house on the night of the 7th April, in an apparently almost dying condition. After a fortnight's rest and tender nursing, he became, however, sufficiently recovered to bear the journey to Sir F. Maude's cottage at Murree, the nearest hill station. Here he improved rapidly till the 15th June, when erysipelas appeared in his wounded arm. From this time he gradually sank, and eventually died, tenderly nursed to the last by Lady Maude, on the 7th August.

In a Divisional Order bearing date 12th August, 1880, Sir Frederick Maude wrote with reference to the death of Colonel Cleland (whom—to use his own words—he mourned as a brother) as follows: "Not only have the ever-glorious 9th Lancers lost a gallant soldier worthy of being at the head of such a distinguished regiment, but the Army and country an officer whose sole aim was to do his duty." And in a Field Force Order, issued by Sir Frederick Roberts on the same melancholy occasion, the following words occur: "By the death of Lieut.-Colonel Cleland, Sir F. Roberts, in common with a large number of officers and soldiers, has lost a valued friend, whilst Her Majesty's Army has been deprived of the services of a most promising and gallant officer."

Much beloved by his men, to whose welfare and comfort he was devoted, and in each and all of whom he took a strong personal interest, Colonel Cleland will long be mourned in the ranks of the 9th Lancers, not only as a just and appreciative commanding officer, but also as a warm-hearted and sympathetic friend.

LIEUT. DUNCAN COLE, STAFF CORPS,

JACOB'S RIFLES.

HE subject of this memoir, who was born on the 8th May, 1859, was the second son of Charles D. Cole, Esq., Retired Paymaster of the late Indian Navy, and some time Consul and Agent for the Government of India at Jiddah, Red Sea; and was descended in the maternal line from the late Rear-Admiral William Holt. He was educated at the Royal Naval School, New Cross, and from thence proceeded, in July, 1876, to Sandhurst. At the expiration of the usual course at the College, he passed out with a first-class certificate, and was gazetted to the 83rd Foot. Proceeding to join that regiment, then in Bombay, he was informed, on arriving in India, that several appointments on probation had been made to the Bombay and Madras Staff Corps direct from Sandhurst; and was almost immediately attached for duty to the 1st Grenadiers. On passing the examination in native languages—which he did several months before the expiration of the allotted time, and for his success was highly complimented by the President of the Committee—he was temporarily attached to H.M. 15th Regiment. A few months afterwards he was again transferred to the 14th Bombay Infantry, with which regiment he proceeded to Aden. Almost immediately after arriving at that station, however, he was yet once again transferred—this time to fill a vacancy in Jacob's Rifles, then on field service in Afghanistan. He joined that regiment—his connection with which, alas! was destined to be brief—at Kandahar in the month of May, 1880, and accompanied it to Girishk in the following July. In the fatal encounter with the enemy at Maiwand on the 27th of that month, he commanded two companies of the left wing of the regiment under Major Iredell, which, early in the engagement, were sent to cover the left flank of the Grenadiers. It was at the moment before the two companies under his command—after working over ground absolutely denuded of cover, and being exposed, after four hours' continuous fighting, to the fierce rush of the encircling hordes of the enemy—were driven in, that Lieutenant Cole fell, killed by a round shot, at the same time that two of the native officers out of the three with him were wounded.

Duncan Cole was not the first of his race who has fought in his country's service, his father having been present in the Chinese War in 1839-42, and the Burmese War in 1852 ; and four of his uncles in the maternal line having individually or collectively fought in the Crimean War and the Indian Mutiny, in addition to both the wars last named.

LIEUT.-COLONEL J. J. COLLINS,

2ND BATTALION, 60TH (KING'S ROYAL RIFLE CORPS).

JAMES JOSEPH COLLINS, who died of dysentery at Nari Bank, near Sibi, on the 8th October, 1880, was the fourth son of William Collins, of Knaresborough, Yorkshire, Esquire, and was born at Knaresborough, February 3rd, 1837. He was gazetted Ensign, by purchase, to the 60th Royal Rifles, August 25th, 1854, at the early age of seventeen years, and was posted to the 2nd Battalion, in which he obtained his Lieutenancy, 23rd March, 1855. He shortly afterwards joined the Head-Quarters at the Cape, remaining there until the close of 1857, when he returned to England on private affairs. Soon after his arrival in this country, he found himself posted to the 4th Battalion of the regiment, on its formation; and in this battalion he obtained his company, by purchase, 19th July, 1859. He accompanied it to North America in 1861, and returned to England with it on the completion of its tour of Foreign Service in Canada and New Brunswick. He was gazetted Brevet-Major, 5th July, 1872, and promoted, May 24th, 1873, to a Majority in the 3rd Battalion, which had recently returned from India. On the 21st August, 1878, he was appointed, as Lieutenant-Colonel, to the command of the 2nd (his original) Battalion, then serving in India, which he proceeded to join, reaching India too late to accompany it in its march to Afghanistan, where it had, in the meantime, been ordered. Immediately on landing he hastened up country, and in February, 1879, took over, at Kandahar, the command of this fine battalion, which he found in splendid order and in a most efficient state, and which he commanded with pride during the campaign of 1879-1880.

Colonel Collins remained at Kandahar during the occupation of that city by Sir Donald Stewart's army, and accompanied it, in the spring of 1880, in its advance on Ghazni and Kabul, taking part in the actions fought at Ahmed Khel, on the 11th, and at Arzu on the 23rd April, and was favourably mentioned in despatches for his services on these occasions.

After a short stay at Kabul, the 2nd Battalion of the 60th was one of the three European Regiments selected to accompany Sir Frederick Roberts in his now historical march to the relief of Kandahar, and was attached to the 3rd Brigade

(Macgregor's), which formed the reserve at the Battle of Kandahar, where Ayub Khan's army was totally routed. For his services Colonel Collins was again mentioned in despatches.

The battalion was now ordered to return to India with Macgregor's Brigade, by way of the Marri country; and a few days after leaving Quetta, while marching through the Bolan Pass, Colonel Collins, for the first time in a service of upwards of twenty-six years, found himself, on the 2nd October, placed on the sick list with what at first appeared to be a slight attack of dysentery. The fatigues and hardships of the campaign, assisted by the bad water supplied on the line of march, had undermined his constitution. He suffered so severely from the heat and the shaking of the dhooli in which he accompanied his battalion through the Bolan Pass, that he sank quite suddenly and unexpectedly at Nari Bank, near Sibi, on the 8th October, after an illness of six days, to the regret and consternation of his battalion, officers and men, by whom no commanding officer was ever more beloved and respected.

On the day following his decease, he was followed by his battalion to the grave, and buried at Sibi with military honours. Subsequently his remains were, at the urgent wish of his widow and relations, exhumed and conveyed to England, where they found a last resting-place in the churchyard of Leatherhead, Surrey, on the 3rd February, 1881, by a curious coincidence the forty-fourth anniversary of his birth.

The following extract from a notice, headed " In memoriam," that appeared in the " Celer et Audax Gazette," of the 3rd Battalion, 60th Rifles, shows how highly Colonel Collins was esteemed in the regiment :—

"We regret greatly having to record the death of Lieut.-Colonel Collins, from dysentery at Sibi, Beloochistan, on the 8th October. . . . . . Most of us knew him well, and deeply shall we mourn his loss. He was a good soldier, and a kind-hearted, steady friend ; ever ready to give advice to those who sought it, and always striving to promote the well-being and comfort of his brother officers and of the men under his command. And now on his way home after months of toil and hardship and victory, has a fell disease carried off one with whom we have lived on terms of intimacy for twenty-six years, without ever hearing from his lips one unkind word. We cannot better perpetuate his memory than by striving to follow his example."

Lieut.-Colonel Collins married, in 1874, Constance Edith Emma Utterton, the youngest daughter of the late Bishop of Guildford, who, with three young daughters, survives him.

BT. MAJOR JOHN COOK, V.C., STAFF CORPS,

5TH GOORKHA REGT. (HAZARA GOORKHA BATTALION).

"HER MAJESTY has lost the services of an officer who would, had he been spared, have risen to the highest honours of his profession." Such are the words used by Sir Frederick Roberts in his Divisional Order of December, 1879, in announcing the death of the subject of this memoir.

John Cook was born at Edinburgh in August, 1843, and was the second son of Alexander Shank Cook, a well-known Scottish Advocate and Sheriff; and grandson of George Cook, D.D., who was for many years leader of the moderate party in the Church of Scotland. He received his early education at the Edinburgh Academy, and subsequently proceeded to Addiscombe, where he was among the last of the cadets who studied there, and who entered the college under the old nomination system. The boy's future profession was decided at a very early age, his father having received a nomination to Addiscombe for him when he was only eleven years old.

At the age of seventeen years he went to India, and soon after his arrival was posted to the 3rd Sikhs, with which regiment he went through the Umbeyla campaign. He was mentioned in despatches for his distinguished conduct during the operations, and was specially thanked by his Colonel for his gallantry in leading a very effectual bayonet charge. In 1868 he took part in the Hazara expedition. For these services he received the India medal with two clasps.

After ten years' service he took the furlough to which he was entitled, and spent a year at home, returning to India in 1871. In 1872 he was promoted to the rank of Captain, and in 1873 was transferred to the 5th Goorkhas as Wing Commander. In 1877 he took another year's furlough, returning to India in 1878. When the Afghan War broke out, the 5th Goorkhas joined the Kuram Field Force under General Roberts, and during the whole war followed the fortunes of that distinguished commander. At the battle of the Peiwar Kotal on the 2nd December, 1878, this regiment had the honour of leading the attack, and it was on this occasion that Captain Cook won his Victoria Cross. After the first stockade of the enemy had been brilliantly carried, he "charged out of the entrenchment"—

to quote the record of the incident given in the number of the "London Gazette" which announces the bestowal of the decoration—"with such impetuosity that the enemy broke and fled. Perceiving at the close of the *mêlée* the danger of Major Galbraith, Assistant Adjutant-General, Kuram Field Force, who was in personal conflict with an Afghan soldier, Captain Cook distracted his attention to himself, and aiming a sword-cut which the Durani avoided, sprang upon him and grasping his throat, grappled with him. They both fell to the ground. The Durani, a most powerful man, still endeavouring to use his rifle, seized Captain Cook's arm in his teeth, until the struggle was ended by the man being shot through the head." A fortnight afterwards he again distinguished himself by the gallantry he displayed whilst in command of a wing of the 5th Goorkhas in the Sapiri Defile on the 13th December. For nearly five hours the regiment maintained a rear-guard fight over most difficult ground with a bold and active enemy thoroughly acquainted with the locality; and though the two officers with him—Captains Goad and Powell—were mortally wounded, he succeeded, with Major Fitz Hugh, in beating off the Mangals and in bringing the convoy safely into camp.

When the Kabul insurrection broke out in the autumn of 1879, the 5th Goorkhas were among the troops who accompanied General Roberts in his march to the scene of the massacre. At the battle of Charasiab on the 6th October, Captain Cook, in command of two companies of the regiment, again on two occasions performed signal service—firstly, while forming part of the reinforcement of the flanking company of the attacking columns operating on the enemy's centre; and secondly in the assault on the main ridge. A sketch of him at the head of his gallant little men in the act of carrying one of the heights appeared in the "Graphic" of the 6th December, 1879.

While quartered in the Bala Hissar the 5th Goorkhas lost many men by the exploding of the powder magazine. In a letter describing the occurrence, Captain Cook referred to it as being the most appalling sight he had ever witnessed, and spoke highly of the gallantry of our soldiers in entering the burning building and rescuing their injured comrades. Shortly afterwards he had the pleasure of meeting his younger brother, Lieutenant Walter Cook, 3rd Sikhs, when that officer's regiment entered Kabul after its spirited defence of the Shutargardan Pass; and the two, as may be imagined, keenly appreciated each other's society during the short time that elapsed before the beginning of the stern work with which the year drew to a close. On the 11th of December, detachments of the 5th Goorkhas and 3rd Sikhs were fighting shoulder to shoulder, and more than once the brothers were side by side. On that day Walter Cook received a ball in the chest which came within an inch of touching his lungs; and barely twenty-four hours afterwards, John received his death wound.

The following is an extract from a letter of a brother officer of Major Cook's (the latter, it should be mentioned, had received brevet promotion in recognition of his services a few weeks before his death) written to Major Cook's sister, and giving the particulars of the manner in which he fell:—

"On the 12th of this month our regiment was ordered by General Macpherson to storm a high conical hill about three miles from this city, on which the enemy was strongly posted, and we were supported by three companies of John's old regiment, the 3rd Sikhs Infantry. John led the advance with two companies of our regiment, and we soon came under the enemy's fire, which occasioned a few casualties among the men. We got about half-way up the hill, but the enemy's fire became so galling that it was found impossible with our small numbers to get on any farther, and it was determined that we should take shelter under some rocks and wait for reinforcements from cantonments. Whilst lying under these rocks, your brother observed large bodies of the enemy coming up a spur to help those already on the top of the conical hill, and he went back about fifty yards to inform Colonel Money, of the 3rd Sikhs, who was in command of us, of what he had seen. No one could show the smallest part of his body from behind the rocks without having several bullets fired at him; and in going back to Colonel Money a heavy fire was kept up on John, but he escaped untouched. In returning, however, he had to run the same gauntlet, and just as he reached the rock under which we were lying, a bullet struck him, passing through the bone of the left leg just below the knee."

Major Cook received immediate surgical attendance on the field, but nearly twenty-four hours elapsed before he could be conveyed into shelter. For two days his wound did well, but mortification then set in, and on the 19th of the month (December, 1879) he died.

In Major Cook the Punjab Frontier Force lost one of its representative men, and the Indian Army an officer it could ill spare. His name—to quote one of his brother officers—was synonymous with all that is true and brave and chivalrous. He was modest to a degree. In a letter written to one of his sisters after the battle of the Peiwar, in which he tells of his having been recommended for the Victoria Cross, he adds, with characteristic generosity, "I think the dead deserve it most." Such was the disposition which endeared him to a wide circle of relatives and friends who watched with interest and admiration his progress in the profession he had adopted, and who, while mourning his loss, will never cease to be proud of his memory. It is some consolation to them to feel that, in the words of Sir Frederick Roberts, "he ended a noble career in a manner worthy even of his great name for bravery."

SURGEON-MAJOR HENRY CORNISH, F.R.C.S.,

ARMY MEDICAL DEPARTMENT.

ENRY CORNISH, an officer who, after performing most valuable service in the Afghan War, was mortally wounded at Majuba Hill, Transvaal, on the 27th February, 1881, was the second son of Charles Henry Cornish, F.R.C.S.E. He was born on the 4th June, 1844, at Taunton, and was educated at King William's College, Isle of Man. After attending as a pupil at the Taunton and Somerset Hospital, and passing through the curriculum of the University and Surgical Schools at Edinburgh, and Netley, he was appointed, in 1866, Assistant-Surgeon to Her Majesty's Forces, and was sent almost immediately afterwards to Mauritius, in consequence of an outbreak of malarious fever in the island. In 1868 he proceeded to the Cape in charge of invalids; and after reaching his destination was detailed to, and did duty with, the force engaged in quelling the Kaffir outbreak on the Orange River.

In 1872 he returned to England, and was appointed Assistant-Surgeon to the 10th Royal Hussars, then stationed at Colchester. On the embarkation of the regiment for India in 1873, he accompanied it; and was with it at Delhi at the time of H.R.H. the Prince of Wales' grand review of the army. In October, 1878, he was gazetted Surgeon-Major.

He accompanied the 10th Hussars in its advance into Afghanistan after the outbreak of hostilities with that country in the autumn of 1878; and was with the two squadrons of the regiment in the disastrous fording of the Kabul River, when forty-seven troopers and one officer were drowned. It is affirmed that he owed his own safety on this occasion mainly to the experience he had acquired in former days whilst serving in Africa.

In June, 1879, he took part in the return of the 10th Hussars and the 4th Battalion Rifle Brigade through the Khyber Pass, to India, "which," to quote words used in General Orders by the Commander-in-Chief, "with cholera on the line of March, excessive heat, entire absence of shade, and a scarcity of water . . . . must be considered one of the most trying operations of the war." For the services he rendered on this occasion he was specially commended; and in a Regimental

Order bearing date the 15th July, 1879, Colonel Newdigate, Commanding 4th Battalion Rifle Brigade, says: "The Officer Commanding cannot allow Surgeon-Major Cornish to leave the battalion without expressing the thanks of all belonging to it, for the unremitting attention, and care, by him of the sick, during the late very trying march."

He continued with the 10th Hussars till near Christmas, 1880, when, having been nearly eight years in India, he decided to avail himself of permission to return to England. Just after he had completed his arrangements for the voyage, however, he received on the 30th December a telegram from Colonel Luck, 15th Hussars, intimating that the regiment was ordered to the Cape, and expressing a hope that Cornish would accompany it The latter, ever ready where active service was concerned, instantly wired back, "Delighted to go with you."

On the 2nd June, 1881, he embarked at Bombay with the 15th in the "Euphrates," and landing in February at Durban, marched to the camp at Mount Prospect. He was there attached to the 92nd (Gordon Highlanders), and subsequently accompanied that distinguished regiment in Sir George Colley's ill-fated occupation of the Majuba Mountain. It was in the retreat, whilst, assisted by the Piper of the 92nd, he was in the act of carrying a wounded man of the regiment, whose bearer had fled, that he was mortally wounded, "fearlessly," as the Surgeon-General reports, "doing his duty."

He was removed to O'Neil's Farm, where he died on the 1st March, 1881, and was buried in the cemetery at Mount Prospect, in which the remains of Sir George Colley and Commander Romilly have also found a last resting-place. Thus after nearly sixteen years of foreign service, closed the career of a gallant officer, beloved by all who knew him.

LIEUT.-COLONEL G. B. CRISPIN, STAFF CORPS,

4TH BOMBAY N.I. (RIFLES).

GEORGE BELL CRISPIN, who died at sea from illness contracted whilst on field service in Afghanistan, was the son of the late General Crispin of the Bombay Army, and nephew of the late Captain William Crispin, R.N., A.D.C. He entered the service in the year 1852. Serving with the 4th Bombay Rifles in the Persian Campaign of 1856-57, he was present at the landing at Hallelah Bay and surrender of Bushire (for which he received the medal with clasp) and was subsequently employed for some time as Postmaster to the Forces. At the close of the Persian Campaign he proceeded to the Punjab, and served on the North-Western Frontier for many years with the 2nd, 3rd, and 5th Cavalry Regiments. During this period, when doing duty at Bhawalpur, where he was the only European officer, he succeeded in suppressing the mutiny that broke out at Ahmadpur, thirty-two miles distant; the troops under his command consisting of two companies of the 4th Sikhs, and a troop of the 2nd Punjab Cavalry. For the services he rendered on this occasion he received the thanks of Colonel Minchin, the Political Agent of Bhawalpur. Together with most of the troops, he suffered severely from fever contracted on the expedition. He subsequently returned to the Bombay Presidency, and after doing duty with the 28th and 13th Regiments, was appointed Wing-Officer of his own corps, the 4th Rifles. He commanded two companies of the regiment in the suppression of the riots in Bombay, and was thanked for his services on that occasion by General Gell, commanding the division.

Colonel Crispin left Karachi with the 4th Bombay Rifles as second in command on its receiving orders to proceed, in February, 1880, on field service to Afghanistan. He remained in command of two companies on detachment in the Bolan for nearly four months, being the only European officer during that time stationed in the Pass. At the expiration of that period he proceeded by forced marches to Quetta, from thence convoying ammunition and treasure to Kandahar, where he arrived safely only the day before the investment of the city commenced. After serving with the regiment throughout the siege, he took part with it in the victory gained by Sir Frederick Roberts over Ayub Khan's army on the 1st September.

From the hard work and exposure he underwent previous to and during the siege, his health now became greatly impaired. Though he continued for a time to set a bright example by his untiring zeal, he was, at last, having become completely prostrated, compelled to proceed to Europe on medical certificate. The change of scene and climate came, unfortunately, too late to repair his wasted strength, and he died at sea during the voyage home, between Aden and Suez, on the 24th October, 1880.

Colonel Crispin leaves a wife and three children to bitterly mourn his loss, and many relations and sincere friends, by whom his memory will always be held in the highest esteem.

CAPTAIN E. W. H. CROFTON,

4TH BATTALION, 60TH (KING'S ROYAL RIFLE CORPS).

EDWARD WALTER HOME CROFTON, who died of cholera at Landi Kotal, Afghanistan, on the 19th October, 1879, was the only son of the late Colonel E. W. Crofton, C.B., and Frances Amelia, daughter of John Home, Esq., his wife, now one of the residents of Hampton Court Palace. He was born on the 12th May, 1842, and was educated at Woolwich. Gazetted, in June, 1861, to an ensigncy in the 2nd Battalion, 60th Rifles, he served for a time at the Depôt at Winchester. In May, 1865, he became Lieutenant by purchase, and two years afterwards embarked with the battalion for India. On his arrival in Bengal (November, 1867) he was placed by the late Brigadier-General Buchanan, R.A., in command of the company of local Infantry at Fort William—an appointment which he held, and the important duties of which he carried out to the General's satisfaction, till he was invalided home in the summer of 1869. Throughout the drill season of 1867 and 1868 he acted as Orderly Officer on all brigade field days, and at all inspections, and acquitted himself, according to the testimony of the General, with zeal and ability. For some time, too, during this period of his Indian service, he performed the duties of Assistant Musketry Instructor in the battalion in a manner which evoked the commendation of his Colonel.

After spending some months in England, Crofton again embarked for India to join his regiment. Proceeding with drafts under Colonel Forde, R.A., to Bombay in H.M.S. "Crocodile" and "Malabar," he acted during the voyage out as Adjutant of the Troops, and for the assistance he rendered was favourably recommended. Rejoining his regiment in the Punjab, he became its Musketry Instructor in January, 1871, and during a three years' incumbency of that appointment, "contributed greatly," in the words of his Commanding Officer, "to the very fair position the battalion held."

In July, 1873, he was promoted to a company in the 4th Battalion, which he joined in England a few months afterwards. During the period of its home service, he held the appointment of Deputy Assistant Adjutant and Quartermaster-General in the Western District, and during his tenure of the office the ability he displayed again caused him to be singled out for commendation. He returned with the battalion to India in the autumn of 1876, and after serving for two years at Agra, was appointed, by the Governor-General, Adjutant of the newly-raised Agra and Masuri Volunteer Corps, a post he was eminently qualified to fulfil. At this time he was in possession of a first-class Hythe certificate (Musketry), had been through a four months' course (at the School of Military Engineering, Chatham) of Reconnaissance and Field Works, Engineering, and Pontooning, had passed the Lower Standard examination in Hindi and Persian, and had been acting Staff-Officer at the Landaur Depôt.

Captain Crofton had long been eagerly desirous of seeing active service. On the second outbreak of hostilities in Afghanistan in the autumn of 1879, he volunteered for the front, and was appointed extra Aide-de-Camp to General Bright, whom he joined at Peshawar, and subsequently accompanied to Landi Kotal. His term of service was destined to be, alas! of but short duration. On the 18th October he was seized with cholera, to which fell disease he succumbed on the following day, to the deep regret of all who knew him.

Captain Crofton's memory is perpetuated by a monument erected over his grave in the little cemetery at Landi Kotal by his brother-officers as a token of the esteem and love in which they held him; and further testimony of his worth is given by General Bright, who laments that in him he had lost a most distinguished Staff-Officer, and one who had endeared himself to all by his unselfishness and great consideration for others.

Sprung from a family of soldiers, he was not the first of his race and name who distinguished himself in Her Majesty's service. His father, Colonel Crofton, C.B., R.A., besides serving in the first Carlist War (for which he received the Order of the First Class for San Ternado), commanded the Osmanli Horse Artillery at Scutari in 1855, and was appointed Brigadier-General in the China War of 1860, and Colonel on the Staff at Malta, where he died; and his grandfather, Captain Crofton, served as Brigade-Major to Sir Colin Halkett, and was slain in June, 1815, at Waterloo.

CAPTAIN G. M. CRUICKSHANK,

ROYAL (LATE BOMBAY) ENGINEERS.

EORGE MACDONALD CRUICKSHANK was the third son of the late Major James John Farquharson Cruickshank, Bombay Engineers. He was educated at Wimbledon School, and obtained his commission from Addiscombe at the age of sixteen years, following in the footsteps of his two elder brothers, who had both joined the corps previously. Shortly after his arrival in India, he was employed in the Public Works Department, and remained so till he was ordered to join the Field Force at Kandahar in 1880.

Captain Cruickshank was appointed to take charge of the Sappers detailed to General Brooke's attacking columns for the ill-fated sortie from that city on the 16th August, 1880, and in this capacity the duty devolved on him of forcing, one after another, the gateways in the houses of the village of Deh Khwaja, being all the time exposed to a plunging fire from the roofs of the adjoining houses. Finally, in breaking into one courtyard, he was severely wounded and became unconscious. Immediately on hearing of his fall, General Brooke, who had by this time worked his way through the village to its northern outskirts, made a gallant effort to save him. He succeeded in getting him into a dhoolie, and conveying him some fifty yards beyond the village walls. At this point the dhoolie-bearers appear to have fled. "Then General Brooke"—thus runs the touching report given by one of Cruickshank's friends—"would not leave him, and they died side by side."

The following extract is taken from a letter written by Colonel Hills, C.B., R.E., from Kandahar, bearing date 10th October, 1880:—

"Poor Cruickshank well deserved the Victoria Cross over and over again, and would, had he survived, certainly have been recommended for it. His pluck, readiness of resource, and quiet energy, won him many friends, and had he been spared, his services would have been rewarded, for he came splendidly to the front on every occasion.

"Quiet, but invariably in the very front of everything, wherever any dangerous work was to be done, one found him there, keeping the men at their work by his thorough pluck and coolness. No man was better known or more respected than he was.

"When we heard he had been left behind, all the Wing Engineers went out to try and get his body in, but he was too far away from the walls, and too close to the village to get there. On the first opportunity we went out, and buried him under a green tree near where he fell, service being read over him and General Brooke and others by the Rev. Mr. Cane, who was a personal friend of his. No one respected him more than I did." .

Captain Cruickshank married Sophie, daughter of Major Reynolds, Bombay Staff Corps, who predeceased him. He leaves issue four children.

CAPTAIN F. J. CULLEN,

66TH (BERKSHIRE) REGIMENT.

FRANCIS JAMES CULLEN, who was killed in action at Maiwand on the 27th July, 1880, was the fourth son of the late Francis Nesbitt Cullen, Esq., J.P., of Corry, County Leitrim, and grandson of the late Colonel James Cullen, of Shreeny House, in the same county.

Born at Corry on the 7th September, 1844, he was educated in Dublin at Dunbar's Academy, from whence he passed direct into the Royal Military College, Sandhurst, in September, 1863. Passing out in February, 1865, he obtained a free commission for the ability he displayed at the previous examination, and was gazetted in the same month to an Ensigncy in the 1st West India Regiment. He shortly afterwards joined that corps at Kingston, Jamaica, where he served under the late Governor Eyre in the rebellion which broke out immediately after his arrival.

In 1867 he accompanied his regiment to Africa, where he served for two years in Senegambia. In the autumn of 1869 he obtained his Lieutenancy without purchase, and was posted to the 66th Foot. He joined that gallant corps some months afterwards in Bombay, and continued to serve with it, with one interval of furlough, till the day of his death. In October, 1879, he obtained his company.

Captain Cullen accompanied the regiment on its being ordered up to Kandahar in February, 1880, and shared with it the duties which fell to its lot after arriving at its destination. In the first week in July he took part in the advance of Burrows' Brigade to the Halmand, and commanded the company of his regiment, which, acting as the General's rear-guard, crossed the river in the neighbourhood of Girishk on the 14th of the month to observe the movements of the Wali's mutinied troops. A fortnight afterwards, in the disastrous encounter with the enemy at Maiwand, he fell fighting gallantly at the head of his company, in the field in front of the Nullah, close to the spot where Colonel Galbraith and his brother officers, McMath, Garratt, and Barr, rendered up their lives. "Your son," wrote the late Major C. V. Oliver, (a gallant officer of the 66th, who survived that fatal day, and subsequently commanded the scanty remnant of the regiment at General Roberts' defeat of Ayub

Khan's army on the 1st September) to Captain Cullen's bereaved mother, "was seen to fall . . . . . doing his duty as a gentleman and a soldier. I was standing by his company for some time only a little while before he fell, and nothing could have been cooler or better than his behaviour. Amongst the many friends I lost on that day there are few I regret so much."

The brief record of the manner in which Captain Cullen faced his death reads as an echo of the anticipations formed after the first tidings of the disaster reached them by the many friends to whom, during his life, he had endeared himself.

LIEUTENANT R. E. L. DACRES,

ROYAL ARTILLERY.

RICHARD EDMUND LYONS DACRES, who died of typhoid fever at Landi Kotal, Afghanistan, on the 13th May, 1879, was the fourth son of Admiral Sir Sydney Colpory Dacres, G.C.B., Visitor and Governor of Greenwich Hospital, and nephew of General Sir Richard Dacres, G.C.B., Constable of the Tower. He was born at Haslar Hospital, Gosport, on the 18th February, 1856, and was educated at Cheltenham College, from whence he proceeded to Woolwich. Quitting the Academy after the usual course, he was gazetted, in August, 1875, to a Lieutenancy in the Royal Artillery.

In January, 1877, Dacres was ordered out to India. Posted to 6/11, R.A., he joined that battery at Rawal Pindi, and did duty with it until it was ordered down country, when he was transferred, at his own request, to Battery 11/9, R.A., which took its place.

On the outbreak of the Afghan War in the autumn of 1878, he accompanied the Battery in its advance, in the 1st Division Kyber Field Force, into the enemy's country. Taken ill with typhoid fever, on the march to Ali Musjid, he had to be sent back to Peshawar, and to suffer the keen disappointment of not being present at the attack and capture of the Fort; but partially recovering, he rejoined his battery, and subsequently took part with it in the Bazar Valley expedition in the last days of January and the beginning of February, 1879, in the affair at Deh Sarak on the 25th March, and in the operations against the Mohmands at Kam Daka on the 22nd and 23rd April, gaining credit throughout for the ability he displayed as an officer, and particularly distinguishing himself in his management of the two guns of which he was in command in the operations last named. It was after a toilsome march back to Landi Kotal on the return of the expedition against the Mohmands, that he was a second time attacked with typhoid fever, to the effects of which he succumbed after an illness of twelve days' duration, in the twenty-fourth year of his age, universally mourned by his comrades, whose admiration he had gained by his conduct both in the field and in camp, and whose affection he had won by his sociability and the friendliness of his disposition.

LIEUT.-COLONEL A. G. DAUBENY,

2ND BATTALION, 7TH (ROYAL FUSILIERS).

ALFRED GOODLAD DAUBENY, second son of the late Rev. Andrew Alfred Daubeny, of Redland Lodge, near Bristol, and of Frances Elizabeth, his wife, daughter of Richard Goodlad, Esq., was born on the 28th May, 1834, and was educated at Cheltenham and Sandhurst. He entered the Army in November, 1852, being gazetted to an ensigncy in the 90th Light Infantry. Two years afterwards he proceeded with that regiment to the Crimea, and there served with it from the 5th December, 1854, till the termination of hostilities, having been present, in the interim, at the capture of the Quarries, the siege and fall of Sebastopol, and the attack on the Redan on the 18th June, and having formed one of the storming party on the 8th September. For his services on these occasions he received the medal with clasp, and the Turkish medal.

On the reduction of the Army he was temporarily placed on half-pay; but in 1857 was brought into the 7th Royal Fusiliers, with which regiment he served in successive grades, at Gibraltar, in Canada, England, Ireland, and India.

In September, 1879, he obtained the command of the 2nd Battalion, and in February, 1880, proceeded with it in its advance to Kandahar. Here he commanded it through the siege till the 16th August, the date of the ill-starred sortie to Deh Khwaja, in which he greatly distinguished himself by his gallant behaviour in leading the charge across an open space near the north end of the village. This space (about 150 yards across) was surrounded on all sides by houses and walls held in force by the enemy, the fire from which was terrific. For his conduct on this occasion he was specially mentioned in General Primrose's despatch, as also for his behaviour throughout the siege.

General Brooke having fallen in the sortie, Colonel Daubeny was selected by General Primrose for the command (temporary) of the brigade thus rendered vacant. He subsequently received orders to proceed in his new capacity to the field of Maiwand to bury the dead, recover lost guns and rifles, and draw up a report on the subject of the field and the battle. For his services on this occasion, and more especially for the masterly nature of the treatise he prepared in fulfilment of the last-named of the duties apportioned to him, he received the thanks of Government.

It was about the time these acknowledgments reached him that Colonel Daubeny was seized with small-pox, and a few days afterwards, on the 21st November, 1880—to the heartfelt grief of every officer and man of his regiment, to the command of which he had reverted on his return from Maiwand—fell a victim to the virulent complaint to which so many of his countrymen in Afghanistan had already succumbed.

Colonel (then Major) Daubeny married, at Poona, in October, 1875, Emma Mackenzie, daughter of A. Rogers, Esq., of the Bombay Civil Service, by whom he had two daughters who survive him.

The deceased officer's commissions bear date as follows :—

Ensign by purchase	23rd November, 1852.
Lieutenant „	8th September, 1854.
Captain .	30th November, 1855.
Major by purchase	23rd June, 1867.
Lieut.-Colonel	25th September, 1878.

LIEUTENANT G. G. DAWES, STAFF CORPS,

1st BENGAL CAVALRY.

GEORGE GRAHAM DAWES was the eldest son of the late Colonel Michael Dawes, of the Bengal Artillery, by his marriage with Louisa, daughter of the Rev. John Burdett, Rector of Banagher, King's County, Ireland. He was born at Meerut, Bengal, on the 17th May, 1846, and remained in India till in his ninth year, when he was taken to England. After receiving some preliminary education at Brighton, he proceeded to the Blackheath Proprietary School, then under the management of the Rev. J. Matheson, and entering eagerly into both work and play, won the approbation of his masters by the steadiness with which he pursued his studies, and the affection and admiration of his young contemporaries by his cheery disposition and by his prowess in the cricket-field, the play-ground, and as a member of the Volunteer Corps. It was his father's wish that he should adopt the Indian Civil Service for his career, and with the object of doing so, he underwent, on leaving Blackheath, a course of private tuition; the sedentary life which close study necessitated soon, however, began to tell severely on his health, and he was unsuccessful at the examination for which he eventually went up. He then determined to enter the Army; and competing, in May, 1868, at the examination for direct commissions, succeeded in taking first place in the list of candidates, easily distancing all competitors. While awaiting his commission, he turned the time at his disposal to profitable account, occupying himself with the study of Oriental languages. In December, 1868, he was gazetted to the 4th (Light) Hussars, then serving at Mirat, whither he shortly afterwards proceeded to join head-quarters. Finding, on arrival at his destination, an examination in languages being held, he sent in his name as a competitor, and taking excellent marks, passed the lower standard within a fortnight of his setting foot in India. In December, 1869, he passed the higher standard examination, and received the appointment of Interpreter to the regiment.

After doing duty for a twelvemonth as a probationer, the subject of this notice entered the Bengal Staff Corps. In November, 1872, he was gazetted to the

1st Cavalry, then stationed at Cawnpore, and was selected shortly afterwards to fill the post of Officiating Adjutant to the regiment—an appointment which he held, and the duties of which he continued to discharge with zeal and ability, for a period of three years.

Falling ill in the autumn of 1876, he applied for and obtained his two years' furlough, and proceeded to England. The period passed rapidly and pleasantly in foreign travel. Although, at its expiration, Dawes cannot be said to have been completely restored to health, he nevertheless abstained from applying for an extension of his leave: rumours of war, and of his regiment being ordered to the front, had reached him; and hurrying out, he rejoined the head-quarters at Sialkot in November, 1878, when his appointment to the Adjutancy was at once confirmed.

In March, 1879, the 1st Bengal Cavalry was ordered to Kohat to form part of the Reserve Division of the Kuram Valley Field Force. A few months after it had been in garrison at this post, cholera broke out in its ranks; and to this virulent disease—at midnight, on the 7th June, 1879—the subject of this notice fell a victim.

Most loving and unselfish in his family circle, generous and true in his friendship, witty, humorous, and with a spontaneous gaiety of disposition that age could never have dulled, George Graham Dawes was ever a welcome companion and guest. His cheery presence will long be missed in the places which knew it. Of the many who had the privilege of claiming friendship with him, it may truly be said that there is not one who does not mourn his untimely death.

LIEUTENANT A. E. DOBSON,

ROYAL ENGINEERS.

LFRED EDMUND DOBSON, who died at Safed Sang, Afghanistan, on the 20th July, 1881, was the eldest surviving son of the late Rev. William Dobson, M.A., for fifteen years Principal of the Cheltenham College. He was born on the 14th July, 1849, at Cheltenham, and was educated at the College, entering it in 1857 at the age of eight years, and remaining in it till 1865. During the greater portion of the interval he studied under the Rev. T. A. Southwood, the head of the Military Department, from whom he received the highest testimonials for conduct, diligence, and proficiency. In 1865 he entered Woolwich, his name appearing fourth in the list of successful candidates at the midsummer examination; and passing out of the Academy after the usual course, he succeeded in again taking fourth place. Gazetted to the Royal Engineers, he did duty for two years at Chatham, and then proceeded to India. After serving for a twelvemonth at Bangalore, he was employed for nearly six years on Public Works in the Wainad District, and during the period approved himself a zealous and accomplished officer, winning praise for the able manner in which he performed much important work. He was subsequently sent to Burmah, from whence, after a few months, he was recalled for service with the Field Force in Afghanistan.

Proceeding in command of the I Company Madras Queen's Own Sappers and Miners, which had been detailed to the 2nd Division Kabul Field Force, Dobson reached Jalalabad in November, 1879. "During the march up," writes one of his brother officers, "he was the life of the party, never sparing himself, always ready and cheerful." He took part with his company, in December, in the expedition to Barikot, and in January, 1880, in the expedition to the Lughman Valley, and rendered important service in the construction of a bridge over the Kabul River, the improvement of the defences of Fort Sale, and the construction of a road over the southern barrier of the Daronta Gorge. A month afterwards he commanded his company in the reconnoitering expedition along the right bank of the Kabul River, penetrating into unknown country, and mapping a portion of the new route to the capital. These duties, and others of a like nature which were subsequently allotted to him in his capacity of Assistant Field Engineer, necessitated constant exposure and great hardship, and eventually began to tell upon his health. In March he was sent to Lachipur, and a few weeks afterwards to Safed Sang. While stationed at this post his health completely broke down, and on the 20th July, 1880, he succumbed to the deadly malarial fever, to which so many of his countrymen fell victims.

Lieutenant Dobson's remains, followed to the grave by the Generals both of the Division and the Brigade with their respective staffs and all the other officers at the post, were buried with military honours in the cemetery, and a headstone, subsequently erected to his memory by the Sappers of his company, by whom he was greatly beloved, marks the place where he rests. Among the many expressions of sorrow and of regard called forth by his death, feeling allusion is made in a Division Order issued by General Bright on the occasion, to the loss the Service had sustained in him, "a loss which," to quote the words of Major Ross Thompson, R.E., under whom he had long served, "is felt not only by his brother officers, but by every one who knew his good and kind and manly character."

The deceased married, in October, 1871, Florence Henrietta, fourth daughter of William Barnett, Esq., formerly M.P. for Maidstone. He leaves a widow and three children.

CAPTAIN JAMES DUNDAS, V.C.,

ROYAL ENGINEERS.

THE following notice, with the exception of a few trifling alterations, was penned by Captain W. Broadfoot, R.E., one of Captain Dundas's oldest friends, and appeared in the "Royal Engineer Journal" of the 2nd February, 1880. The writer has so ably recorded the various incidents of Captain Dundas's life, that the Editor of this work takes the liberty of transcribing the memoir *in extenso*.

James Dundas was the eldest son of the late George Dundas, one of the Judges of the Court of Session in Scotland, and of Elizabeth his wife, eldest daughter of the late Colin Mackenzie, Esq., of Portmore, Peebleshire. He was born on the 12th September, 1842, and was educated at the Edinburgh Academy, Trinity College Glen Almond, and Addiscombe College, from which he was appointed Lieutenant in the Royal (late Bengal) Engineers in June, 1860.

After passing through the usual course of study at Chatham, he sailed for India in March, 1862. On arrival he was posted to the Head-quarters of the Sappers and Miners at Rurki, and after a short service there was transferred to the Public Works Department in Bengal. His talent and sound judgment being recognized he was, after a short service, promoted to the grade of Executive Engineer and entrusted with the charge of one of the most responsible divisions in that Presidency.

In 1865 he accompanied the expedition to Bhutan under General Tombs C.B., V.C., and so distinguished himself as to be recommended by that officer for the Victoria Cross. The official report of the circumstances is as follows :—

"A party of the enemy, from 180 to 200 in number had barricaded themselves in the block-house, which they continued to defend after the rest of the position had been carried, and the main body was in retreat. The block-house, which was loopholed, was the key of the enemy's position. Seeing no officer of the storming-party near him, and being anxious that the place should be taken immediately, as any protracted resistance might have caused the main body of the Bhoteas to rally, the British forces having been fighting in a broiling sun, on very steep and difficult ground for upwards of three hours, the General ordered these two officers (Major Trevor and Lieutenant Dundas) to show the way into the block-house. They had to climb up a wall which was fourteen feet high, and then to enter a house, occupied by some 200 desperate men, head foremost through an opening not more than two feet wide, between the top of the wall and the roof of the block-house."

Major-General Tombs states that on desiring the Sikh soldiers to swarm up the wall, none of them responded to the call until these two officers had shown them the way, when they followed with the greatest alacrity. Both officers were wounded.

After the termination of the Bhutan expedition, Lieutenant Dundas rejoined the Public Works Department. He returned to England on leave in 1870, and again in 1877, rejoining his appointment in India early in 1878.

During the summer of that year he saved the life of a native under circumstances which showed that in addition to the high chivalrous courage which won for him the V.C., he possessed that calm and cool determination which is perhaps the highest form of human courage.

A house in the Simla bazaar was on fire, and the roof had partly fallen in and buried a native, to such an extent that he could not get out and would infallibly have been burnt to death or suffocated. Captain Dundas, who was passing, made an attempt to rescue the man, but was driven out of the place by the falling rubbish and by the smoke. He called for a volunteer from the crowd to help him, when a gallant officer of the Royal Artillery responded, and again he attempted the rescue, and this time his efforts were successful. He received some severe burns about the hands.

Captain Dundas was for a number of years associated with General Sir Alexander Taylor, K.C.B., R.E., in charge of one of the principal branches of the Public Works Department; the estimation in which his services were held is shown by the following passages which occur in a letter written by that distinguished officer shortly after Captain Dundas's death:—

"James Dundas having been my personal assistant from 1871 to 1879, there is probably no one better entitled than I am to say, from experimental knowledge, that in him the Corps has lost one of its 'very best.'

"A man of high abilities, well cultivated—a modest, high-minded English gentleman, brave, gentle, and courteous, I do not know that he ever gave offence to any one; far less do I believe that he had an enemy. To me he was an invaluable professional assistant; and I owe much to his varied and accurate engineering knowledge, to his trustworthy and universal popularity. But he was much more to me than a highly talented assistant, he was a greatly valued and respected personal friend.

"In the spring of 1879, he was specially selected for transfer to the Secretariat of the Government of India in the Public Works Department, but service in the field was more acceptable to his chivalrous disposition, and after a short tour of duty at Head-quarters of Government he found his way to the front last summer, on the fresh outbreak of war in Afghanistan."

When General Roberts advanced on Kabul in the autumn of 1879, he selected Dundas to accompany the Field Force as Commanding Royal Engineer, believing that Colonel Perkins had left Kuram; but the latter subsequently rejoined the Division. The manner in which the Engineers carried out the duty of providing shelter for the troops after the retirement into the Sherpur cantonments at the close of the year received the warm acknowledgments of the General. "No body of officers," he writes in his Division Order issued on the subject, " could have worked more zealously, or with better results."

On the afternoon of the 23rd December, Captain Dundas, with Lieutenant Nugent, was ordered to join General Macpherson's force to aid in the destruction of the line of forts held by the enemy on the south side of the British position at Sherpur. It was while carrying out this duty, through a fatally premature mine explosion which has been attributed to the use of a home-made quick-match in lieu of one of the fuzes which had been sent out and were found to be worthless, that he lost his life. His body was recovered by his comrades on the same day, and at their hands received a soldier's burial.

James Dundas succeeded, in 1877, to the estate of Ochtertyre, in Perthshire, on the death of his uncle, the Right Hon. Sir David Dundas.

LIEUT.-COL. HALFORD FELLOWES, STAFF CORPS,

32ND (PUNJAB) BENGAL N.I. (PIONEERS).

THE subject of this notice was born at the Leigh, Bradford, Wilts, on the 16th October, 1833, and was the youngest son of the late Rear-Admiral Sir Thomas Fellowes, K.C.B. He entered the Indian Army in 1851 as Ensign in the 31st Regiment (now 2nd Queen's Own) Light Infantry, with which he served through the Santal campaign of 1855-56. During the Mutiny in 1857, and in the subsequent operations in 1858-59 in the Saugor district and Central India (for which he received the medal with clasp), he served as Adjutant of the regiment, which was one of the very few Bengal corps that remained faithful throughout. He was Brigade-Major at Allahabad and Umballa from 1865 to 1867, and during the Abyssinian campaign of the latter year (for his services in which he was mentioned in despatches and received a second medal) he served as Brigade-Major under Sir Donald Stewart. From 1871 to 1877 he was second in command of the 23rd Pioneers, on the expiration of which period he was transferred to the 32nd Pioneers, and succeeded to the command of the regiment in November, 1878.

The 32nd Pioneers had been stationed at Quetta, Baluchistan, for ten months before the Afghan War broke out, and had suffered greatly from the unhealthy climate. In the month of November, 1878, the regiment was detailed to General Stewart's division of the army of invasion, and subsequently took part in General Biddulph's advance from Kandahar to Girishk, losing many of its number from dysentery during the month it stayed there. On the return march it formed part of the Thal-Chotiali Field Force, which succeeded in opening up the new route. It was in the course of the return journey that Colonel Fellowes was seized with the disease which proved fatal to him. The marches were very long, the heat was excessive, and there was often either an absence of water, or the water obtained was so bad as only to accelerate the disease. On the 6th April, 1879, at the urgent request of the surgeon of the regiment, General Biddulph allowed him to be left behind under a strong guard, in the hope that moving by easy stages might save his life; but it was not to be. At noon on the 9th of April, at a place called Kala

Chupri, in the Hun Pass, he quietly passed away, and the next day his body was carried on to Legari Barkhan, where the force had halted, and was buried the same evening with full military honours, every officer from the General downwards following it to the grave. Six commanding officers bore the pall—a Union Jack—and the service was read by Major Crookshank, 32nd Pioneers, amidst the tears of many of the men of the regiment, by whom their Colonel was greatly respected and beloved. A roughly carved cross was placed at the head of the grave, which was protected with large stones and planted with willows.

In his General Order of the 10th April, 1879, General Biddulph wrote that "He had not been closely connected with the regiment for five months without learning to appreciate the zeal, ability, and tact with which Lieut.-Colonel Fellowes discharged the onerous duties which from time to time devolved upon him; and he desired to place on record the high opinion he had formed of the gallant officer. By Colonel Fellowes' death, the 32nd Pioneers had sustained a deplorable loss, and General Biddulph in sympathizing with the corps, and his friends, recorded with deep regret that Her Majesty's Indian Army had been deprived of a good and faithful soldier, while he was to all appearance in the full vigour and usefulness of life;" and Major Crookshank, in his Regimental Order of the same date, paid the following tribute to his memory:—"Colonel Fellowes' high character, both professionally as a soldier, and socially as a Christian and a friend, soon secured for him the love and esteem of the officers of the regiment, who will long mourn the loss of a kind, self-denying, and sympathizing commanding officer and comrade."

LIEUT. T. O. FITZGERALD, STAFF CORPS,

27TH (PUNJAB) BENGAL N.I.

DESCENDED from a family whose name has from time immemorial been associated with the Army Service, a son of the late and brother of the present Knight of Glin, Thomas Otho Fitzgerald, the subject of this memoir, is not the first of his gallant race who has laid down his life at his country's call.

He was born at Glin Castle, co. Limerick, on the 23rd February, 1849, and after receiving his education at Kingstown School, entered Sandhurst. His course at the college was a notable one: not only did he display, as a smart under-officer, a special aptitude for his profession, and win a more than local reputation by his prowess in all kinds of athletic sports, but by his largeness of heart and the never-failing geniality of his ways he endeared himself to his contemporaries to an extent to which few before or after him have succeeded in doing; and it is not too much to say that there are few regimental ante-rooms in which his death is not mourned as that of a brother.

Quitting Sandhurst in 1869, he was gazetted, in the month of November of that year, to the 19th Foot; and in October, 1871, obtained his Lieutenancy. In due course he entered the Bengal Staff Corps, and was posted to the 27th Punjab Infantry, with which regiment he served continuously till the day of his death. For the Jowaki campaign of 1877-78, in which he took part throughout, he received the medal.

On the outbreak of hostilities with Afghanistan in the autumn of 1878, the 27th Punjab Native Infantry formed part of the 3rd Infantry Brigade, under Brigadier-General Appleyard's command, of the Khyber Field Force; and taking part with the regiment in the advance of the Division into the Khyber Pass, Fitzgerald was present in the direct attack on Ali Masjid, on the 21st November. As darkness was closing in on that day, some one hundred men of the 14th Sikhs under Captain Maclean, supported by seven companies of the Punjabis under Major Birch, were fighting their way up the steep slope, above which impended the Afghan left flank position, against the stone breastworks so obstinately held by the enemy—their advance enfiladed by a heavy artillery fire. A few moments before the order to retire was sounded, Captain Maclean had rushed forward with a handful of his men into a position in which he found himself in urgent need of support; and Major Birch, gallantly responding to his call for assistance, fell shot dead as he advanced to succour him, his companies being at the same time swept back by the hail of lead with which they were met from the breastworks. Fitzgerald's opportunity had now come; and with reference to one of his soldierly instincts it is superfluous to say that he availed himself of it.

The Afghan fire can only be described as murderous; but he would not have it that his chief's body should be left to the mercy of the enemy. Rushing forward with his gallant orderly, he succeeded in reaching and raising it. At this moment a bullet struck him in the wrist. With the characteristic remark, "Oh, that's nothing!" he lifted Major Birch's body in his arms, and carried it to a more sheltered spot. Laying it down, he was in the act of tying a handkerchief round his wounded arm when a second bullet struck him, passing through his chest, and killing him instantaneously. The Afghan fire was no more to be faced, and the bodies had to be left where they lay; on the morning of the morrow, however, they were recovered, both of them having been left untouched by the enemy. They were conveyed, by the General's orders, to Peshawar; and on the 24th November, 1879, were buried in the cemetery at that station with full military honours.

LIEUTENANT ST. J. W. FORBES,

92ND (GORDON HIGHLANDERS).

ST. JOHN WILLIAM FORBES was the third son of Lieut.-Colonel John Forbes and Lucy Georgina his wife, youngest daughter of Thomas Whitmore, Esq., of Apsley, Shropshire. He was born at Malvern Link on the 20th January, 1856, and was educated at Eton, where his father and mother resided. Passing direct from the college, he was gazetted in November, 1873, to the 72nd Highlanders; but a few weeks afterwards was transferred to the 92nd, which he joined at Multan early in 1874. During the brief span of his career in that distinguished regiment, he filled every appointment that a subaltern can hold—that of Adjutant, Quartermaster, Instructor of Musketry, and Interpreter. He went through the garrison course at Sialkot, and was in the first class; and while at home on leave in 1877 he obtained a first-class extra certificate at Hythe. In order that he might act as Adjutant to the detached wing of the 92nd at Benares, he returned to India before the expiration of his leave, and receiving the appointment, retained it till the regiment was reunited in December, 1878, in view of its departure on active service into Afghanistan. With reference to one of Forbes's enthusiastic temperament, with a love for his profession that was little less than a passion, it is superfluous to say that he threw himself heart and soul into the new sphere of activity which now presented itself. He took part in the advance of the regiment in the spring of 1879 to Ali Khel, where it joined the Advance Division of the Kuram Field Force. For two months he acted as Orderly Officer to Brigadier, now Major-General, Hamilton Forbes, and won the approbation of that distinguished officer by the zeal and energy with which he performed his new duties; and subsequently he acted for a short time in the same capacity to General Macpherson. During the battle of Charasiab, on the 6th October, in which the 92nd performed gallant service, the duties of the post of Acting Quartermaster which he held necessitated his remaining in camp; but he was present at the occupation of Kabul, and in the expedition to Maidan in November. It was during the operations of General Roberts' force which marked the close of the year, at the moment of crowning the summit of the Takht-i-Shah at the head of his breathless company on the 13th December, that he rendered up his life in a heroic personal attempt to save the body of his Colour-Sergeant (gallant James Drummond, who had fallen at his side) from mutilation. To the 92nd General Baker had given the post of honour on that day, viz., to lead the attack. The four companies of the regiment—two in advance, two in support—swept over half a mile of swamp at the double, under a heavy fire from the Beni Hissar spur. Barely waiting a moment at the base of the Takht-i-Shah to take breath, they commenced ascending the heights, the men straining every nerve to gain the crest before the enemy could collect in numbers to resist them. "Your son," writes one of Forbes's brother officers to Colonel Forbes, "was at this time leading his company in the most gallant manner, his company being then on the right. Before reaching the top we had lost our compact formation, as, owing to the extreme steepness of the ascent, many men were quite out of breath; and a few of the most active only, headed by your son, led the advance. On reaching the spur, without a moment's hesitation, your son, accompanied only by his Colour-Sergeant, with some eight or ten men behind, with the most determined bravery charged up the ridge where one of the enemy's standards was waving. Before he had gone far, Colour-Sergeant Drummond, a most gallant and splendid non-commissioned officer, fell shot through the body; and immediately several of the enemy, who had until this moment remained concealed, rushed down upon your son, who stood to defend his Colour-Sergeant, and give up his life in his defence. He was overpowered by numbers, not, however, before he had killed the first man who attacked him, and still fought bravely until he fell shot through the head." So runs the brief record. We have to turn elsewhere to ascertain how the gallant writer of the letter, with a few men of his company, himself avenged the death of his comrade, bayonetting or shooting down every man of the band of ten who had not fled.

The body of St. John Forbes was recovered, and buried on the morning of the 15th December, 1879, in the little cemetery within cantonments. "His character,"—to quote the words of a distinguished officer under whom he served—"does not end with his life, but remains an influence on the side of right and goodness, quickened into warmer life, in the hearts of all who valued him, by his gallant and noble death."

CAPTAIN ST. J. T. FROME,

72ND (DUKE OF ALBANY'S OWN HIGHLANDERS).

ST. JOHN THOMAS FROME, who was killed at the battle of Kandahar on the 1st September, 1880, was descended from the old Dorsetshire family of that name, and was the only son of General Frome, Colonel Commandant Royal Engineers, and Jane, his wife, daughter of the late Colonel Alexander Light, 25th King's Own Borderers.

He obtained his first commission in the 72nd as Ensign, by purchase, in 1861; became Lieutenant, also by purchase, in April, 1864; and obtained his company in April, 1872.

Captain Frome served with his regiment through the whole of the two Afghan campaigns. At the assault of the Peiwar Kotal he commanded the leading company of the 72nd, which was sent in advance to support the 5th Goorkhas, and for his services on this occasion was favourably mentioned in despatches. He was with the force at Ali Khel during the winter of 1878-79; in the subsequent advance upon Kabul; at the battle of Charasiab (for his conduct in which action he was again recommended); at the capture of Kabul; the occupation and defence of the Sherpur cantonments; in the memorable march from Kabul to Kandahar; and at the battle of the 1st September, in which he fell at the head of his company, when clearing the fortified enclosures covering Ayub Khan's position.

Sir Frederick Roberts, in his Field Force Order issued after the battle of Kandahar, speaks of Captain Frome as "a gallant and distinguished soldier"; and in his address to the 72nd and 92nd Highlanders, delivered on leaving for India, after paying a just tribute to the memory of Colonel Brownlow, late commanding the 72nd, he adds: "With him fell an equally gallant spirit, Captain Frome." Similar testimony is borne by his brother officers, by whom his loss as "a proved friend and true soldier" is sincerely regretted; and one of high rank, under whom he served during the Afghan campaign, thus writes of him:—"He was an excellent officer, and the coolness and gallantry with which he always led his company into action was the admiration of all who were ever with him under fire."

LIEUTENANT C. H. GAISFORD,

72ND (DUKE OF ALBANY'S OWN HIGHLANDERS).

CECIL HENRY GAISFORD, who fell in action before Kabul on the 14th December, 1879, was the eldest son of Lieut.-Colonel Gaisford, of The Grove, Dunboyne, late of the 72nd Highlanders. He was born at Galway on the 20th September, 1856, and was educated at Eton. Entering the army in September, 1876, he proceeded, twelve months afterwards, to India; and on the 30th November, 1877, joined, at Sialkot, the head-quarters of the 72nd Highlanders, his father's old regiment, to which he had been gazetted.

On the eve of the outbreak of the Afghan War, in the autumn of 1878, Gaisford was on detachment at Ranikhet in command of a company, his Captain having left for England. The responsible duty of marching his men and followers a distance of 500 miles to overtake the regiment, then en route for the front, consequently fell to him. He accomplished this in two months; and, joining the right wing, served with it in the whole of its subsequent operations till the day of his death. He was one of those who took part in the successful and gallant assault of the Peiwar Kotal on the 2nd December, 1878, which was carried in spite of the desperate resistance of the enemy; a few days afterwards he took part, with 250 of the 72nd, in General Roberts' reconnaissance to the Shutargardan; and on the 15th December he was present at the repulse of the Mangals in the Sapiri defile. During the spring and autumn of 1879 he acted as Adjutant to his regiment, and as Brigade Major at Ali Khel. On the renewal of hostilities, in September, 1879, he was again at the Shutargardan, in General Baker's Brigade; and at the battle of Charasiab, on the 6th October, was with the two companies of the 72nd when they so splendidly carried the Red Ridge, the enemy's right centre.

On the 14th December, 1879, Gaisford commanded one of the companies of his regiment, which, under Colonel Brownlow, stormed the Asmai heights. The operations on this occasion have been variously described, but all accounts agree that the capture of the highest peak by the 72nd and Guides was "splendid." Of this there can be no doubt, for it was in full view of Sherpur. It was in the evening of the same day, on the orderly retirement from the hill which had been so bravely won, that Gaisford received his death-wound. The awful suddenness of the shock could not, however, quell the gallantry of his spirit. Indicating his sword, he called on his comrades to take care of it, "because it was his father's."

"He died like a soldier, full of courage," wrote Colonel Brownlow, his Commanding Officer, in a letter to Colonel Gaisford. "I never saw anyone more cool or self-possessed under very trying circumstances. He was a most promising officer, and you already know I thought very highly of him. During the whole of the day and during the retirement, accomplished under the heavy fire of the enemy, he was hardly a moment out of my sight, and he could not have behaved better than he did"—testimony of his worth joined in by Major Stockwell, who wrote: "Under fire he was as brave as the best." It will perhaps not be out of place here to add that before he was eighteen years of age he had gained the Royal Humane Society's medal for gallantry in saving life, and that in his own home circle he was lovable and beloved, having ever a bright smile and a kindly word for all. The peasantry in the neighbourhood appreciated his rectitude so fully that his decision used invariably to be accepted as final in the adjustment of the little differences they were in the habit of referring to him.

Lieutenant Gaisford was buried with military honours in the cemetery near Sherpur, at the extreme west end of the Bemaru heights, where his comrades have placed a marble slab over his grave.

LIEUT.-COLONEL JAMES GALBRAITH,

66TH (BERKSHIRE) REGIMENT.

HE subject of this memoir was the fifth son of Samuel Galbraith, Esq., of Clanabogan, in the County of Tyrone, Ireland, and of Susannah Jane, his wife, daughter of the Rev. Robert Handcock, D.D., of Dublin and of Lacken, Co. Roscommon, and granddaughter of William Handcock, Esq., for many years M.P. for Athlone. In Burkes' "Landed Gentry" the Galbraiths of Clanabogan are stated to have been of Scotch descent, and to have settled in Ulster in the reign of Charles I.

Educated at home, James Galbraith passed his examination at Sandhurst for a commission in the Army, and was gazetted in December, 1851, to an Ensigncy, by purchase, in the 66th Regiment, with which gallant corps to the last his life was identified. He proceeded, on appointment, to the Depôt, then stationed in Guernsey; and after serving there for some eighteen months embarked for Canada to join the Head-quarters. While in that country he was promoted (June, 1854) to a Lieutenancy. The regiment was ordered home in the autumn of the same year, and a few months after its arrival in England was sent to Gibraltar. In the spring of 1855 Galbraith was sent home to the Depôt (which had been transferred to Leeds), to act as Paymaster and Quartermaster. In February, 1856, he obtained his company, by purchase.

Captain Galbraith sailed for the East Indies in the year 1857, with two companies of the regiment, under command of Major Benson, in H.M.S. "Gloriana," and joined the Head-quarters at Cannanor, where the 66th was stationed for over four years. For some part of this period he commanded a detachment at Calicut. Returning to England with the regiment for its term of home service, he did duty with it at Devonport, Aldershot, Guernsey, Jersey, the Curragh, and Dublin, and obtained while stationed in Ireland (August, 1869) his Majority.

On the regiment being ordered a second time to India, in 1870, Major Galbraith commanded a wing, during the voyage out, in one of Her Majesty's troopships; and three companies while stationed at Haidarabad, Sind. He subsequently commanded the regiment at Belgaum during parts of the years 1874 and 1875, and again at Haidarabad from the spring of 1879 till he succeeded to the permanent command at Karachi, in November, 1879. In the interval (October, 1877) he obtained his Brevet Lieutenant-Colonelcy.

In February, 1880, the 66th was ordered to Kandahar, and arrived there under his command on the 25th March, 1880, four days before the departure of the Bengal troops for Kabul under command of Sir Donald Stewart. Colonel Galbraith commanded the regiment on the 14th July, when the mutineers of the Wali's army were defeated near Girishk and his guns retaken. It was on the 27th July, 1880, on the fatal field of Maiwand, that he fell, fighting manfully against the overwhelming numbers of Ayub Khan's followers. "He was last seen," writes General Primrose in his despatch, "on the nullah bank, kneeling on one knee, with a colour in his hand, officers and men rallying round him." When the battle-field was revisited by the force under command of Brigadier-General Daubeny, in September, his body, and that of his old friend Captain McMath, were found together, with those of many of their gallant comrades.

Colonel Galbraith was a gallant soldier and a true friend. His even temper and calm judgment peculiarly fitted him for command; and those who served under him will ever respect and honour his memory.

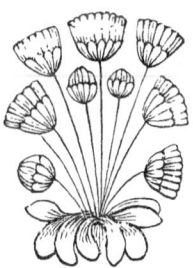

CAPTAIN J. H. GAMBLE,

1ST BATTALION 17TH (LEICESTERSHIRE) REGIMENT.

JOHN HENRY GAMBLE, who died at Landi Kotal, Afghanistan, on the 14th July, 1879, from illness contracted while on field service, was the eldest son of Clarke Gamble, Esq., Q.C., of Pinehurst, Toronto. He was educated at Upper Canada College and Cheltenham College, England, where he remained a student until July, 1860, when he proceeded to Sandhurst. Passing out of the Royal Military College after the usual course, he was gazetted, in July, 1862, to an Ensigncy in the 1st Battalion 17th Foot, which he shortly afterwards joined in Quebec, where it was then stationed. After returning with the battalion to England in 1864, he was promoted, in September, 1865, to a Lieutenancy, and subsequently served with the 2nd Battalion of the regiment in Jamaica, Canada, England, and Ireland. On the 2nd Battalion being ordered to India in the spring of 1877, he remained for duty at the Depôt, but in the autumn rejoined Headquarters at Mhow; almost immediately afterwards, however (November, 1877), he was gazetted to a company in the 1st Battalion, then in cantonment at Murree, and immediately rejoined his old friends at that station.

On the outbreak of hostilities with Afghanistan in the autumn of 1878, Captain Gamble took part, in command of his company, in the advance of the battalion into the enemy's country and in the operations which ensued; was present with it in the flank march over Rhotas heights in reverse of Ali Musjid, 20th to 22nd November, 1878; the affairs at Chinar, 9th and 10th December; the first and second Bazar Valley expeditions; and the affairs at Maidanah, 18th to 21st March, 1879. After the signing of the treaty of peace at Gandamak, the battalion retraced its steps from the advanced position of Safed Sang, where it was at the time stationed, to Landi Kotal, where it arrived, with its ranks sadly thinned by disease, after a most trying march. The situation of the camp was very unhealthy, the heat intense, and the water supply bad and difficult of access. Cholera and fever broke out among the troops; and day after day the number of victims increased, till it was found necessary to shift the camp. The new position was found to be a little cooler. "After the heat we have had," wrote Captain Gamble in one of his letters, "92° feels delicious." During the march he had been greatly weakened by an attack of dysentery. In the last letter he wrote (bearing date 4th July, 1879), he spoke cheerfully of his condition; but four days afterwards, on the 9th, a renewed attack completely prostrated him. Worn out with fatigue and anxiety, he now sank rapidly, and on the 14th of the month passed away peacefully, amid the deep regrets of his brother officers and the men of the regiment, by all of whom he was greatly beloved.

Captain Gamble was a man of singular sweetness and gentleness of disposition, who attracted towards him all who knew him, and bound them to him by such tender cords that he never lost a friend or made an enemy. We may fittingly close this brief notice with extracts from two regimental orders issued on the occasion of his death, which will serve to show the esteem in which he was held by the Commanding Officers under whom he served. In the first, which bears date Landi Kotal, 15th July, 1879, these words occur:—"He (Captain Gamble) was a most able officer, zealous and conscientious in the performance of his duties, and a good friend to all, in whatever position they might be. In the death of Captain Gamble the 17th Regiment loses an officer whom it will be hard to replace, and the Commanding Officer feels sure that every man in the regiment joins in mourning the loss sustained." The second Order, publishing a memorandum received from Colonel (Brigadier-General) Cobbe, bearing date 2nd August, 1879, is as follows:—"It is with feelings of the deepest sorrow that Colonel (Brigadier-General) Cobbe has heard of the death of Captain Gamble, of the 1st Battalion, at Landi Kotal. Although this officer has only served for some few months under Colonel Cobbe's immediate command, the period was quite sufficient to enable him to form a most high estimate of his character and capabilities, and to appreciate his value as a most useful and excellent officer, and for whom he had contracted a strong personal friendship. Colonel Cobbe requests the officer commanding the battalion to allow this memorandum to be published in Regimental Orders, as a record of his personal feelings, as well as his sympathy with the officers and soldiers of the 1st Battalion 17th Regiment, at the sad loss sustained by them all in the death of Captain Gamble."

CAPTAIN E. S. GARRATT,

66TH (BERKSHIRE) REGIMENT.

ERNEST STEPHEN GARRATT was the eldest son of the Reverend Samuel Garratt, Honorary Canon of Norwich, and Vicar of St. Margaret's, Ipswich, and Lœtitia Sarah Bathsua, his wife, daughter of the Reverend Bowater James Vernon, who was Senior Chaplain to the Forces in St. Helena at the time of the death of the Emperor Napoleon I., when the 66th Regiment happened to be stationed in the island.

The subject of this memoir was born on the 28th September, 1845, and was educated at Marlborough, and under private tutors at Geneva and elsewhere. In 1865, when nineteen years old, he obtained a direct commission as Ensign in the 66th Regiment, then lately returned from India. In July, 1867, he became Lieutenant; and during the five years the regiment was on home service, was quartered at Aldershot, the Channel Islands, Plymouth, and the Curragh. He embarked with the regiment in the spring of 1870, on its again being ordered to India, and obtained his company while on the voyage out.

General Barclay, formerly Lieutenant-Colonel of the 66th, giving the opinion he formed of him during the period of his Indian service, writes: "I first made his acquaintance at Belgaum in 1875; he was then in command of a detachment at the fort, and I was much struck, on inspecting his company, with the thoughtful manner in which all arrangements for the comfort of his men were carried out. No care or even expense was spared. His company, from his Colour-Sergeant to the youngest soldier, would have done anything for him." And a brother officer, who lived on terms of great intimacy with him, writes: "One thing which always struck me about him was his great kindness of heart. I never remember to have heard him speak a harsh or unkind word of anybody, and if a disparaging word was said of anyone in his presence, he would always put in a kind word for the subject of the remarks." It is perhaps worthy of mention, too, that during this period of his service he nursed his brother officer, Captain McMath, through a long and dangerous illness—the result of an encounter with a wounded panther—and was instrumental, as his patient was wont to affirm, in saving his life.

After serving for some years at various stations in Bombay, he returned on leave to England, married, and rejoined the regiment at Ahmadnagar; and after another voyage home, where he held for eighteen months an appointment at the Depôt, at Reading, was once more ordered to India in the autumn of 1879, three months before the departure of the 66th from Karachi to Kandahar.

While at Kandahar he was very much occupied with experiments in telegraphy. "He was a first-rate electrician," writes Lieutenant Hamilton, of the 2nd Queen's, Aide-de-Camp to General Primrose, to whose quarters Garratt was in the habit of resorting to test his telephones; and the General himself says: "I have always heard him spoken of in high terms by those who knew him; and I was particularly struck with the amount of intelligence he always displayed. He was considered a very good officer, and scientific in his pursuits, which made itself prominent by his knowledge and practice of telegraphy and the telephone."

"We are all like brothers," is one of his own expressions in a letter written at this period to his wife respecting the officers in the regiment, between whom and himself there evidently existed a very strong feeling of friendship—the more pleasant to think of, since "in their deaths they were not divided." Before this letter closed, the action with the Wali's troops, near Girishk, had taken place. After describing the pursuit and capture of the guns, he continues: "Then, as the enemy still held the valley to which they had retreated, we were ordered to clear it; and in this three of our men were wounded badly. One or two shots came so close to me that my horse shied"—he was senior Captain on active service, and doing Field Officer's duty—"and nearly threw me, as I was acting galloper between the General and the Regiment."

A fortnight afterwards, on the 27th July, 1880, the battle of Maiwand was fought. "When they were surrounded at the end," writes one of the officers of the 66th, in a private letter, "he turned the rear-rank of his company about to fire to the rear as well as to the front." His death took place when the regiment was retiring to the garden where the last stand was made. One of the men of his company gives the following particulars:—"I saw Captain Garratt fall. I stopped to see if I could render him any assistance. I then noticed that he had a bullet wound between the temple and the jaw bone, and that his eyes were closed. I raised his arm and found that he was dead." And General Primrose, making reference to him and his brother officer, Captain Cullen, in his letter to the Adjutant-General, published in the "Gazette" of the 31st December, 1880, tells how they "were both killed on the field in front of the nullah, up to the last moment commanding their companies and giving their orders with as much coolness as if on ordinary regimental parade."

A large pile of stones marks the place where the Afghans themselves buried those whom they found dead on the field. There his body lies with the rest of those with whom he fell. The burial-place of the 66th was left undisturbed by either friend or foe.

CAPTAIN F. T. GOAD, STAFF CORPS,

5TH INFANTRY REGIMENT, HAIDARABAD CONTINGENT.

FREDERICK THEOPHILUS GOAD, who received his death-wound in the Mangior Pass, Kuram Valley, on the 13th December, 1878, was the second son of Major Samuel Boileau Goad, 3rd Bengal Cavalry, and of his wife Emma Gordon, daughter of John Leith Davidson, Esq. He was born on the 25th August, 1842, at Simla, and after receiving his education in England was gazetted, on the 12th March, 1861, to H.M. 72nd Highlanders. Joining that regiment in Bengal, he did duty with it at various stations in the Presidency until it was ordered home, when, being anxious to prolong his Indian service, he exchanged into the 45th Foot. He subsequently accompanied that corps to Abyssinia, and, serving with it throughout the campaign, was present at the storming and capture of Magdala, for which he received the medal and clasp, and was also highly commended by Lord Napier for the zealous and most useful service rendered by him in the Transport Department, in which he had been specially selected to serve at a time when Transport officers were much needed.

In 1865 he passed second out of seventy-two in the competitive examination for the Bengal Staff Corps. Two years afterwards he returned to England, and while in this country underwent a course of training at the School of Musketry at Hythe, where he came out with an extra first-class certificate, also winning, as the best shot in the right wing, a handsome silver cup. He was in the Haidarabad Contingent when he obtained his company in August, 1873, and was second in command of the 5th Infantry Regiment in the contingent when he volunteered for the Transport service at the opening of the Afghan War.

Captain Goad was at once detailed for service to the Kuram Valley Field Force, in connection with which he rendered, according to the testimony of the General, most valuable aid in the difficult task of organizing the Transport trains. It was in the march of the brigade of troops under Sir Frederick Roberts from Ali Khel to Fort Kuram in December, 1878, while in charge of the long baggage train which was treacherously attacked by a horde of Mangals, that he received his mortal wound. The incident is thus related by the "Standard" correspondent:—

"Captain Goad was marching along at the head of a long string of camels, which were attended by five soldiers of the 72nd Highlanders, besides their own drivers. Suddenly there came round the rock, close to the road in the defile, a band of some one hundred Mangals. The Highlanders mistrusted them and wanted to fire, but they put up their hands and signalled they were friendly, whereupon Captain Goad told the soldiers to lower their rifles. The Mangals came within thirty yards. They saw an immense number of camels and a quantity of baggage defended by only half-a-dozen men. The temptation was too great for them. With extraordinary rapidity they unslung their guns from their backs and commenced to fire. Captain Goad was the first to fall. He was hit by a ball delivered from a long bell-mounted gun. The ball went through his sword and penetrated both thighs a little above the knee. The charge in the blunderbuss must have been enormous. Four Highlanders stood round him where he lay, the fifth ran back to tell the 5th Goorkhas to come on. These four men stood shoulder to shoulder and again and again repulsed the shrieking Mangals, who could not stand the terrible fire of the breechloaders.

"Even poor Goad lying on the ground with his legs shattered gave the Mangals three shots from his revolver, at the same time encouraging the men to stand firm. At last the 5th Goorkhas came up, but not before the four brave fellows had shot away every round of their seventy cartridges. Even on his deathbed Goad remembered with gratitude the generous bravery of the four soldiers who stood round him and defied a Mangal to touch him."

On the following day, the 14th, Captain Goad's left leg was amputated. The hope that the operation might save his life proved, however, futile; he rapidly sank, and died a few hours afterwards. His remains were buried close to the Kuram Fort, being followed to the grave by a large number of officers, including the General and his staff.

The following is an extract from Sir Frederick Roberts' despatch of the 18th December, 1878:—

"It was about this time that Captain Goad, who had been most active in keeping order in the baggage train, received the wound from the effects of which, I deeply regret to say, he subsequently died. I desire to record the high value which I had placed on the services of this officer.

"Belonging to the 5th Infantry of the Haidarabad Contingent, Captain Goad volunteered for active service, and owing to his experience of Transport work, and to his natural ability, he had already rendered most valuable aid in the difficult task of organizing the transport trains. I much deplore his death, both personally, and on account of the loss which the public service has sustained."

A thorough soldier, ready to undergo any fatigue or hardship, self-sacrificing to a degree, Captain Goad was greatly beloved by all who knew him. His love of sport was little less than a passion, and much to his amusement caused him to be alluded to in the Indian journals on more than one occasion as "The Nimrod of the Deccan." He was a good linguist, speaking Hindustani in several dialects with ease and fluency.

The deceased officer married, in July, 1877, Katherine, daughter of the late Robinson Elsdale, Esq., of Moulton, Lincolnshire, and it was during the enforced absence of his wife, sent home with fever, that he volunteered for the campaign. He leaves one son, an infant two months old at the time of his death.

MAJOR JOHN GODSON, MADRAS STAFF CORPS,

4TH MADRAS NATIVE INFANTRY.

HE subject of this notice, who died on the 25th December, 1880, from illness contracted while on service in Afghanistan, was born in London on the 11th December, 1834. Passing, after due preparation, the examination for an Indian cadetship, he entered the service in his twenty-first year. Gazetted to an Ensigncy in the 52nd Regiment N.I. in July, 1855, he immediately proceeded to India, and joined that regiment at the latter end of the September following. Twelve months afterwards he obtained his Lieutenancy. He performed regimental duty, at various stations, from September, 1855, till January, 1863, at the expiration of which interval he was given the charge of pensioners and payments at Vizagapatam and Vizianagarum—an appointment he continued to hold for upwards of ten years. During this period he entered the Madras Staff Corps, and was promoted (July, 1867) to the rank of Captain.

Reverting to regimental duty in August, 1873, Captain Godson was attached for some time to the 12th Madras N.I. In July, 1875, he obtained his Majority, and was transferred to the 4th Madras N.I., with which regiment—holding successively the appointments of Officiating Wing Commander, Wing Commander, Officiating Second in Command and Wing Commander, and Second in Command and Wing Commander—he served continuously till the day of his death.

On the formation of the Madras Brigade for field service, after the renewal of hostilities with Afghanistan in the autumn of 1879, Major Godson accompanied his regiment, which was detailed to the Khyber Line Force, to Peshawar, and advancing with it into the Pass, shared with it at Ali Musjid, and eventually at Jalalabad and Safed Sang, the various duties which fell to its lot. Commanding a detachment of 100 rank and file, he took part in the expedition under Colonel Hodding, 4th Madras N.I., which proceeded on the 26th March, 1880, from Jalalabad to Lachipur to support the British nominee for the government of the district against a threatened attack, and returned on the 31st idem. In April, 1880, he was given the command of Fort Battye, and retained the appointment for a period of six weeks. He also took part in the operations in Kamah in the early days of June, commanding the detachment of the regiment which was engaged.

During the term of service of the 4th Madras N.I. in Northern Afghanistan, Major Godson's duties were frequently of a trying nature, entailing protracted exposure to the vicissitudes of the climate and considerable privation; and towards the latter end of the war his health began to fail him. After the conclusion of hostilities and the evacuation of the northern line, the regiment was moved down country to Bangalore. This station Major Godson reached only to die. In the forty-sixth year of his age, on Christmas Day, the 25th December, 1880, he fell a victim to the rigours of the recent campaign, deeply regretted not only by his brother officers and the men of his regiment, amongst whom he left a high reputation for every manly quality, but also by a wide circle of private friends who held him dear.

THE REV. G. M. GORDON, M.A.,

CHURCH MISSIONARY SOCIETY.

GEORGE MAXWELL GORDON, second and youngest son of the late Captain J. E. Gordon, R.N., M.P. for Dundalk, of Hadlow Park, Tonbridge, and of Barbara, youngest daughter of the late Samuel Smith, Esq., M.P., of Woodhall Park, Herts, was born in 1838. After receiving a private education, he graduated at Trinity College, Cambridge. He was then ordained. After holding two curacies, he offered his services to the Church Missionary Society in 1866, and remained a missionary at his own cost for a period of fifteen years, until his death. The following particulars of his missionary work have been supplied by the Editorial Secretary of the Society for this notice.

In 1867 Mr. Gordon went to Madras to join the Itinerant Mission which had been started by the late Rev. D. Fenn among the villages surrounding that city, and living in tents, travelled continually from place to place. His health breaking down, he took a voyage to Australia to recruit it. Returning to India, he resumed his itinerations in Madras. Subsequently, when in this country, he was offered, and declined, an Australian bishopric.

In 1871, travelling through Persia *en route* to India, on missionary work, he proceeded to the Punjab, and joining the Rev. T. V. French, now Bishop of Lahore, assisted him in establishing the Divinity College at Lahore, where he continued to work till 1874. He then set up an Itinerant Mission in connection with that College on the banks of the Jhelum, with Pind Dadan Khan as centre. His zeal and self-denial in the years that followed are described by General Maclagan in a contribution to the "Church Missionary Intelligencer" for October, 1880.

In 1876 he visited Dera Ghazi Khan, on the Indus, and established, at his own expense, a mission among the Baluch tribes within the British frontier.

Meanwhile, the Afghan War broke out, and Mr. Gordon volunteered to act as Chaplain to the force under General Sir Michael Biddulph, K.C.B. He proceeded with it to Quetta, and thence to Kandahar, in the winter of 1878-79. Returning to the Punjab, he resumed charge of the Church Missionary Society's stations at Pind Dadan Khan and Dera Ghazi Khan. Then he accompanied Bishop French to Quetta, and again joined the Forces as Chaplain at Kandahar, where he did good work among the soldiers in the citadel, and was most constant in his attention to the sick and wounded in hospital. He fell in the disastrous sortie on the 16th August, 1880. The event is thus described by an eye-witness, his fellow Chaplain, the Rev. A. G. Cane:—

"On that morning he was in the hospital, seeing the wounded as they were brought in. About 7 a.m. he left the hospital, and went to the Kabul Gate. There he heard that a number of wounded lay in a ziaret, some 400 yards from the walls. He was incorrectly informed that no one would venture out to bring them in, since four officers had already gone out there. Mr. Gordon, accompanied by Major Adam, at once set out with a dhoolie and bearers for the ziaret; they were under a most galling fire from both flanks, and as Mr. Gordon stood in the doorway of the little hut, a bullet from the village of Kairabad pierced his arm and entered his side, and the dhoolie which he took out brought him in. He suffered considerably in the morning, but about 3.30 passed away quietly, as if in sleep. He was buried the same evening along with several officers and men in a little cemetery within the city walls, and now rests, as he would have wished, beside those to whom he had faithfully ministered and amongst whom he fell."

SURGEON H. A. C. GRAY, M.B., C.M.,

BENGAL MEDICAL DEPARTMENT.

ENRY ALFRED CHATHAM GRAY, who died of cholera on the 4th July, 1879, at Peshawar, on the return march of troops from Afghanistan, was the eldest son of Honorary Surgeon Daniel Henry Gray, of the Madras Medical Establishment, and was born at Mercara, in Coorg, on the 23rd October, 1849. After receiving private tuition from his father, he entered Bishop Corrie's Grammar School in Madras, and subsequently, in 1866, matriculated at the University. A few months afterwards he obtained a Government Scholarship in the Madras Medical College, where—having abandoned, under the circumstance, his intention of continuing his University course—he commenced his studies in October 1867. In the following year he passed his Preliminary Scientific examinations, and two years later, the first examination for M.B. and C.M. Having, however, a predilection for the higher branches of medical science, he resolved to prosecute and complete his studies in an English university, with the view of obtaining a commission in the Indian Medical Service; and proceeding to England in May, 1871, in medical charge of a passenger ship, was enrolled shortly after his arrival as a medical student in the Edinburgh University. Here he distinguished himself by obtaining first-class honours in medical subjects; and in August, 1873, took his degree. During his collegiate career he devoted his leisure hours to the study of science and general literature, and published a poem which has been favourably reviewed by the Press in Scotland and Madras. After leaving the University, he officiated for a time, for friends, at Scarborough, Melrose, and other places.

In August, 1874, he obtained a commission in the Indian Medical Service, passing sixth in the list of successful candidates; and in October proceeded to Netley. In February, 1875, he was found qualified, and in the following May arrived at Calcutta, where he was employed in the Presidency General Hospital, and with the 25th Bengal Native Infantry. He was ordered to assume medical charge of the 18th Bengal Native Infantry at Agra in October, and a month afterwards marched with the regiment to Baxar Dewar. Summoned to England on urgent private affairs in the spring of 1876, he took six months' leave, at the expiration of which period he returned to Bengal, and was ordered to proceed in medical charge of convicts to Port Blair. On completion of this duty he went back, in December, 1876, to Calcutta.

The Madras Presidency being threatened at this time with a severe famine, Gray volunteered his services. On arriving in Madras in April, 1877, he was appointed Sanitary Medical Officer of the Chingleput district; his duties, which included the inspection of the villages and the direction of the medical and sanitary arrangements of the relief camps, involving much travelling and a considerable amount of exposure and hardship. He was subsequently ordered to the Karnul districts, and while there contracted malarial fever. His services in the famine campaign ranged over a period of eighteen months.

In October, 1878, in view of the impending Afghan War, he was recalled to Bengal, and was detailed for service to Sir Sam. Browne's Division. In the course of the campaign he had charge of the Native Field Hospital at Ali Musjid, and did valuable work at Dakka, Jalalabad, Safed Sang, and Gandamak, receiving the commendation of the principal medical officers under whom he served for his energy and for his attention to the sick under his care. It was on the return march of the troops to Bengal, at Peshawar, that he was seized with cholera; and his strength having been exhausted by his recent severe work, he succumbed almost immediately to the disease.

The Commander-in-Chief, in placing on record his appreciation of the valuable services rendered to the Army by the Medical Department mentions the subject of this memoir by name.

Mr. Gray was a frequent contributor to the "Indian Medical Gazette" and other scientific journals. By his untimely death the Madras Medical College lost one of its ablest and most distinguished students.

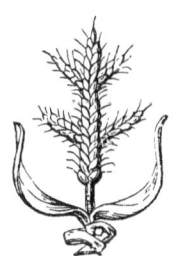

LIEUT. W. R. P. HAMILTON, V.C., STAFF CORPS,

QUEEN'S OWN CORPS OF GUIDES.

E had a brilliant career before him; he understood well the business in which he was engaged, and he was not afraid of the consequences which his duty entailed upon him." Such were the words used by Viscount Cranbrook, Secretary of State for India, with reference to the subject of this memoir in announcing to the House of Lords the disaster which had overtaken the Kabul Embassy.

Walter Richard Pollock Hamilton was the fourth son of Alexander Hamilton, Esquire, J.P., of Inistioge, Ireland, and Emma his wife, daughter of the late Right Hon. Sir Frederick Pollock, Bart., for twenty-two years Lord Chief Baron of Her Majesty's Court of Exchequer; and was great grandson of the Right Rev. Hugh Hamilton, D.D., Lord Bishop of Ossory. He was born on the 18th August, 1856, and was educated at Eagle House, Wimbledon, and Felsted School, Essex. In January, 1874, he obtained twenty-first place in the open examination for the Army, and was gazetted to the 70th Regiment. After serving for a few months at the Depôt, he embarked for India in October, 1874, and on arriving, joined the Head-quarters at Rawal Pindi.

On obtaining his Lieutenancy, Hamilton was offered, and accepted, a commission in the Corps of Guides. Within three months of joining that distinguished regiment, he passed the higher standard examination in languages, and was detailed to the Cavalry. Throughout the Jowaki-Afridi expedition of 1877-8 under General Keyes, he served as Aide-de-Camp to the commanding officer; and on the 14th March, 1878, was present at the operations against the Ranizai village of Skhakat.

In October, 1878, in view of the impending hostilities with Afghanistan, the Corps of Guides was moved to Jamrud at the mouth of the Khyber, and for a period of six weeks was employed in reconnoitering the mountains about the Pass. In the first of the two campaigns which followed, Hamilton participated throughout with the cavalry of the corps in the heavy work which fell to its lot. He was present in the front attack at the capture of Ali Musjid. In March, 1879, he commanded a troop on escort duty with a surveying party under Lieutenant Leach, R.E., which succeeded in beating off an attack of the Shinwari tribe. Taking part, in the last days of March, 1879, in the advance of General C. Gough's Brigade to Futtehabad, he was present at the engagement in that place—in which his dear and gallant friend Wigram Battye met his death—on the 2nd April; and his heroic bravery on the occasion won for him the Victoria Cross. The record which appears against his name in the "London Gazette" announcing Her Majesty's intention to bestow the decoration runs as follows:—" For conspicuous gallantry during the action . . . . in leading on the Guide Cavalry in a charge against very superior numbers of the enemy, and particularly at a critical moment when his Commanding Officer (Major Wigram Battye) fell, Lieutenant Hamilton, then the only officer left with the regiment, assumed command and cheered on his men to avenge Major Battye's death. In this charge Lieutenant Hamilton, seeing Sowar Dowlut Ram down, and attacked by three of the enemy whilst entangled with his horse (which had been killed), rushed to the rescue, and followed by a few of his men, cut down all three, and saved the life of Sowar Dowlut Ram." A few days after the action he marched with the Head-quarters of the corps to Gandamak, and was one of the officers who subsequently escorted Yakub Khan into the British Camp.

When it was determined to send an Embassy to Kabul, and Sir Louis Cavagnari was selected to act as Minister and Plenipotentiary, he chose Lieutenant Hamilton to accompany him as Political Assistant, as well as to command his escort of seventy-five men of the Corps of Guides. As is related elsewhere, the entire Embassy and escort, with the exception of one or two members of the latter, were foully massacred after a six weeks' residence in the capital, on the 3rd September, 1879. That portion of the official account of the tragedy which refers to the subject of this memoir states, "that at his final charge to silence a gun, which he did silence, Lieutenant Hamilton fell where he said he would fall, killing on his way to inevitable death three men with his pistol and two with his sword." Thus ended the brief career of as gallant a young officer as ever held Her Majesty's commission, regretted with a deep regret—which found expression in the words of his Sovereign, of Cabinet Ministers, and of the heads of the British and Indian Armies—as a loss to the service and the country.

We close this notice with some lines—dealing with a subject which, by a strange fatality, was on the eve of recurrence—penned by Walter Hamilton late in August, and posted by him eight days before the massacre of the Embassy took place:—

THE VILLAGE BÉHMARU: SCENE OF THE OUTBREAK OF THE KABUL DISASTER, 1841.

REVISITED, AUGUST, 1879.

  Though all is changed, yet remnants of the past
   Point to the scenes of bloodshed, and alas!
  Of murder foul; and ruined houses cast
   Their mournful shadow o'er the graves of grass
  Of England's soldiery, who faced a lot
   That few, thank heaven! before or since have shared;
  Slain by the hand of treachery, and not
   In open combat, where the foe ne'er dared

To show themselves. The fatal, honest trust
   Placed in an enemy who loved a lie,
And knew not honour, was a trust that cost
   The lives of those that gave it. Yet to die
Game to the last, as they did, well upheld
   Their English name. E'en now their former foe
Frankly avers the British arms were quelled
   By numbers only, and the cruel snow.
'Tis forty years since British soldiers turn'd
   To look their last on this now peaceful scene,
Whose lingering gaze spoke volumes as it yearn'd
   For vengeance due to treachery so mean.
And vengeance true did Pollock, Sale, and Nott
   Deal with a timely and unerring hand,
As they with victory effaced the blot
   Which just had dimmed the annals of our land.
And now while standing here, where side by side
   Fell many fighting with a fruitless bent,
Regret were uppermost, were't not for pride
   Which gives no place for weaker sentiment.
And Pride might well be foremost if one thought
   That though fair Fortune smiled not for a while,
How England's fame shone brighter as she fought,
   And wrench'd lost laurels from their funeral pile,
And rose at last from out misfortune's tide
Supreme—for God and right were on her side.

LIEUTENANT EDWARD HARDY,

ROYAL HORSE ARTILLERY.

THE subject of this memoir, who was killed in the action in the Chardeh Valley, near Kabul, on the 11th December, 1879, was the youngest son of the Rev. Charles Hardy, Vicar of Hayling Island, Hampshire. He was born on the 25th July, 1853; was educated at Blundell's School, Tiverton; and after a short preparation with Mr. Frost of South Kensington, passed into the Royal Military Academy, Woolwich, as Cadet, in January, 1872. He received his commission as Lieutenant in October, 1873. In 1874 he joined Battery G/3 Royal Artillery, then serving in India. During a severe epidemic of cholera which subsequently occurred, Hardy, as senior subaltern, was commanding the battery, owing to the illness of his senior officer. Writing of his conduct at this trying time, Captain Rooke says: "He threw all his heart into attending to the amusements and welfare of his men. We were camped out during the rainy season, and if he had been an officer of long standing in the service, he could not possibly have carried out the work better than he did." He returned to England on sick leave in 1876, and early in 1877 was appointed to the Depôt at Sheffield. Subsequently he was appointed to Battery H/6 Royal Artillery: and in October, 1878, went again to India, and was stationed at Lucknow. In the following spring, having volunteered for active service, he was appointed to Battery F/A, Royal Horse Artillery, then with the force under General Sir F. Roberts in Afghanistan. Accompanying the battery over the difficult Shutargardan Pass on the second outbreak of hostilities, he was present with it in October, 1879, at the occupation of Kabul.

On the 11th December, as subaltern to Major Smith Windham, Hardy was ordered out with four guns of the battery, escorted by two squadrons 9th Lancers and one squadron 14th Bengal Lancers, the whole under General Massy, to join General Macpherson on the Ghazni road; the object being for the two brigades to make a combined attack upon the Kohistanis who were reported to be assembling in force. Before, however, this movement could be effected, the enemy attacked the small force in overwhelming numbers, and owing to the swampy nature of the ground the guns got into difficulties. In spite of two desperate charges made by the cavalry, the enemy pressed on with great determination, and finally closed upon the guns, which were now abandoned and fell into their hands. Hardy was killed on the last gun, which was some distance behind the others, and on the limber of which lay a wounded officer of the 14th Bengal Lancers, who had been made over to his charge, and whom he refused to desert. This officer—Lieutenant Forbes—twice wounded before, had again been hit after he had been placed on the gun, and was now perfectly helpless. Hardy was last seen standing over him, surrounded by the enemy and using his revolver. The revolver was found, some days afterwards, near the spot, with three barrels still undischarged, and with the steel extracting-rod completely severed by a sword-cut; showing that the enemy had closed upon him, as he nobly stood his ground to defend his wounded comrade.

Under the heading "Martyrs to Duty," mention is made of Lieutenant Hardy's death in Major Mitford's book, "To Kabul with the Cavalry Brigade." After describing incidents of the action, the writer continues as follows : "Shortly afterwards, the guns took a wrong turning, and some delay occurred, during which the enemy swarmed down in overwhelming numbers. The drivers cut the traces, and one of the men called to Hardy to gallop away with them, but the gallant young fellow said, 'No! I won't desert my guns; besides, I can't leave that youngster' (alluding to Forbes). So they both met their deaths."

Lieutenant Hardy was buried with military honours in the Bemaru cemetery on the 31st December, and a wooden cross, erected by his brother officers, marks his grave.

His Commanding Officer, writing to announce his death, expresses " The great sympathy of the battery and deep regret at the loss they had sustained : also their admiration of one who died after fighting his guns very manfully under most trying circumstances."

The deceased officer married, in February, 1878, Emma Lennard, only daughter of Henry Downes, Esq., of Tiverton, Devon, who survives him.

SUB-LIEUTENANT F. H. HARFORD,

10TH (P.W.O. ROYAL) HUSSARS.

FRANCIS HARVEY HARFORD, who was drowned in the Kabul River on the night of the 31st March, 1879, was the second son of William Henry Harford, Esq., D.L., J.P., of Barley Wood, Somersetshire, and Old Down, Gloucestershire, and was godson and nephew in the maternal line of the late Lieut.-Colonel Harvey Tower, of the Coldstream Guards.

The subject of this notice was born in March, 1858, and having passed his early years at Laurence Weston, entered Winchester in 1871. Leaving the college in December, 1873, he proceeded to Bonn to study under Dr. Perry for Sandhurst, having been destined from his earliest youth for the Army. In 1876, before he had attained eighteen years of age, he succeeded in passing with credit the entrance examination for Sandhurst, obtaining full marks for German, in which language he was proficient. Addicted to all manly pursuits, he approved himself while at the college a keen sportsman and an accomplished hand at polo, for which game he retained his fondness to the last, being engaged in a match at Jalalabad only a few hours before his death.

Passing out from Sandhurst in 1877 in the first class, he was gazetted to the 16th Foot, then serving in Ireland. It was but for a short time, however, that he did duty with his first regiment; H.R.H. the Prince of Wales conferring on him an appointment to the 10th Hussars, then serving in India, he was transferred to that corps in October, 1877.

He left England in the following December, and joined the Head-quarters at Rawal Pindi. On the outbreak of the Afghan War in the autumn of 1878, he accompanied the regiment into the Khyber, and was present with it, on the 21st November, at the taking of Ali Musjid.

During the events which immediately succeeded, the 10th Hussars were stationed at Jalalabad. It was in the neighbourhood of this post, in the accident which consigned in the space of a few moments forty-six men of the regiment to one common grave, that Harford met his death. Forming one of the ill-fated squadron which was told off to accompany the force directed to co-operate with General

Macpherson's column in the second Lughman Valley expedition, he was swept away with the rest of the squadron, during the night of the 31st March, 1879, in the disastrous fording of the Kabul River at Kala-i-Sak, and was one of those found missing when the roll was called after the accident. On the 4th April his body was found lying untouched, and was buried with military honours on the evening of the same day, the General and all the officers in garrison following it to its last resting-place.

Few young soldiers have gone to an early grave more deeply regretted than the gallant but ill-fated subject of this brief memoir. His life was one of the finest promise, and there are none who knew him who could doubt that that promise would have been fulfilled to the utmost had he lived.

LIEUTENANT C. J. R. HEARSEY,

9TH (QUEEN'S ROYAL) LANCERS.

CHARLES JOHN RUMBALL HEARSEY, who was killed in action in the neighbourhood of Kabul on the 11th December, 1879, was the eldest son of the late Sir John Bennet Hearsey, K.C.B., by his marriage with Emma, daughter of Charles Rumball, Esq. He was born at Sialkot in the Punjab on the 7th February, 1856, and was educated at Boulogne, under the Rev. J. Bewsher, and at Ockbrook, Derbyshire, under the Rev. Joseph Jackson Shawe. In 1875 he entered the Army with an Indian Cadetship, and shortly afterwards joined the 9th Lancers, then serving in Bengal.

Immediately prior to the outbreak of hostilities with Afghanistan in the autumn of 1878, Hearsay proceeded with his regiment to Taru, on its being ordered up into the neighbourhood of Peshawar to form part of the Reserve Division. He subsequently accompanied the head-quarters and two squadrons which, under Colonel Cleland, were moved into the Khyber in the spring of 1879, on the forward concentration of the Northern Division of the Army of Invasion, sharing, at various stations in the Pass, the duties which fell to their lot, and returning with them into British territory after the signing of the treaty of peace at Gandamak. On the second outbreak of hostilities, in September, 1879, he served in the regiment in the force under Sir Frederick Roberts, taking part in the advance of the 2nd Division on Kabul, and being present at the operations in the second week in December. In the action of Killa Kazi on the 11th December, while gallantly charging with his troop against overwhelming numbers of the enemy, in the desperate effort made by the Lancers to save the surrounded guns, he fell shot through the heart. His body was subsequently recovered, and with that of his brother officer Ricardo, was buried with military honours in the cemetery at Sherpur.

The cool self-possession with which young Hearsey rode to almost certain death is of itself evidence of the fact that he was not wanting in one at least of the soldierly qualities which distinguished his late gallant father.

CAPTAIN P. C. HEATH, STAFF CORPS,

BRIGADE MAJOR, KANDAHAR FIELD FORCE.

PERCY CHARLES HEATH, who was killed in action on the 27th July, 1880, at Maiwand, was the third son of Major-General Heath, of the Bombay Army. He was born on the 11th April, 1847, and was educated at Sydney College, Bath, from whence he proceeded to Sandhurst. Passing out of the college after the usual course, he was gazetted to the 45th Sherwood Foresters, and proceeded to India, where the head-quarters were then stationed. He served with his regiment throughout the Abyssinian campaign of 1868-69, being present at the storming and capture of Magdala, and obtaining the medal. On the termination of the war he returned to India as Aide-de-Camp to Major-General Sir George Malcolm, commanding the Mhow Division. In July, 1869, he entered the Bombay Staff Corps, and was appointed Adjutant of the 17th Native Infantry. In June, 1874, he was transferred to the Adjutancy of the 5th Native Light Infantry. He subsequently served in the Quartermaster-General's department of the Bombay Army, and on the formation of the Bombay column for service in Southern Afghanistan, he was appointed Brigade-Major to the 1st Infantry Brigade under the command of Brigadier-General Burrows. This brigade formed part of the Girishk Column which was sent out to co-operate with the Wali's army on the Halmand against Ayub Khan, who was advancing from Herat. At the time the force left Kandahar, Captain Heath was prevented by a severe attack of illness from accompanying his brigade, but taking advantage of the despatch of a convoy of commissariat stores, he rejoined it at Khushk-i-Nakhud on the 18th July. Towards the close of the action at Maiwand, and shortly before the Native Infantry broke, he was with Brigadier-General Burrows on the left of the line, when a rifle bullet struck him in the head, and he fell dead from his horse.

LIEUTENANT THOMAS RICE HENN,

ROYAL ENGINEERS.

THE subject of this memoir, who perished on the field of Maiwand, Afghanistan, on the 27th July, 1880, was the third son of Thomas Rice Henn, of Paradise Hill, in the County of Clare, Esquire, J.P. and D.L., one of Her Majesty's Counsel and Recorder of Galway, by Jane Isabella, his wife, daughter of the Right Honourable Francis Blackburne, Lord Chancellor of Ireland. He was born on the 2nd November, 1849, in Dublin, and was educated at Windermere College, and the Royal Military Academy, Woolwich, into which he passed at the early age of seventeen years—without any special preparation, and having attended the examination solely in order that he might understand its character and be prepared for it on a subsequent occasion—second in the list of successful candidates. He obtained his commission in the Royal Engineers in July, 1869, and after serving for a period at Chatham, was ordered out to India. On arrival, he was posted to the Bombay Sappers and Miners, and passing through successive grades, serving at various stations, and winning approbation from all with whom he was associated by the zeal and ability he displayed in the discharge of his duties, he continued in that corps till the day of his death.

For some little time prior to the outbreak of the Afghan War, Henn had been stationed at Kirki, where he held the appointment of Officiating Quartermaster of the Corps. In January, 1879, he took part, in command of No. 2 Company, in the advance into Baluchistan of the detachment which was ordered up to form part of the Reserve Division of the Kandahar Field Force, and for several months was employed in the Bolan Pass on the road-constructing and other duties upon which it was engaged. He subsequently proceeded in command of his company to Kandahar, where, shortly after his arrival, he was selected to fill the staff appointment of Brigade Major of Engineers. It will perhaps be not out of place here to record the high estimation in which his talents and energy were held by Major-General Phayre, C.B., who recommended him in his despatches, and was at one time anxious to make him an Assistant Political Officer, and who, in his Field Force Order of the 22nd October, 1880, has paid a deserved tribute to his memory. In the first days of July, 1880, he took part in the advance of Burrows' Brigade to the

Halmand, and in the disastrous encounter with the enemy at Maiwand on the 27th of the month, he rendered up his life in an act of heroism which his country will be slow to forget. As regards his conduct on that fatal day, some interesting details have been given in a letter addressed to Sir Michael Roberts Westropp, Chief Justice of Bombay, by Lieut.-Colonel Hills, C.B., R.E., late Commanding Engineer at Kandahar, who writes as follows :—

"When I was appointed Commanding Engineer, I at once requested that he and his company of Sappers might be sent up to the front. On the move forward of the Brigade to Girishk, he and forty-four men and non-commissioned officers accompanied the force, and did excellent service during the long and trying marches. On the battle-field of Maiwand he and his Sappers were posted alongside the battery of Horse Artillery, and I am glad to say that they were the last of all the troops to leave the line of battle. Captain Slade, commanding the Horse Artillery (Major Blackwood having been severely wounded), told Henn he was going to limber up, and when he started off, he says, Henn made his men stand up and fire a volley into the crowd of Ghazis and regular troops pouring down upon them, and then gave the order to retire quietly and steadily. He had been wounded in the arm some time before this, but remained with his men to the last. He followed the line of retreat of the 66th towards the wall of the first garden, across the large nullah, and in a small water-channel in that garden he and the remains of his men took their stand with some men of the 66th and Grenadiers, and here he fell, using a rifle to the last : as far as I can ascertain, he was finally shot through the head and suffered little. Around this place were found, lightly buried, Henn and 14 Sappers, 23 men of the Grenadiers, and 46 men of the 66th : the mound in front was found strewn with horses of the mullahs and cavalry of the enemy, proving that our poor fellows had died hard and gallantly."

Lieut.-Colonel Hills then states that of his 44 men 8 to 10 were wounded, "so that his men under his noble example did their duty grandly." Again—"Their steadiness and admirable conduct is greatly attributable to his example and teaching. All I can add is, that he was a general favourite and greatly esteemed for his talents, and had he been fortunate enough to have survived, would have thoroughly earned his Brevet on the attainment of his Captaincy. In him I have lost a warm coadjutor and friend, and our Service an excellent soldier : one of the men of the 66th brought in his sword, which had been presented to him by his uncle. He had served under me for seven years, and no one could more thoroughly appreciate his sterling qualities and cheerfulness under trying circumstances."

Lieut.-General Primrose, in his despatch of the 1st October, 1880, giving details of the battle, states, on the authority of a Colonel of Artillery of Ayub Khan's army who was present at the time, that a party, estimated by the latter to consist of 100 officers and men, made a most determined stand in the garden. "They were surrounded by the whole Afghan army, and fought on until only 11 men were left, inflicting enormous loss upon the enemy. These 11 charged out of the garden and died with their faces to the foe, fighting to the death. Such was the nature of their charge and the grandeur of their bearing, that although the whole of the Ghazis were assembled around them, not one dared approach to cut them down. Thus standing in the open, back to back, firing steadily and truly, every shot telling, surrounded by thousands, these 11 officers and men died ; and it was not until the last man had been shot down, that the Ghazis dared advance upon them."

From an examination of the ground, from corroborative evidence, and from the position in which the bodies were found, it has now been clearly ascertained that this last stand was made by a party made up of the 66th Regiment, the Bombay Grenadiers, and the Sappers; and that the achievement of the eleven was the achievement of Henn, Hinde (of the Grenadiers), and Blackwood of the Horse Artillery (who had been carried, earlier in the action, a wounded man, to the ground on which he died), together with eight soldiers of the gallant 66th, whose officers, ten in number, had all fallen previously, as is minutely described in General Primrose's despatch, striving to save the colours of their regiment.

It only remains to be added, that Lieut.-General Sir Garnet J. Wolseley, K.C.B., who has examined such existing evidence as bears upon the disastrous battle of Maiwand, has stamped a distinguished soldier's approbation upon the conduct of the lamented subject of this memoir, and in a letter written to Lieutenant Henn's father, with a soldier's sympathy for the dead and for the living, has pronounced an eulogium upon him which may well remain graven upon the hearts of his family. "No hero," writes Sir Garnet, "ever died more nobly than he died; and I only wish it were possible for the country, for which he died, to properly evince its gratitude to his memory. I did not have the advantage of knowing him; but I envy the noble manner of his death. If I had ten sons, I should be indeed proud if all ten fell as he fell." And again he writes: "Had your son lived, he would, I presume, have been decorated by the Queen as one of her bravest soldiers." That, had he lived, he would have upheld the military fame of his gallant countrymen, and the honour of the profession which his life adorned and which he loved so well, his friends may rest assured, and in the assurance find consolation.

LIEUT. W. F. HENNELL, STAFF CORPS,

1st PUNJAB CAVALRY.

WILLIAM FREDERIC HENNELL, who fell a victim to cholera on the 21st July, 1879, at Kandahar, during the occupation of that city by our troops, was the youngest son of Colonel Samuel Hennell, formerly Resident in the Persian Gulf, and of Anne Inman Orton, his wife. He was born at Bushire in October, 1850. His parents soon afterwards returning to England, his early years were spent at Springfield, in the village of Charlton Rings, Gloucestershire. He was educated at Cheltenham College; and after passing through Sandhurst, received, in February, 1870, his commission in the 36th Regiment, then serving at Rawal Pindi, and afterwards at Mian Mir in the Punjab. Early in 1874 he entered the Bengal Staff Corps, and was at first appointed Officiating Wing Subaltern in the 23rd Pioneers, joining that regiment at Jhelum.

Having served his probationary year, he entered the Punjab Frontier Force, and was appointed Officiating Squadron Subaltern of the 1st Punjab Cavalry, stationed at Rajanpur, on the frontier. His regiment was one of the first ordered on active service in the Afghan War, and formed part of General Stewart's Division of the Army of Invasion.

During the greater part of the march to Kandahar Hennell filled the post of Acting Adjutant; and to the efficiency with which he performed the duties of his office, Major Maclean, who commanded the regiment, has testified in the very highest terms. After being present at the action of Takht-i-pul, he entered Kandahar with the regiment on the 9th January, 1879, and remained there till he succumbed to cholera, on the 21st July. He was universally beloved in the camp, and in his death everyone felt he had lost a personal friend.

2ND LIEUTENANT ARTHUR HONYWOOD,

66TH (BERKSHIRE) REGIMENT.

THE subject of this notice, who was killed in his twentieth year at the battle of Maiwand on the 27th July, 1880, while defending the Queen's colour of his regiment, was the fourth son of the late Sir Courtenay Honywood, and Anne Maria, his wife, second daughter of the late W. Paynter, Esq., of Richmond, and of Belgrave Square, London.

Arthur Honywood was born in the year 1860 at Evington Place, Ashford, and received his education in Hertfordshire. Proceeding to Sandhurst, he passed out of the college after the usual course, and was gazetted, in August, 1879, to a second Lieutenancy in the 66th Regiment. He embarked shortly afterwards for India, and joined the Head-quarters at Karachi, in time—to his infinite satisfaction—to take part with the regiment in its march to Kandahar. His term of service was destined, alas! to be of short duration. In the first days of July, 1880, he accompanied the 66th in its advance in Burrows' Brigade to the Halmand, and was present, on the 14th of the month, at the dispersing of the Wali Shere Ali Khan's mutinied troops in the neighbourhood of Girishk. At the battle of Maiwand, on the 27th, he was struck with a bullet early in the engagement. "I met him," writes one of his brother officers in reference to the last sad act of the drama of that day, "in one of the gardens, wounded through the leg." It is known that he reached the garden where the last desperate stand was made—that spot which has become sacred to the memory of the little band of heroes who, in their determination to sell their lives dearly, watered it so copiously with their blood. The sequel—in so far as the subject of this notice is concerned—is supplied in General Primrose's despatch: "Lieutenant Honywood was shot down whilst holding a colour high above his head, shouting, 'Men, what shall we do to save this?'"

WILLIAM JENKYNS, M.A., C.I.E., BENGAL C. S.,

SECRETARY TO THE BRITISH EMBASSY AT KABUL.

THE subject of this memoir, who rendered up his life in the last desperate charge from the gates of the burning Residency at Kabul on the evening of the 3rd of September, 1879, was the eldest son of his father, a gentleman bearing the same name, and occupying the office of Inspector of Buildings in the city of Aberdeen. Born on the 23rd August, 1847, he was educated partly at the Aberdeen Grammar School, and from thence proceeded, in 1864, to the University, gaining, by open competition, the Udny Duff Bursary. In 1867, during the third session, he capped his first success by carrying off the £10 prize for the best essay on a given subject; and in 1868 he graduated. With reference to his career as a student, which was throughout a notable one, we cannot do better than quote some passages from the interesting inaugural address delivered by Professor Geddes, from his Chair at the University, to one of the Arts classes, at the opening of the winter session of 1879. "In the year 1864," observed the Professor, in the course of his remarks, "I first became acquainted with William Jenkyns. He stood 4th in the Bursary List of that year, and I was therefore prepared to find in him a good scholar. I early became sensible that he was that, and much more, an earnest student, one that loved duty for its own sake, rejoiced in it, and devoted himself to it. His personal appearance was prepossessing .... and there was a light in the eye giving evidence of a fine spirit dwelling within—*mens pulchra*, to change the common quotation, *in corpore pulchro*. His course at College was one of great distinction. In every class of the curriculum he was a 'prizeman,' except in Natural Philosophy, where he was 1st O.M.; in that of Logic he stood second, and similarly in all the other classes. He studied for the Indian Civil Service, and came out 4th in the list of successful candidates at the examination—an ordeal far more difficult then than now,—having to contend, still a stripling, with men twenty-one or twenty-two years old, that being the age in those days up to which competition was allowed. The position he even then attained was so notable that I referred to it in a published address, now exactly ten years ago, at the opening of the session, in the following words:—'Another fact which I recall with the utmost pleasure on this occasion is the circumstance that one of our most promising classics only the other day, in 1868, in the month of his graduation at Aberdeen, came in 4th in the Indian Civil Service competition. To stand as high as 4th in that ordeal, while still what we call a 'Magistrand,' and wearing the scarlet gown, is, in my judgment, a feat equal to standing 1st with the usual addition of two years' special training, customary after the Magistrand year. You all know his name—no less amiable he was than accomplished—William Jenkyns.'"

After passing into the Indian Civil Service, the subject of this memoir spent two years in London, training for the work of the Judicial Department; and that he turned the time at his disposal to good account is attested by the fact that he took, during this period, no less than three of the money prizes offered for competition by the authorities. On the 7th October, 1870, he left Aberdeen for Bombay, embarking on the new phase of his career which was rapidly to bring him to the front in the ranks of Indian civilians. His first station was Multan, where he acted as Assistant Commissioner. In 1872 he was sent to Dera Ismail Khan, where, in addition to other work, he discharged the duties of Inspector of Schools. His next station was Mianwali. In the course of his service in the trans-Indus, he set himself to acquire the languages of the frontier—Pushto, the Afghan language, and Baluchi, the Baluch language. In both of these he passed distinguished examinations, and received handsome rewards; and it is perhaps worthy of record that he was the only British officer who, at the time, had succeeded in accomplishing this linguistic feat. He next set himself to the acquisition of Persian, and subsequently passed with high honour an examination in that language at Calcutta, receiving a prize of £200. In Arabic, too, he was prepared to pass a similar examination, but the exigencies of the public service prevented him from getting leave of absence from his post to attend for it. The fact of his having passed all these linguistic tests now brought him prominently into notice; and when Sir Lewis Pelly was despatched, in 1876, to Peshawar, as the British representative at the conference with the Amir of Afghanistan, Jenkyns received the appointment of Interpreter and Secretary to the Embassy.

After the dissolution of the conference, the subject of this memoir was selected to fill the post of Political Agent in Ladak, a distant province of the Kashmir Government, bordering upon Yarkund. He subsequently held various other appointments, including the Assistant-Commissionership of Peshawar. That in the tenure of one and all of these offices he discharged his duties with zeal and ability, is evidenced not only by the fact of his steady progress, but by the testimony of those under whom he worked and with whom he served.

On the outbreak of the Afghan War in the autumn of 1878, William Jenkyns was appointed a political officer with Sir Sam. Browne's Division of the Army of Invasion, and served with the force on the Northern line through the whole of the first campaign. In the negotiations which were consummated by the treaty of peace at Gandamak, he rendered material aid; and it is a pleasant picture which has been drawn of the delight expressed by his gallant and revered chief, Cavagnari, as the latter slung the precious document over the back of his able coadjutor, and despatched him at daybreak on his now historical journey to Simla and back. For thirteen hours Jenkyns remained continuously in the saddle, covering in that space of time, in the month of May, the 120 miles of broken ground which lies between

Gandamak and Peshawar, hurrying on to Simla, obtaining the Viceroy's ratification of the treaty, returning to Peshawar, taking again to the saddle, and eventually riding in to Gandamak on the third day after he had started on his errand. For this feat and for his services prior to it, a Companionship of the Order of the Indian Empire—a decoration which, alas! was destined never to reach him—was conferred upon him by Government.

During the wintering of the troops at Jalalabad, the subject of this notice occupied himself with collecting information specially with a view to revenue administration in the event of the district being annexed. For the mass of data he gathered together and subsequently published, he received the formal thanks of the Government of India. In sending a copy of his book to Professor Geddes, of Aberdeen University, with a letter from which most of the incidents detailed above have been gathered, he makes allusion to the little volume in a characteristic sentence. "It is nothing," he writes, "in itself, and can have no interest for you; but I send it merely to show I have been working"—and further on, adds:—"and that my thoughts are still of King's College."

On the despatch of the British Embassy under Sir Louis Cavagnari to the Court of Kabul, Mr. Jenkyns was "specially selected, in recognition of his proved merits and abilities,"—to quote the words of Government—to fill the post of First Assistant Political Officer. Incessantly active, he found time to address, after the arrival of the Embassy at its destination, a series of interesting letters to the "Pioneer" newspaper, descriptive of the capital in its physical, social, and political aspects, and presenting a vivid picture of the every-day life of the Embassy itself—the paying of ceremonial visits, the attendance at the parade-ground for public sports, the rides in the neighbourhood of the city, and the like. So matters went on, comparatively quietly, till the fatal 3rd of September—that day on which, in violation of almost the only law which Afghans profess to hold sacred, was re-enacted, after an interval of thirty-eight years, the ghastly tragedy which has stamped the name of its perpetrators in letters of blood on the page of history to be held up to everlasting execration. Of the little band who, after many hours' continuous fighting, sallied out, sword in hand, from the gates of the burning Residency, William Jenkyns was the last officer seen alive. In the thirty-second year of his age, in the hour when his manhood was fulfilling the splendid promise of his youth, he fell at his post, dying as a hero dies. Though destined, like many a hero, to be short-lived, he discharged during the brief span of his career, with a rare ability, multifarious and varied duties, and he has left behind him a name which his countrymen will not willingly let die.

LIEUTENANT W. N. JUSTICE,

PROBATIONER, STAFF CORPS.

WILLIAM NAPIER JUSTICE, who was killed in action at Maiwand on the 27th July, 1880, while serving with Jacob's Rifles as a probationer for the Bombay Staff Corps, was the eldest and only son of Lieut.-Colonel H. A. Justice, of the Madras Staff Corps, and of Isabella Caroline, his wife, daughter of Dr. Thomas Oxby, of the Bengal Medical Service. He was born at Singapore on the 6th January, 1858, and was educated at Cheltenham College. Gazetted, in September, 1876, to a Lieutenancy in the second Battalion 17th Foot, he embarked with that regiment a fortnight afterwards for Bombay, and proceeded with it to Mhow. After passing the necessary examinations, he was attached to the 21st Bombay Native Infantry (Marine Battalion) as a probationer for the Staff Corps.

In August, 1879, Lieutenant Justice was transferred to Jacob's Rifles, and in the month of October joined the Head-quarters at Quetta, Baluchistan. Appointed shortly afterwards to the Quartermastership of the regiment, and performing the duties of the post in a manner which called forth warm acknowledgment from his commanding officer, he accompanied the Rifles to Kandahar, and in July, 1880, took part with them in the advance of Burrows' Brigade to the Halmand. It is perhaps worthy of record that on the 23rd of the month he despatched from Khushk-i-Nakhud a letter to a friend in Bombay, showing a peculiarly correct appreciation of the position of affairs as they then were, and giving evidence of a power of observation which, had he been spared, would have stood him in good stead in his profession. His career, however, was destined to be cut short at its outset. In the disastrous encounter with the enemy at Maiwand, at the moment when he was attempting to rally his men at the most critical juncture of the battle, he fell mortally wounded, and a few moments afterwards expired in the arms of his brother officers, Captain Harrison and Lieutenant Rayner, of the 66th, as they were attempting to carry him into a less exposed position.

SURGEON A. C. KEITH, M.B.,

ARMY MEDICAL DEPARTMENT.

ALEXANDER CROMBIE KEITH was born on the 11th December, 1849, and was the youngest son of the late William Keith, Esq., M.D., of Aberdeen, and Burnette, his wife, daughter of James Silver, Esq., of Netherley, Kincardineshire. Educated at the Gymnasium, Old Aberdeen, and the Aberdeen University, where he took his degree, he entered the Army Medical Department in February, 1877, and went out to India the following year.

Till proceeding into Afghanistan on active service, Dr. Keith was stationed at Attock, where for some time he performed the duties of Civil Surgeon, and during an outbreak of cholera organized a camp hospital, for which he received the commendation of the authorities.

On the second outbreak of hostilities with Afghanistan in the autumn of 1879, he was detailed for service to Sir Frederick Roberts's Division of the Army of Invasion, and accompanying it in its advance, was present at the battle of Charasiab, the occupation of Kabul, and the defence of the Sherpur cantonments. Shortly after the reassertion of British supremacy in the capital, however, his career was brought to an untimely close. A chill caught by him during a reconnaissance was followed by an attack of pneumonia, which ended fatally on the 13th January, 1880.

Dr. Keith's kindly disposition, and his devotion to the sick committed to his charge, made him a general favourite, and caused his death to be deeply and widely regretted. He was a keen and excellent sportsman, and his genial companionship will long be missed by the friends with whom he was wont to make excursions with gun or rifle against the game of the country.

SURGEON A. H. KELLY,

BENGAL MEDICAL DEPARTMENT.

AMBROSE HAMILTON KELLY, who was killed in the defence of the British Residency at Kabul on the 3rd September, 1879, was the eldest son of William Russell Kelly, of Dublin, Solicitor. He was born on the 30th September, 1845, and was educated at the Rathmines School, then under the management of the Rev. Roger North. His studies in Medicine and Surgery were pursued at Dr. Steevens' Hospital, Dublin, where he was a resident pupil for two sessions, and obtained the highest prize awarded by the Governors. His diploma as Licentiate in Surgery from the Royal College of Surgeons, Ireland, is dated 26th January, 1869; and in the month of March following he obtained the diploma of the King and Queen's College of Physicians. On the 1st October, 1869, he gained his commission as Surgeon in the Bengal Medical Service, and proceeding to Calcutta in the spring of the following year, settled down to the uneventful life of ordinary professional routine in an Indian cantonment till the despatch of the Lushai punitory expedition gave him an opportunity for seeing active service and earning a medal and clasp. In the interval between the date of his arrival in Bengal and the winter of 1871-72, he did duty at the Presidency General Hospital (from the 7th June to 4th August, 1870), was attached to the 13th Bengal Cavalry and the 2nd Central India Horse (from the 4th August, 1870, to the 29th May, 1871), held medical charge of the Bengal Sappers and Miners (from 29th May to the 7th August, 1871), and officiated with the 3rd Bengal Native Infantry (from the 7th August to the 18th October, 1871). On the date last quoted he was placed in medical charge of the 22nd Punjab Infantry, and proceeding with that regiment into Lushai territory, was present with it throughout in the various operations of the Cachar Column.

On the return of the Expeditionary Force in the spring of 1872, Dr. Kelly was transferred for duty to the 1st Punjab Infantry, in the medical charge of which regiment he officiated for some twelve months. On the expiration of that period, the credit he had gained and the skill he had exhibited on various occasions secured him the coveted post of Surgeon to the Guides—a corps in which his eminent predecessors Bellew and Courtenay had performed distinguished service before him. From March 1873, till the time of his death, he was intimately associated not only with this famous regiment, but also, in his capacity of Civil Surgeon of Hoti-Mardan, with the entire Eusufzai district; and the peculiar facilities he enjoyed of intercourse with the inhabitants gave him considerable influence and gained him much respect amongst them. We next find him taking part in the expedition against the Afridis under General Keyes—for which he obtained a second clasp—in the winter of 1877-78, and in March, 1878, present at the surprise of the Ranizai village of Skhakat and the attack on the Utman Khel villages. The outbreak of the Afghan War once more called the Guides to the front; and from the memorable 21st September, 1878, till the signing of the peace of Gandamak and the close of the first campaign, Dr. Kelly was present with his regiment, adding to his high reputation by the success with which he coped with the heavy work which fell to his hand. There are many officers and men of the late Peshawar Valley Field Force who, amongst other reminiscences, will not soon forget the humanity and self-abnegation with which he devoted his abilities to the care of the sick and wounded Afghans and Kugianis at Gandamak.

On it being decided by Government to despatch a mission to the Court of Kabul, Dr. Kelly was selected to fill the post of Medical Officer to the Embassy, and in that capacity accompanied Sir Louis Cavagnari to the capital, in the month of July, 1879. Besides finding time, during his short residence in Kabul, to write home a series of deeply interesting letters—some of which have been made familiar to the public by their insertion in the columns of the "Times" newspaper—Dr. Kelly opened a dispensary in the city, which was daily thronged with applicants anxious to secure the skill of the "Feringhi" for their various ailments, which was freely bestowed on all. On the ill-fated 3rd of September, 1879, he met his untimely and tragical death, fighting manfully in the defence of the Residency with his gallant comrades in arms.

The subject of this memoir, Ambrose Kelly, was a man remarkable alike for his spirit of adventure and his high social gifts. Tall in stature, powerful in physique, a keen sportsman, something of a naturalist, and possessed of a great knowledge of horticulture, he was eminently qualified for the career he had chosen. It seems fitting that one whose life had been spent as his had, should have been found ministering to the last to the needs of the afflicted. Cut off in his prime, and, like his predecessor Lord in the first Afghan War, an ornament to his profession, his loss is deeply felt, not only by his brother officers, but by the Bengal Medical Service in general.

In Sandford Church, Dublin, a very handsome and interesting memorial of Dr. Kelly has been erected. It consists of a richly engraved mural brass tablet, and of a pair of stained-glass figure windows—the former, a tribute of the love and esteem of his brother officers, and the latter of the affection of his family.

SURGEON-MAJOR HENRY KELSALL,

ARMY MEDICAL DEPARTMENT.

THE name of Kelsall is not unknown in Her Majesty's Service, the father of the subject of this memoir having been a Surgeon in the Navy, and no less than three of his uncles—including Colonel Joseph Kelsall, who formerly commanded the 70th Regiment—having served with distinction in the Army.

Henry Kelsall, who was an only son, was born at Plymouth on the 28th March, 1834, and received his education at Orchard Hill, Northam, Frankfort-on-the-Maine, and University College, London. After subsequently pursuing, for a time, the study of Medicine at Guy's Hospital, and with Dr. Grouse in Suffolk, he entered the Army in September, 1855.

Gazetted to a troop of Royal Horse Artillery, then under orders for the Crimea, he was about to proceed to the seat of war, when his departure was arrested by the arrival in England of the news of the conclusion of peace. He continued to serve with this troop until appointed Assistant Surgeon to the 20th Foot, with which regiment he remained during the whole of its last term of Indian service, sharing the heavy and important work which fell to its lot. In the Mutiny campaign he was present at the affairs of Chanda, Umipur, and Sultanpur, under General Sir T. H. Franks, the taking of the Fort of Dauraha, and the siege and final capture of Lucknow; in the subsequent operations in Oudh, at the affairs of Mianganj, MorarMow, the Fort of Simri, Birah, and Baxa Ghat; and in the later campaign, under Lord Clyde, at the affairs of Chardu, the Fort of Masjidia, and Banki. For his services he was honourably mentioned in General Evelyn's despatches, and received the medal with clasp for Lucknow.

On the return of the 20th Regiment to England Kelsall was appointed, at his own request, to the Staff, in order that he might have leisure to prepare for his promotion to the rank of Surgeon, which he obtained in March, 1870. He was soon afterwards gazetted to the 2nd Battalion 1st Royal Scots, and remained in medical charge of that regiment until recent regulations abolished all such appointments.

Promoted Surgeon-Major in November, 1872, he did duty for a time at the

General Hospital, Devonport, and as Principal Medical Officer at Pembroke Dock.

On the outbreak of the Afghan War, Surgeon-Major Kelsall applied to serve in India, and was sent to take charge of Battery I/C, Royal Horse Artillery, which he joined on the 28th of March, 1879, direct from England, and continued with until the return march from Afghanistan. The strain of severe duties and the amount of exposure he underwent in a trying climate, proved, however, too much for a constitution already impaired by long residence in India and a recent severe illness, and on the 6th June, 1879, he fell a victim to an attack of pleurisy at Daka. His heroic fortitude and the disinterestedness he displayed throughout this illness in bestowing his entire attention on those around him, were of a piece with the broad humanity of his life: to the last all his care and thought were for others. Thus, not unworthily, ended the career of an officer whose professional attainments frequently gained for him recognition from those under whom he served both in quarters and in the field.

Surgeon-Major Kelsall's accomplishments were not few. He spoke several modern languages with fluency, possessed a considerable knowledge of drawing and of music, was an excellent horseman, and proficient in most field sports; these attributes, added to his more sterling qualities, gained for him the respect and esteem of all with whom he was associated in the different appointments he held.

The deceased married, in 1862, Annie, daughter of Mr. John Milne, of Montrose, who, with one son, survives him.

CAPTAIN J. A. KELSO,

ROYAL ARTILLERY.

JOHN ANDREW KELSO, who was killed at the Peiwar Kotal on the 2nd December, 1878, was the only son of the late John Kelso, Esq., of the Indian Civil Service, a gentleman who for many years had charge of the Government Revenue Survey in the Province of Assam.

The subject of this memoir was born on the 22nd February, 1839. After passing the earlier portion of his life with his parents in India, he proceeded to England, and studied for several years at King's College, London, from whence he entered Woolwich. Passing out from the Academy after the usual course, he was gazetted, in November, 1860, to the Royal Artillery, and, joining his battery in India shortly afterwards, did duty with it at various stations in the Bengal and Madras Presidencies for a period of seven years.

In March, 1868, Kelso was posted Subaltern to No. 2 Light Field Horse Battery, Haidarabad Contingent, and continued to serve with it until April, 1873, when he received his promotion and reverted to the regular service. After a twelve-months' interval, he was appointed Commandant of No. 2 Light Field Horse Battery, Punjab Frontier Force, which in January, 1877, was converted into No. 1 Mountain Battery, mules being substituted for horses. With this he served throughout the Jowaki campaign of 1877-78, obtaining the medal with clasp, and receiving honourable mention in Brigadier-General Keyes' despatches for the zeal and activity he displayed during the operations. Shortly after the conclusion of hostilities a severe attack of fever necessitated his proceeding on sick leave to the hill station of Murree.

In October, 1878, the battery was ordered up to Jamrud in view of the impending outbreak of war with Afghanistan, being detailed to Sir Sam. Browne's Division of the Army of Invasion, and Captain Kelso at once rejoined and resumed command of it. General Roberts, however, applying for its services, it was sent, a month later, to join the Kuram Force at Kohat, and proceeding from thence to Thal, took part in the subsequent advance of the division into the enemy's country. It was during the assault of the Peiwar Kotal on the 2nd December, in the hour of victory, that Captain Kelso met a soldier's death, being shot through the head at the moment when—to quote the words of an eye-witness—he had "moved up the steep slope with incredible rapidity, and, wheeling to the right, formed up on the left of the Highlanders, and opened fire."

Captain Kelso was an officer of high repute in the service, and the sorrow caused by his death was both deep and wide-spread.

After referring in his despatch to the assistance rendered by the battery in the advance, and to the determined manner in which the guns were fought, General Roberts, coupling the name of the deceased with that of the late Major Anderson of the 23rd Punjab Pioneers, wrote as follows:—"The death of these officers is mourned by the whole force, for both were well known as brave and excellent soldiers;" and in a private letter, after expressing his great admiration for Captain Kelso's very soldierly qualities, the General added: "Few men could have done what he did with his battery in so short a time, and I considered myself extremely fortunate in having him with my column."

Captain Kelso married, in January, 1867, at Trichinopoly, Marion, third daughter of the late W. H. Ranking, M.D., F.R.C.P.L., of Norwich. He leaves a widow, with one son and three daughters.

LIEUT. F. G. KINLOCH, STAFF CORPS,

5TH BENGAL CAVALRY.

FRANCIS GARDEN KINLOCH, who was killed in the Kuram Valley, Afghanistan, on the 29th September, 1879, was the third son of Colonel Grant Kinloch, of Logie, Forfarshire, and Agnes Garden, his wife (of Troup and Glenlyon). He was born in the year 1852, and was educated at Brighton College, and under the Rev. E. A. Claydon, at Blackheath. In 1872 he was appointed to the Highland Light Infantry Militia, with which he served as Musketry Instructor after receiving an extra first-class certificate at Hythe.

Gazetted to a lieutenancy in the Gordon Highlanders in February, 1874, he joined that regiment at Multan, and did duty with it at various stations in the Bengal Presidency. After acquiring, and passing in, the necessary Oriental languages, he was admitted to the Bengal Staff Corps. In 1877 he joined the 5th Bengal Cavalry, and in the following year was appointed Adjutant of the regiment.

Shortly after the outbreak of hostilities with Afghanistan young Kinloch volunteered for active service, "in any capacity so that he might go to the front." His application was supported by his Commanding Officer. "I have much pleasure," wrote Colonel Charles Gough, "in recommending him as an intelligent and active young officer, who would work hard and do well whatever he may be put to." Scarcely was the requisite permission gained, however, before an attack of fever laid him prostrate, and necessitated his being sent on sick leave to Simla. Shortly aftewards the massacre of the British Embassy took place, and an immediate advance on Kabul by the Kuram and Khyber armies was ordered. Though scarcely convalescent, Kinloch again volunteered "for the front," and was ordered to join the 12th Bengal Cavalry, then with General Roberts at the Shutargardan. Starting immediately, he proceeded by way of Kohat to Thal. Having joined Dr. Bellew, he accompanied him into the Kuram Valley, *en route* for Kabul. On the morning of the 29th September, 1879, finding that his baggage bullocks had not kept up, he turned back a short distance to hurry them on, when some forty men of the Orakzai tribe, who were lying in ambush behind some rocks near the road, fired a fatal volley, which, according to the testimony of his Sowar orderly, who escaped, killed him instantaneously. His body was recovered the same afternoon, and was buried next day in the cemetery at Thal—every officer and soldier in the garrison following it to its last resting-place. His sword and revolver, which were carried off by the enemy, were recovered some months afterwards by Brigadier-General Tytler's avenging column, and restored to his family.

Lieutenant Frank Kinloch's untimely and tragical end was deeply regretted by the officers of the different corps in which he had served, and by all others who had known him. The estimation in which he was held is attested by many warm expressions of regard which occur in letters written after his death to members of his family. "He was as promising a young soldier as ever I saw," wrote Sir Charles Brownlow, K.C.B., who had made his acquaintance while commanding at Rawal Pindi. "I often said he would be heard of if he saw any service." In a letter written by Major Shakspeare, his Commanding Officer, the verdict is concurred in in the following words :—"The regiment will feel his loss the more as time rolls on. The service has lost a good officer, and the 5th Bengal Cavalry a good Adjutant. I shall find it hard to replace him."

LIEUTENANT S. E. L. LENDRUM,

ROYAL ARTILLERY.

THE subject of the following brief memoir, who died of typhoid fever at Kokaran, near Kandahar, on the 30th April, 1879, aged twenty-three years, was the youngest son of the late James Lendrum, D.L., of Magheracross, Co. Fermanagh, and of Anne, his wife, daughter of the late Samuel Vesey, D.L., of Derrabard, Co. Tyrone.

Samuel Edward Latham Lendrum was born on the 10th September, 1855, and received his early education at Portora Royal School, in his native county. In September, 1873, he entered the Royal Military Academy, Woolwich, and after undergoing the ordinary course of three years, was gazetted to Battery 4/5 Royal Artillery. His commission bears date September 2, 1876. His home service, chiefly at Woolwich, extended over about eighteen months In the autumn of 1877 he embarked with his battery for India, and proceeded with it to Morar (Gwalior), where it was stationed for upwards of a year.

On the outbreak of hostilities in Afghanistan, Lieutenant Lendrum's battery was not among those selected for active service; he succeeded, however, in effecting a transfer to Mountain Battery 11/11, which formed a portion of Sir Donald Stewart's command. Joining his new battery at Simla, he accompanied the division in its laborious march through the Bolan Pass and across the Khoja range, reaching Kandahar on the 8th January, 1879. After a brief stay here, he took part with the battery in General Stewart's advance to Kalat-i-Ghilzai, from whence, with two guns, accompanied by 100 sabres of 15th Lancers and 50 Goorkhas, he was despatched for the purpose of collecting grain stored by the Amir. He was absent with this party just a month, having advanced up the Arghesan Valley as far as Maruf, when, their object being accomplished, they received orders to return to Kandahar. Here Lieutenant Lendrum remained till the middle of April, when he was seized with the fever which ultimately proved fatal to him. On the symptoms becoming serious, he was removed to the neighbouring village of Kokaran, and here, after thirteen days' illness, he died, tended to the last with extreme kindness by Surgeon-Major H. Skey Muir, M.D., as well as by two gunners, who had volunteered to nurse him.

Lieutenant Lendrum's ardent devotion to his profession, and the high opinions expressed of him by his Commanding Officers, had seemed to give earnest of a bright career. He was possessed of a gallant spirit that had never failed him, and was of a nature the most open, frank, and generous. These were his salient qualities, and they had gained for him, to an unusual degree, the warm affection of all among whom he was thrown. On his leaving Morar for active service the gunners of his old battery presented him with a mark of their regard; and over his last resting-place within the citadel of Kandahar a marble slab has been erected "by his brother officers in token of their esteem."

2ND LIEUTENANT E. D. LOS,

1ST BATTALION, 25TH (KING'S OWN BORDERERS).

ERNEST DANIEL LOS was the eldest son of Peter Roland Los, Esq., of the Hague, formerly for many years Consul for the Netherlands at Sunderland, and of Harriett, his wife, eldest daughter of the late Thomas Gray, Esq., of Balbirnie, near Montrose, N.B. He was born at Sunderland on the 6th January, 1860, and after receiving his earlier education abroad, was transferred, in compliance with his wish to enter the Army, to the United Services College, Westward Ho, North Devon, where for two years he had the advantage of studying under the head-mastership of Mr. Carmell Price. Energetic alike at work and at play, he won the hearts both of his masters and his young contemporaries by the manliness of his character and the geniality of his ways, and in course of time became prefect of the college. At midsummer, 1878, he entered Sandhurst, his name appearing thirteenth in the list of 160 candidates. Passing out from the college after the usual course, he succeeded in obtaining eighth place and taking honours. In August, 1879, he was gazetted to the 1st Battalion, 25th King's Own Borderers, then stationed in the Punjab on its return from active service in Afghanistan; and embarking for India a month afterwards, he joined the Head-quarters at Peshawar.

In December, 1879, in consequence of the serious events which were happening at Kabul, the regiment was a second time ordered to the front, and proceeded to Landi Kotal in half battalions. Taking part in the advance, Los was present, under Captain Dixon, with Colonel Boisragon's column, which, co-operating with General Doran's brigade, dispersed the Mohmands at Kam Daka on the 15th January, 1880, wresting the Gara heights from a force ten times its number. "He commanded the left flank of the front line of skirmishers," writes his senior officer, "and showed great courage in the bold way in which he climbed the hillside under a dropping fire." He subsequently took part with the regimental head-quarters in the Lughman Valley expedition, holding successively the appointments of Head Quartermaster and Transport officer, and the command of a company. In the tenure of these offices he showed, according to the testimony of his Commanding Officer, "an aptitude for and love of soldiering." In the first days of April he took part in the operations against the Wazir Kugianis; and in the middle of the month marched with the head-quarters to Pezwan. At this post he was seized with enteric fever, to which he succumbed on the 31st May, only a few hours before his friend and brother officer Lieutenant Herbert Spoor fell a victim to the same fatal disease.

Lieutenant Los's remains rest in the little cemetery at Pezwan. A headstone, erected by his brother-officers in token of the love and esteem they bore him, marks his grave.

LIEUTENANT G. H. LUMSDEN,

PROBATIONER, BENGAL STAFF CORPS.

GORDON HUGH LUMSDEN, who was assassinated in the Kuram Valley, on the night of the 19th February, 1880, was the younger son of Captain J. T. Lumsden, who was killed during the Mutiny, while with Lord Clyde's force advancing to the relief of the Residency, Lucknow; was a grandson of the late Henry Lumsden, Esq., of Auchindoir, Aberdeenshire; and a cousin of Sir Peter Lumsden, K.C.B., C.S.I., late Adjutant-General of the Army in India.

The subject of this notice was born on the 2nd February, 1857, and was educated at the College School, Taunton, under the Rev. W. Tuckwell, M.A. Being desirous to enter the Indian Civil Service, he commenced preparation for the examination at the age of sixteen years, with Mr. Scoones of London; but his health twice failing him while studying, necessitated a change of plan. Obtaining an Indian cadetship in consideration of his father's services, he entered the Army, and was gazetted to a Lieutenancy in Her Majesty's 43rd Light Infantry, then serving in India. After doing duty with that regiment for a twelve-month at Bellary, Madras, he proceeded in June, 1877, to Bangalore for the course of Garrison Instruction, and obtained a first-class certificate. Posted, in May, 1878, to the 8th Bengal Cavalry as a probationer for the Staff Corps, he subsequently served with that regiment throughout the Afghan Campaign of 1878-1879, accompanying the head-quarter wing to Kandahar and Kalat-i-Ghilzai, and being present with it in the expedition into the Arghæsan Valley, and in the defeat of the body of the enemy which attacked the British camp on the 10th February, 1879. On the return of the 8th Cavalry to Multan after the close of the campaign, he proceeded to Calcutta for the study of the oriental languages, and after a few months' preparation succeeded in passing with credit the Higher Standard examination.

In January, 1880, Lumsden was posted to the 13th Bengal Lancers, and full of eagerness and hope at the prospects of a continuation of active service, joined that regiment in the Kuram Valley. His expectations, alas! were destined never to be fulfilled. On the night of the 19th February, he retired, after mess, to his tent, and the next morning was found by his servant lying dead at the foot of his bed, covered with dagger-wounds, the attitude of his body denoting that a struggle with his assassinator had taken place. A man who subsequently came into the camp stated that he had met, many miles distant in the Mangal country, a professional thief, who boasted that for two nights he had prowled about the camp marking the positions of the tents, and that on the third, after lying hidden in a nullah till after midnight, he had crept up to and entered the one which appeared to be easiest of access; that while in the act of retracing his steps after collecting a number of articles, he had knocked something down; that the sahib who was sleeping within, awakened by the noise, had jumped up and seized his sword; and that he had sprung upon him and stabbed him till he died.

Thus, at its very outset, was cut short a career full of promise—a life which, notwithstanding the shortness of its duration, had given evidence of a development sufficient to satisfy the wide circle of friends who held it dear.

LIEUTENANT HECTOR MACLAINE,

ROYAL HORSE ARTILLERY.

THE subject of this memoir, whose quite recently murdered body was found in the camp of Ayoub Khan near Kandahar, by the victorious troops of General Sir Frederick Roberts on the 1st September, 1880, was the eldest son of William Osborne Maclaine, Esq., J.P., D.L., of Kyneton, Gloucestershire, and his wife Anna, only surviving child of the late John Thurburn, Esq., J.P., of Murtle, Aberdeenshire; was grandson of Colonel Hector Maclaine, who served with distinction in the Peninsular War; and was a grand-nephew of Major John Maclaine, who fell at Waterloo; of Captain Murdoch Maclaine, the only British officer killed at Maida; and of General Sir Archibald Maclaine, K.C.B., who was knighted for his defence of Matagorda,

Hector Maclaine was born on the 24th November, 1851, at Murtle, and was educated by private tutors at home until January, 1865, when he went to Eton. In January, 1870, he entered the Royal Military Academy at Woolwich. His commission in the Royal Artillery bears date 6th January, 1872. After serving for a time with the 5th Brigade at home, he proceeded, in October, 1873, to India, and joining Battery B/18, served with it at Haidarabad and Karachi. In 1874 he returned home with the battery (which after its arrival in England was transformed into I/2) and did duty with it at Woolwich, Preston, Coventry, and Athlone, until July, 1878, when he was appointed to the Horse Artillery. Two months afterwards he proceeded to India in charge of drafts for E/B, R.H.A., which battery he joined at Mhow, and subsequently proceeded with it to Kirki.

In December, 1879, owing to the Artillery losses sustained by our Army in the neighbourhood of Kabul, orders were received from Simla for a Lieutenant from a Horse Artillery Battery in the Bombay Presidency to be sent to the front. Maclaine at once volunteered to go, and on Christmas-day was despatched to the Khyber Pass to join Battery I/C, with which he subsequently served at Daka until it returned to India, when he left it to rejoin his old Battery (E/B) which had left Kirkee in February, 1880, for active service at Kandahar. Overtaking it a little way beyond Sibi, where it was delayed for want of transport, he marched with it through the Bolan Pass to Kandahar, which was reached on the 10th April, 1880.

In June, 1880, Maclaine, having been laid up for five weeks with fever, was sent in charge of invalids and convalescents to Baba Wali, and while there received notice that E/B was ordered out to join General Burrows' force in support of the Wali Shere Ali. Though no serious fighting was at this time expected, he left Baba Wali in the highest spirits at the prospect of any active service, and rejoined the battery. In the pursuit of the Wali's mutinous troops in the neighbourhood of Girishk, on the 14th July, E/B took an active part, and Maclaine, being allowed to choose his own ground for his guns, did considerable execution with them at comparatively close range. After the action the camp was moved to Kushk-i-nakhud. On the 23rd July there was a slight skirmish with about 500 of the enemy's horsemen, and Lieutenant Maclaine with Colonel Malcolmson was sent to look out for another body of the enemy reported near. In the disastrous action at Maiwand on the 27th of the month Maclaine was the first to get into action, going forward with his two guns to the left front and opening fire. The splendid behaviour of the battery while working the guns under fire for more than three hours, and the tremendous execution done, are testified to by the survivors, and received the highest praise in the despatches. When the native infantry broke, and the cavalry failed to charge, the swarms of Ghazis made a final and determined rush for the guns, and those of Lieutenant Maclaine being slightly in advance of the others, were unfortunately surrounded and taken before he was able to extricate them. From one account it would appear that it was impossible to retire the two guns, the limbers having gone back for more ammunition; and that after firing one last round Maclaine and his gunners had to fight their way out to rejoin Captain Slade and the other four guns of the Battery. Lieutenant Maclaine was slightly wounded in the hand. He assisted Captain Slade in the retreat, the other officers of the Battery being killed or wounded, and was in charge of the advance guns all through the terrible night of the 27th, the horrors and sufferings of which are now so well known. Many officers have testified to his noble and unselfish conduct and care for the wounded who crowded the guns. Early on the morning of the 28th, having been almost without food, water, or rest for nearly thirty hours, he and a non-commissioned officer left the road at the village of Sangiri in search of water for the wounded, who were suffering tortures of thirst. Lieutenant Maclaine was taken prisoner, though how is not exactly known: he never came back; and no trace of the non-commissioned officer has ever been found. It would appear that he must have been overpowered by numbers. Some natives say he went into a house, in search of some vessel in which to carry water to those sinking on the road, and that there he was hemmed in and taken. In the list of casualties he was returned as killed or missing; and the Royal Artillery Regimental List for the month of August was published without his name, his place in his Battery being filled up. Some time after Ayub Khan's army had surrounded Kandahar, it became known, however, that a British officer was a prisoner in his camp, and this prisoner was subsequently discovered to be Lieutenant Maclaine. Efforts were made for his recovery, but without success. Sir F. Roberts, hearing of his captivity, wrote from Kalat-i-Ghilzai to Ayub Khan, demanding his release. Native spies had reported the unfortunate prisoner to be ill of fever some time before this. When General Roberts and his troops had completed their march from Kabul to the relief of Kandahar, the former again endeavoured to obtain the release of Lieutenant Maclaine, but with no result. On the 1st September, in the hour of the crowning victory over the enemy, and with his triumphant brother officers and fellow-soldiers near at hand, he was murdered by his fanatic guard, and his dead body, yet warm, was found outside his little tent near that of Ayub Khan, by the 92nd Highlanders. Some Sepoy prisoners escaped alive; and it is probable that if Lieutenant Maclaine, who was a strong, athletic man, had not been weak from illness, he too might have effected his escape. Three healed wounds were found on his chest, inflicted by Ghazis who had attacked him in his captivity. In his tent was found a small scrap of paper, on which were a few pencilled words in the form of a diary, as follows:—

"July 28th. Kushk-i-nakud.
  „ 29th. Sangiri.
  „ 30th. Given to Cavalry, Sher Ahmed Khan—Imprisoned in Kokaran.
August 4th. Sirdar Noor Mohamed Khan arrived, and I got better treatment in his bungalow.
  „ 6th. Was handed over to Ayoub Khan in camp at Kokaran; well treated.
  „ 7th. Marched to near Kandahar Karez.
  „ 8th. Some shells from city in camp.
  „ 9th. Ayoub Khan moved camp N.W. of old Kandahar hill. City I believe surrounded by troops, but mostly Ghazis. Fighting near city most days.
  „ 14th. Loss of British cavalry and horses.
  „ 15th. Post captured. Two shells burst, well ranged, but wide of camp."

This is all the record of his captivity which exists. He was buried with military honours in Kandahar, together with the three officers who fell in the engagement, and between two of his own gunners.

Lieutenant Maclaine's cruel fate excited a most profound sensation among the troops. When the news of his most pathetic death reached England it created very wide-spread sympathy, and expressions of sorrow reached his family from the Queen, the Duke of Cambridge, and all the officers under whom he had served.

The following was entered in the Orders of his old Battery, I/2, R.A.:—

"It is with deep regret that Major Ward has read the announcement of the murder of Lieutenant Maclaine... By those who knew him he will be remembered as an officer of singularly soldierlike qualities, winning the regard and esteem of all with whom he was associated. All ranks of his old Battery have now to deplore his untimely end; and in paying their tribute of respect to his memory, the Battery would also express their sympathy and condolence with his bereaved relatives. Of the late Lieutenant Maclaine it may be truly said 'he died at the post of duty.'" And Major Ward adds: "Words would fail to express the sorrow felt by his old comrades on hearing the sad intelligence of his cruel fate. By all the men who ever served under him he was greatly beloved. His name will long be held in affectionate remembrance by the Battery in which the earlier years of his military life were spent." Similar testimony of his worth, and of the profound sorrow caused by his untimely fate, is given by Sir Frederick Roberts, in his despatch; by Colonel the Honourable A. Stewart, R.H.A., in a communication addressed to the "Times" newspaper, who says: "He was not only a good energetic officer and soldier, but an active, dashing, powerful, and enterprising man. I had frequent opportunities of seeing and admiring his great energy, his love of soldiering, and excellent military qualities;" by Colonel Hastings, R.A., under whom he had formerly served in India, who writes: "He is most deeply regretted by every one of us who knew him, old and young: all who have served with him confirm the opinion I formed of him—a thorough good soldier and a perfect English gentleman;" and by Major Slade, R.H.A., in a letter in which the assistance he rendered in the hour of defeat is warmly dwelt upon.

It only remains to be added, that beloved and respected as Hector Maclaine was in the Service, he was no less beloved and respected in civilian circles, and that, as an expression of their admiration for his qualities and their sympathy with his parents, the friends and neighbours of his family in Gloucestershire have erected a very handsome window in Thornbury parish church to his memory.

CAPTAIN W. H. M^cMATH,

66TH (BERKSHIRE) REGIMENT.

ILLIAM HAMILTON McMATH was the second son of Hamilton McMath, Esq., of Thornford, Co. Monaghan, Ireland, and of Mary his wife, eldest daughter of James Parker, Esq., of Mount Kearney, Co. Down. He was born on the 4th February, 1845. After some early training in the Grammar School, Dundalk,—where he was elected Captain by his companions, and won twice running the silver medal, the highest prize awarded,—he was removed to King William's College, Isle of Man, where, in 1861, he studied under the Rev. Gilmour Harvey and Dr. Dixon, the then Head Masters. He subsequently underwent a short special preparation for Sandhurst under Mr. De Burgh, of Dublin; and after passing through the usual course at the College was gazetted, in August, 1865, to an Ensigncy in the 66th Foot.

Joining the regiment at Davenport, he proceeded with it in January, 1867, to Aldershot, and subsequently to Jersey and Guernsey. In August, 1868, he purchased his Lieutenancy, and in October of the same year obtained a first-class certificate, extra, at the School of Musketry at Hythe.

After serving for twelve months at the Curragh and Dublin, he embarked with the 66th, in 1870, for India. While in Bengal he was temporarily attached to the 25th Native Light Infantry. On his leaving that corps to rejoin the 66th, a Regimental Order was issued by the Commandant, making warm allusion to the satisfactory manner in which he had performed his duties, and expressing regret for the loss of so promising an officer.

While stationed at Haidarabad in the Spring of 1871, and subsequently while at Belgaum in the years 1874 and 1875, McMath, with whom sport was little less than a passion, found many opportunities for enjoying his favourite pastime. On one occasion, while pursuing the larger game of the country in the district last named, severe injuries were inflicted on him by a wounded panther. He fortunately succeeded in killing the beast after it closed with him, and, holding his lacerated flesh together, managed, with the aid of his native attendants, who kept pouring water on his head, to walk a distance of six miles to his quarters. There he was tenderly nursed by his brother-officer and bosom friend, Captain Ernest Garratt, to whose care, as he was wont to assert, he owed his life. His constitution was excellent, and so thoroughly did he recover his strength that he was able to take part, in January, 1876, in the long march of the 66th, to Poona, a distance of 220 miles.

After holding for a time the Adjutancy of the Regiment, he obtained, in April, 1877, his company. Early in 1878 he availed himself of leave of absence, and visited England. He returned to India the same year, and rejoined the Head-quarters of the regiment at Kolaba. In March, 1879, he was appointed Officiating Adjutant in the camp of Deolali, through which all troops proceeding from and to England had to pass; and in November of the same year he was again at Poona, temporarily doing duty as Brigade Major.

On the 31st January, 1880, he received, to his great satisfaction, orders to rejoin the regiment for service in Afghanistan. He reached the Head-quarters at Nari Bank, and was there detached, with Lieutenant Lynch and his company, for the purpose of taking up to Kandahar a present of a battery of artillery from the Government to the Wali, Shere Ali Khan. In a letter describing this performance, he writes: "We had hard work taking the guns up the Bolan, also through the Gazaband and Khojak Passes. The latter operation took me two days, having had to encamp the first night on the top of the Khoja Amran Mountains, and taking the battery down the mountain was tough work. I, however, did not lose a single man, camel, bullock, or thing, and handed the battery over complete to the Afghans." This was at Chaman. The day the guns were handed over he received a telegram from Sir Donald Stewart, thanking him for bringing the battery forward with so little delay.

After reaching Kandahar he received the appointment of Commandant of the body guard of the General (his former chief, General Primrose), and had quarters in his garden. In the first days of July he took part in the advance of Burrows' Brigade to the Halmand, and acted as Brigade Major to the Field Force during the action on the 14th with the Wali's mutinied troops at Girishk. In a letter describing the operations of that day, he writes: "I was fourteen hours in the saddle on the 14th without having had a meal, and on the night of the 15th the whole of our force fell back upon this place, a march across a desert of twenty-five miles without a drop of water. Left the Halmand at 6 p.m., and did not arrive till 8 a.m., another fourteen hours in the saddle."

At the battle of Maiwand, on the 27th, McMath was seen steadying his company, to the command of which he had reverted, and was heard quietly to remark: "That's right, men; go on giving them volleys like that!" The company was the third from the right of the fighting line. Shortly after it was forced to retire, Captain McMath was struck by a round shot, which frightfully shattered his shoulder. His faithful servant, Haider Beg—a soldier who eventually escaped into Kandahar—ministered to his wants with water until ordered by him to quit the field and save his own life. The end was not far distant. Within a few minutes from the time of his receiving his first wound a bullet pierced his heart, immediately putting an end to his sufferings. Thus fell one of the best of men and most genial of comrades: "one who"—to quote from General Primrose's letter to the Adjutant-General, published in the "London Gazette" of the 31st

December, 1880—"had his life been spared, would have risen to distinction in Her Majesty's Service."

It is moving to record that Captain McMath's little dog "Nellie"—a pet of the regiment—which had followed her master into action, was subsequently found by the burying party lying dead at his side.

2ᴺᴰ LIEUTENANT E. S. MARSH,

2ND BATTALION, 7TH (ROYAL FUSILIERS).

EVERARD SWAINE MARSH, second son of the Rev. William Marsh, Vicar of Wethersfield, near Braintree, Essex, was born on the 8th June, 1858. He was educated at Wellington College, and when he left, in 1875, was a member of the cricket eleven, and the football twenty. From thence he proceeded to Blackheath, for private tuition under Professor Wollfram. After serving one training in the year 1878 with the West Essex Militia, he entered Sandhurst, and after the usual course, passed out from the college at the final examination second in priority, receiving a prize for Military Topography and Reconnaissance. Gazetted to a second Lieutenancy in the 7th Fusiliers in January, 1879, he joined the regiment at Bombay in the following March, and served with it in that Presidency for a period of two years.

In February, 1880, the battalion was ordered into Afghanistan on active service, and the subject of this notice took part with it in its march to Kandahar. In the month of July he accompanied the relieving force which was sent out to cover the retreat of the remnant of General Burrows' Brigade after the disaster at Maiwand, and with twenty of his men succeeded in taking no less than nine of the Ghazis prisoners, besides killing others. His services on this occasion, for which he was publicly praised by General Brooke, formed a fitting prelude to the act of heroism with which, three weeks afterwards, he closed his brief career.

In the fatal sortie to Deh Khwaja on the 16th August, he rendered up his life in the vain attempt to save that of his wounded brother-officer, Lieutenant Wood. His Colonel, in a letter to his parents, gives the following account of the manner in which he met his death:—"It was at the close of the action at Deh Khwaja that he was killed. He had passed through the thick of the fight, and was returning on Kandahar, when he was told that the dhoolie-bearers had left Lieutenant Wood, who was mortally wounded, to the mercy of the enemy. He at once got some men together and led them to the rescue, but in attempting to lift the dhoolie he was shot dead. It was a gallant act, and he died a soldier's death."

LIEUTENANT C. A. MONTANARO,

ROYAL ARTILLERY.

CHARLES ALFRED MONTANARO, who died on the 20th December, 1879, from the effects of a wound received in action before Kabul on the previous day, was the eldest son of Alfred Montanaro, Esq., late Commissary, Ordnance Department, of Great Grimsby, Lincoln, and formerly of Clifton, Somersetshire, by his marriage with Caroline Eliza, daughter of Captain J. Birch, 73rd Regiment, late of Crosby Lodge, Cumberland. He was born on the 20th June, 1855, and was educated at the Southampton College. Passing direct into Woolwich at his first attempt in February, 1872, he remained at the Academy for the usual course, his terms tallying with those of the late ill-fated Prince Imperial. In August, 1874, he obtained his commission, being gazetted to Battery 5/4 Royal Artillery, with which he did duty for eighteen months at Gosport.

Embarking with the battery in January, 1876, for India, he served with it at Allahabad and Morar until the beginning of 1878, when he joined the Punjab Frontier Force, being appointed to No. 2 Derajat Mountain Battery (Major Swinley's) at Abbottabad.

On the breaking out of hostilities with Afghanistan in the autumn of 1878, Montanaro took part in the advance of the battery which was detailed to the Kuram Valley Field Force, into the enemy's country, and was subsequently present with it in the operations in the Khost Valley, and at the action of Matun. On the renewal of hostilities in the autumn of 1879, the battery again formed a portion of the force under Sir Frederick Roberts, and did excellent service in the long train of events embodied in the second campaign. Accompanying it in the advance on Kabul, Montanaro was present at the battle of Charasiab on the 6th October, 1879, and at the subsequent occupation of Kabul and defence of Sherpur. On the 14th December, 1879, in the operations round Kabul, he distinguished himself by the gallant and determined manner in which he fought his guns on the conical hill till the enemy closed upon them, and by the material assistance he then rendered in bringing them out of action. How he stood to them to the last is recorded in the General's despatch of the 23rd December, 1879, which twice mentions his name. Five days afterwards, on the morning of the 19th, the battery was ordered outside cantonments with a small brigade to shell the enemy out of a village lying to the south-east of Sherpur. Scarcely had the guns gone into action in the open, when a heavy fire was poured upon them by the enemy from the front and flank. At the first discharge young Montanaro received his death-wound, a bullet fired at about 800 yards' distance striking him in the side, traversing his chest, and lodging in his spine. He fell immediately and heavily, as if dead, but when being lifted up gave the order, "Run the gun back." Carried at once into the Native Field Hospital, he received every care which the medical skill and devoted attention of Dr. Duke, the Surgeon of the battery, could bestow. His case, however, was, from the first, hopeless; he never rallied, and died quietly in the evening of the following day. As his first thought, when he was stricken down, was for his guns, so his last thought was for the home circle he loved. A few hours before he passed away, even as the death stupor was stealing on him, he dictated to Major Swinley, who was watching over him, a letter to his father. "I did not like to telegraph to you, for fear it should be too great a shock to you all"—so runs one of the essentially characteristic sentences.

In a letter testifying to the blank left by Lieutenant Montanaro's death, his commanding officer deplores the loss to himself, of a friend, and to the service, of a clever and most promising officer; and Sir Frederick Roberts, making reference to the sad event in his despatch of the 23rd December, 1879, recalls his mention of "this promising young officer's gallantry in standing to his guns to the last on the 14th December." That the estimate formed of him, and thus expressed, is not exaggerated, letters received from many unexpected sources after his death bear ample witness.

The subject of this notice was the inventor of a time-fuze that has been favourably reported on, and also of a saddle for carrying Pioneers' tools, which has been for some time in use, and in connection with which his name is perpetuated, it being entered in the equipment table as "Montanaro's Pattern."

CAPTAIN C. S. MORRISON,

14TH BENGAL CAVALRY (LANCERS).

CLAUDE STEUART MORRISON was the youngest son of the late James Colquhoun Morrison, Esquire, of Palermo, Sicily. He was born at Helensburgh, Dumbartonshire, on the 25th September, 1844, and was educated at the Glasgow Academy, the Forest School, Walthamstow, and Addiscombe. Entering the Indian Army in June, 1861, he did duty for two years with the 1st Battalion, 20th Foot; and after passing his examination in Hindustani was attached for a few months to the 6th Punjab Infantry and the 28th Bengal Native Infantry, respectively. In October, 1864, he was posted to the 3rd Goorkhas, and served with that regiment in the Right Column Dwar Field Force, as Officiating Quartermaster, through the whole of the Bhutan campaign of 1864-1866, being severely wounded in the temple at the outset. He received the Frontier medal, with clasp for Bhutan; and Brigadier-General Tytler testified, in his memorandum of the 31st of March, 1865, to the gallantry he displayed on all occasions of contact with the enemy. In the course of the campaign he held the appointment of Detachment Staff Officer to the camp in advance of Baxar.

On peace being concluded, Morrison proceeded for duty with a wing of his regiment to Bareilly; but his health—which had been undermined by fever contracted during his recent field service—giving way, he was sent home to Europe on eighteen months' leave. After returning to India, he continued for about a year to do duty with his old corps. He was then (August, 1869) appointed to the 14th Bengal Lancers, in which regiment — holding successively the appointments of 3rd and 2nd Squadron Officer, Adjutant, and Squadron Commander—he remained till the day of his death.

In March, 1870, he was promoted to the rank of Captain; and a few weeks afterwards was selected to form one of the deputation sent to Karauli. During a three months' residence at that place, he won golden opinions at head-quarters by the tact and judgment he displayed. "I do not think," wrote the Governor-General's Agent for the States of Rajputana, in recommending him for political employment, "that a better man could be selected;" and the Governor-General in Council was also pleased to signify his approbation of the manner in which his recent duties had been performed.

After doing duty with his regiment for a time subsequently to his rejoining it, he went through the short course of garrison instruction at Rawal Pindi, being specially mentioned for Fortification, Surveying, and Military Law; and three years later succeeded in passing for Army Staff employment. Almost immediately afterwards he again found his way to the front on active service, receiving the appointment of Provost-Marshal to the Force under Brigadier-General Ross in the Jowaki campaign of 1877-1878. "For most zealously carrying out the duties entrusted to him," he was favourably brought to notice in the General's despatch.

Accompanying the Right Wing of his regiment in January, 1879, to Thal, Captain Morrison did duty with it on the frontier during the first of the two Afghan campaigns, frequently crossing into the enemies' territory in pursuit of parties of freebooters, and earning the war medal. After the signing of the treaty of peace at Gandamak he remained with the regiment in spite of ill-health during the trying hot weather which ensued; and on the renewal of hostilities in the autumn of 1879, took part in the advance of the force under Sir Frederick Roberts across the Shutargardan. He was present at the battle of Charasiab (for which a clasp has been granted) on the 6th October, and at the subsequent entry into Kabul : there he remained till the end of November, when, yielding reluctantly to the repeated solicitations of the medical officers, he consented to seek rest, and accompanied the first sick-convoy to Peshawar. He arrived in India in so debilitated a state as to necessitate his being at once sent home on twelve months' leave; but the change came too late to save his life, and he died at the residence of his brother within a few months of reaching this country.

Captain Morrison's death is most deeply and deservedly regretted by all in the regiment. He was a most energetic, painstaking, and thorough officer, ever ready to take an extra turn of duty, or to do anything in his power to help or please his companions.

LIEUT. A. R. MURRAY, STAFF CORPS,

11TH (P.W.O.) BENGAL CAVALRY (LANCERS).

ARCHIBALD ROSS MURRAY was the eldest son of Brigadier-General J. I. Murray, C.B., who in the Mutiny raised that distinguished regiment the 14th Bengal Lancers, late "Murray's Jât Horse." Having obtained a Queen's Indian cadetship in recognition of his father's services, he joined the Depôt of the 44th Regiment in 1874. Shortly afterwards he was transferred to the 9th Foot, and accompanied that regiment to India, remaining with it till 1877, when he was attached to the 13th Bengal Lancers as a Staff Corps probationer.

On the outbreak of the Afghan War, Murray accompanied his regiment to Jamrud and into the Khyber Pass, where it formed part of the Second Division of the Peshawar Valley Field Force. He took part, in December, 1879, with the detachment engaged in the Bazar Afridi expedition under Sir Frederick Maude, and for the gallantry he displayed was mentioned in the General's despatch. During the next six months he continued with the regiment at various posts from the Khyber to Jalalabad, and in the month of June, 1879, shared with it the severe return march to India. Shortly afterwards he was permanently transferred to the 11th P.W.O. Bengal Lancers. He did not, however, live to join that corps. On the 18th July, 1879, his bright and promising career was cut short by cholera, to which disease he succumbed, after a few hours' illness, at Tret Punjab, at the early age of twenty-four years.

In a letter expressing his regard for the subject of this memoir, General Maude writes as follows:—"I had professionally a high opinion of him. I had intended, had his regiment not been sent to the front, to have made him my orderly officer, so as to give him an opportunity of seeing more service." And Colonel Low, of the 13th Bengal Lancers, in referring to his death, says: "When he left us we all felt it to be a regimental misfortune. A finer fellow or more promising officer I never saw."

A handsome memorial has been erected in the Church at Rawal Pindi "In affectionate remembrance" of him by his brother officers of H.M. 9th Foot and 13th Bengal Lancers.

BT. LIEUT.-COL. W. H. NEWPORT, STAFF CORPS,

28TH BOMBAY N.I.

ILLIAM HENRY NEWPORT, second son of the late Major Christopher Newport of the Bombay Army, was born at Bombay on the 23rd February, 1837, and was educated at Cheltenham and Addiscombe. Entering the Bombay Army in December, 1855, he was gazetted to the 3rd Europeans, and subsequently served with that regiment through the Indian Mutiny. He was present at the siege and capture of Ratgarh, the action of Baroda, where he carried the Queen's colours, the relief of Saugor, the capture of Garakota, the forcing of the Madenpur Pass, the siege and storming of Jhansi, the battle of Betwa, and the storming of Lohari, where he was severely wounded. At the assault of Jhansi he assisted in carrying out, under heavy fire, a wounded officer, after the order to retire had been given. For this act of gallantry, as also for leading stormers at the assault of Lohari, he was mentioned in despatches. He also took part in the actions at Kunch, Muttra, and Galauli; in the capture of Kalpi, and in the battle and subsequent capture of Gwalior. For these services he received the medal with clasp, and brevet rank on his promotion in 1867.

After the Mutiny, Lieutenant Newport joined the Staff Corps, and was posted for duty to the 18th Bombay Native Infantry. He served with a detachment of that regiment against the Waghirs in Kathiawar in 1865-66, and in Abyssinia in 1867. It was in that year that he was promoted to the rank of Captain and Brevet-Major. After this he served for a short time with the 25th, the 28th, and the 16th Native Infantry. From 1874 to 1876 he officiated as Fort Adjutant at Asurgarh, at the expiration of which period he returned as Wing Officer to the 28th Native Infantry. In the meantime (December, 1875) he had obtained his Majority. In 1877 he became second in command of the regiment, and received his Brevet Lieutenant-Colonelcy.

Lieut.-Colonel Newport returned to England on leave in June, 1878, but was recalled in October, 1879, to join his regiment on its being ordered up for service in Afghanistan. Engaged on varied duty during the spring of 1880, he marched with his regiment to reinforce the garrison of Kandahar on the 16th July of that year, and on the morning of the 16th of August sallied forth to take his part in the sortie which ended so disastrously. The history of that ill-fated attempt to capture the village of Deh Khwaja is well known; suffice it to say, that Lieut.-Colonel Newport led the detachment of the 28th who were with him, together with a company of the 7th Fusiliers, in the most gallant manner into the village. They reached an open space surrounded by walls, whence a deadly fire was at once opened upon them; and finding themselves hemmed in on every side, and cut off from all chance of reinforcements, a retreat was ordered. It was not until the last of this gallant little band were leaving that fatal spot, that Lieut.-Colonel Newport was observed standing, resting on his sword. On being questioned by Captain Adderley of the Fusiliers as to why he did not come on, he pointed to a bullet-wound in his left breast, and ordered him to take the men out of the village as fast as he could. He was carried a short distance by some of his own men, assisted by one or two of their comrades of the Fusiliers, but died in their arms, his body being afterwards recovered and buried with those of the other officers and men who fell at the same time.

As a soldier, Lieut.-Colonel Newport won the esteem and goodwill of all who became associated with him; whilst in private life he endeared himself to a large circle of relatives and friends, by his affectionate solicitude for the one, and the ever-ready hand of friendship he extended to the other.

An extract from a letter of his Commanding Officer, Colonel Nimmo (who was also severely wounded in this ill-fated engagement), may fitly close this short summary of an honourable career: "He won the admiration of all by his gallantry and bravery; and often when lying on my back unable to move, the men used to come and speak to me of him, recounting how splendidly he had behaved, and what confidence they had in him."

Lieut.-Colonel Newport married in November, 1868, Caroline Tunno, youngest daughter of the late Stanley Clarke, Esq., of Charlton Kings, Cheltenham, by whom he had issue four daughters.

LIEUT.-COL. GILBERT NICHOLETTS, STAFF CORPS,

COMMANDANT 2ND BALUCH REGIMENT.

HE subject of this memoir, who died at Kokaran, near Kandahar, of cholera, on the 18th July, 1879, was the eldest son of John Nicholetts, Esq., of South Petherton, Somerset. He was born on the 13th July, 1826; and after receiving an education at Rugby, entered the Indian Army in July, 1848, obtaining a Lieutenancy in 1st Bombay Fusiliers. After serving with that regiment for a period of six years, he was transferred, in 1854, as Adjutant, to the 1st Baluchis.

On the Persian War breaking out in 1856, Gilbert Nicholetts accompanied the late General John Jacob to the Persian Gulf; and serving with the 1st Sind Horse, was present at the attack on and capture of the Mohamra Forts. For his services he received the Persian medal and clasp. When peace was proclaimed, he rejoined the 1st Baluchis, which regiment had been despatched to the Punjab and North-west Provinces, on the outbreak of the Mutiny. In the campaign that followed in 1857-58, he was with the regiment throughout in the conspicuous part it played. While serving against the Fatehgarh rebels, he was present at the action at Gangri on the 14th December, 1857, and took part in the advance on and occupation of the enemy's position at Kasganj. Subsequently, while serving against the Rohilkhand rebels, he was present at the action at Anupshahr, the skirmish at Dinapur, the destruction of the enemy's boats, and at many minor affairs on the banks of the Ganges. In the campaign in 1858 he participated in the attack on the enemy's fortified position at Rampur Kussia, succeeding to the temporary command of the regiment on his Colonel (Farquhar) being disabled, and retaining it through the remainder of the campaign. He was present at the surrender and occupation of the Fort of Amethi, and subsequently with Lord Clyde's column at the occupation of Sankarpur, the action with Beni Madho at Dhundia Keria, and with a movable column detached after the action to drive the enemy across the Gumti. He then rejoined the force with the Commander-in-Chief at Lucknow, and served throughout the operations across the Gogra, including the advance on and occupation of Baraitch, the action with the Nana's force at Brigidia, and occupation of the Fort, the capture of the Masjidia Fort, the defeat of the Nana's force at Banki, and the final expulsion of the rebels across the Rapti, on the 31st December, 1858, earning a second medal.

In 1866 Captain Nicholetts (who had, in the meantime, received his promotion) was specially selected by the Commander-in-Chief of Bombay to command the 2nd Baluchis; and when, in October, 1877, the regiment was ordered up to the frontier, the high state of discipline and efficiency in which it left Karachi, was sufficient to show that Sir Robert Napier's confidence had not been misplaced.

In October, 1878, Colonel Nicholetts proceeded, in command of the regiment, from Dera Ghazi Khan to Quetta, to join the force under General Biddulph which was in course of concentration, in view of the impending hostilities with Afghanistan. He took part with the regiment in the advance into the enemy's country in November, and was present at the action at Takht-i-pul and the subsequent entry into Kandahar on the 8th January, 1879; and afterwards, between January, and July, in the expeditions to Girishk, Har Kalabist, and the Khakrez Valley.

His distinguished career was now drawing to a close. In the second week of July, while in command of the regiment at Kokaran, he was seized with cholera, to the ravages of which disease he succumbed on the 18th of the month.

Lieutenant-Colonel Nicholetts was a thorough soldier, distinguished for the great love he bore his profession. Though he was strict in maintaining discipline in the regiment which he had raised to such a high state of efficiency, his genial manner and kindness of heart rendered him deservedly beloved by all ranks. By his untimely death the Indian Army sustained a heavy loss.

LIEUTENANT CHARLES NUGENT,

ROYAL ENGINEERS.

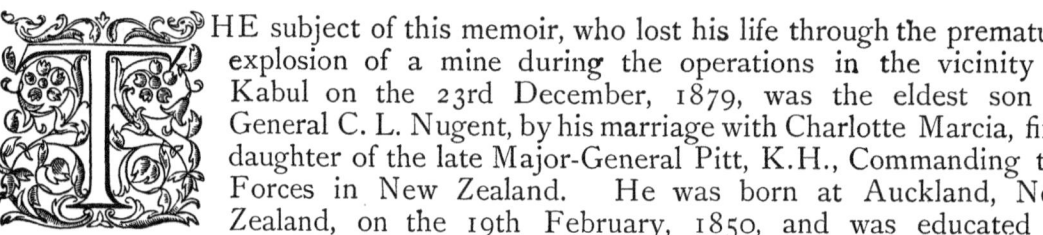HE subject of this memoir, who lost his life through the premature explosion of a mine during the operations in the vicinity of Kabul on the 23rd December, 1879, was the eldest son of General C. L. Nugent, by his marriage with Charlotte Marcia, fifth daughter of the late Major-General Pitt, K.H., Commanding the Forces in New Zealand. He was born at Auckland, New Zealand, on the 19th February, 1850, and was educated at St. Andrew's, Scotland, under Mr. Thomas Hodge, and Dublin, under Mr. H. Basset. He entered the Royal Military Academy in 1869, and passing out twenty-first in priority after the usual course, was gazetted, in August, 1871, to the Royal Engineers.

After serving for three years in England, he proceeded, in September, 1874, to India. On his arrival, he was posted to the Bengal Sappers and Miners, and did duty for four years at Rurki and Rawal Pindi.

On the concentration of the troops on the frontier in the autumn of 1878, in view of the impending hostilities with Afghanistan, Lieutenant Nugent proceeded in command of the No. 7 Company of the Sappers and Miners to join the Kuram Valley Field Force, and taking part in the advance into the enemy's country, rendered important service on the road over the Shutargardan Pass, and in other localities. On the renewal of hostilities in the autumn of 1879, he took part, in command of his company, in the advance of the force under Sir Frederick Roberts, on Kabul, and was present at the battle of Charasiab on the 6th October, and the subsequent entry into that city. During the occupation of Sherpur, he was employed on the works for the defence of the cantonment, in the construction of which he and his brother officers won golden opinions, by the zeal and ability they displayed; and was also previously engaged in the hazardous duty of destroying the large quantity of powder lying loose about the Bala Hissar. On the 23rd December he was directed to join General Macpherson's force with his company, to aid in the destruction of the line of forts held by the enemy to the southward of the cantonment. In performing this duty he entered, in company with Captain Dundas, V.C., Royal Engineers, a fort immediately under the Siah Sang, and before he emerged from it two violent mine explosions took place. On search being made immediately afterwards, his lifeless remains, together with those of Captain Dundas, were discovered by his comrades. Death had apparently been instantaneous, the bodies having been thrown by the explosion—the premature nature of which has been attributed to the too rapid consumption of a home-made quick-match—completely across the enclosure of the fort.

Lieutenant Nugent was buried with Captain Dundas on the 25th December, in the Sherpur cemetery. In a Division Order issued by Sir Frederick Roberts on the day of the funeral, the following words occur:—"Both Captain Dundas and Lieutenant Nugent had gained the esteem and admiration of all by their manly, modest, and courteous bearing. By their death the Corps of Royal Engineers has lost two most valuable officers, and the Kabul Field Force two gallant and much lamented comrades."

COLONEL J. J. O'BRYEN, STAFF CORPS,

COMMANDANT 22ND (PUNJAB) BENGAL N.I.

AMES JOSEPH O'BRYEN was the sixth surviving son of Terence O'Bryen, Esquire, of Glancolumbkill, County Clare, Ireland, a lineal descendant of the ancient royal line of Thomond —the last of whom, Murrough O'Brien, on surrendering his kingdom or principality to King Henry VIII. in 1543, obtained for himself and his heirs permission to change the *i* in the family name into *y*.

In November, 1843, the subject of this notice obtained an Ensigncy in the 16th Native Infantry (Grenadiers) in the Honourable East India Company's Service. Taking part in the Sutlej campaign of 1845-46, he was present at the battles of Mudki, Firozshah, and Sobraon, in the latter of which he was wounded. The gallantry he displayed in action won for him the commendation of his Commanding Officer, Brigadier Maclaren, who was himself mortally wounded in the campaign. For his services he received the medal and two clasps.

Posted to the Adjutancy of the regiment in 1852, O'Bryen continued to hold the appointment till the disbanding of the Grenadiers in the Mutiny of 1857. For the next six years he did duty in different parts of India, being for a time barrack-master of Moradabad and Almorah, and also officiating second in command of the newly-raised 16th, or Lucknow Regiment. He was admitted to the Staff Corps on its formation ; and in 1863 obtained his Majority. In 1864 he became permanent second in command of the 22nd Punjab Infantry, in which capacity he served in the Lushai expedition of 1872, receiving the medal and clasp. In 1874 he obtained command of his regiment as well as his Colonelcy, and three years afterwards served with it during the Jowaki campaign of 1877, the clasp for the same being awarded to him.

In December, 1879, Colonel O'Bryen marched with his regiment into Afghanistan on its being ordered up from the Peshawar district to form part of the 2nd Division of the Kabul Field Force. It was but for a little time, however, that he was able to share with it in the Khyber the duties which fell to its lot. His long service of thirty-six years and upwards had some time since begun to tell on his constitution; but though advised by his medical officer to take a few months' leave and recruit his health, he steadily refused to desert his post at so critical a time. His condition rapidly grew worse; and five weeks after crossing the frontier he succumbed to the effects of exposure and hardship, dying at Safed Sang on the 21st of January, 1880, in the 57th year of his age. By his death, the Service lost a most efficient, active, and zealous officer, conspicuous alike for his gallantry and his great goodness of heart.

Colonel O'Bryen married, in 1851, Louisa, daughter of R. Barnes, Esquire, of Purneah, Bengal, and leaves a large family.

MAJOR C. V. OLIVER,

66TH (BERKSHIRE) REGIMENT.

CHARLES VALENTINE OLIVER was the second son of John Dudley Oliver, Esquire, of Cherrymount, County Wicklow, Ireland, who was the head of a younger branch of the Olivers, of Castle Oliver, County Limerick, a family well known in Ireland for many generations.

The subject of this memoir was born on the 9th March, 1836, and was one of five brothers who entered the Army within a short time of each other. He was gazetted to the 66th Regiment, as Ensign, in 1854, and passed his whole service in that distinguished corps in various parts of the world, including India, Gibraltar, the Channel Islands, Great Britain, and Ireland. Although never purchased over, his promotion was slow, and he only obtained his regimental majority a short time before his death.

Major Oliver was one of the officers sent out to Jamaica in 1866 to serve on the court-martial which tried two officers accused of acts of cruelty in putting down the negro rebellion in that island, and which honourably acquitted them. After his return to England, he served with the regiment at Aldershot, Jersey, Guernsey, the Curragh, and Dublin; and in 1870 proceeded with the head-quarters a second time to India. When the regiment was stationed at Karachi, he was for a considerable time in charge of the Sanitarium of Ghizri.

Major Oliver marched with the regiment to Kandahar in February, 1880, and was present at the action on the Halmand, near Girishk, on the 14th July. At the battle of Maiwand, on the 27th, he was one of the three officers present with the colours who came out unhurt. It is said that he and General Burrows were the two last to leave the field, and they were so hard pressed that he was obliged, in self-defence, to shoot with a rifle two or three of the Afghan cavalry who attacked them on the open plain. It will perhaps not be out of place here to remark on the pain and distress he was subjected to through his name being confused with that of another officer, and being quoted in several of the English journals in a list published by them of the survivors of the battle who were the first to reach Kandahar, thus making it appear that he had ridden on ahead of his men. The officer alluded to was another of the same name belonging to a different service. The fact is, that telegraphic communication had been severed some hours before Major Oliver with the scanty remnant of his regiment reached the city walls. He arrived in a state of great exhaustion from which he never quite recovered.

Although Major Oliver suffered much from weakness during the siege, he nevertheless commanded all that was left of the 66th at the battle of Kandahar on the 1st September. After the defeat of Ayub Khan's army, he continued in a low state of health, and he subsequently fell an easy victim to the disease—small-pox— which eventually carried him off on the 10th October, 1880. His death was thus alluded to in the "Kandahar News:"—"All our readers will receive with feelings of deep sorrow and regret the sad news of the death of Major C. V. Oliver, 66th Regiment, which occurred yesterday morning in the citadel, from small-pox. After bringing back the remnants of his regiment from the fatal and terrible field of Maiwand, and the still more terrible retreat on Kandahar, and passing safely through the perils of the siege, he was on the eve of marching to India, en route to England with his regiment, when the fell disease struck him down, and in little more than a week our Queen and country had to deplore the loss of a faithful servant, and the 66th Regiment, the Kandahar Field Force, and the whole Army, a fine soldier, brave officer, good companion, and staunch friend. Requiescat in pace."

2ND LIEUTENANT W. R. OLIVEY,

66TH (BERKSHIRE) REGIMENT.

HE subject of this notice, who was killed at Maiwand on the 27th July, 1880, while carrying the Queen's colour of his regiment, was the second son of Lieut.-Colonel W. R. Olivey, Chief Paymaster, Army Pay Department (for nearly twenty years Paymaster of the 1st Battalion, 12th Regiment) and Elizabeth, his wife, only daughter of the late R. Goodfellow, Esq., of Falmouth, Cornwall.

Walter Rice Olivey was born at Sydney, New South Wales, on the 19th March, 1860. After receiving a preliminary education, he was prepared for Sandhurst at the Grammar School at Bury, in Lancashire, by the Rev. E. H. Gulliver, the then head-master, and went direct from that establishment to the College. Passing out in December, 1879, fifteenth in the honour list, and taking the prize for Military Topography, he was gazetted, a month afterwards, to the 66th Regiment, and on the 11th March, 1880, left Portsmouth for India, to join headquarters.

Olivey reached Kandahar in time to take part with the regiment in the advance of Burrows' Brigade to the Halmand in the first days of July, and was present on the 14th of that month at the dispersing of the mutinied troops of the Wali Shere Ali Khan in the neighbourhood of Girishk. At the battle of Maiwand, on the 27th, he forfeited his young life with the 300 officers and men of the regiment who fell. Early on that day he was severely wounded, but would not relinquish the colour he was carrying, though urged to do so. "I was speaking to him after he was wounded," writes one of his brother officers. "His helmet was off and a handkerchief was tied round his head." He was last seen in the garden where the final desperate stand was made, encouraging the men around him, and holding his colour aloft as a rallying point.

LIEUTENANT E. G. OSBORNE,

ROYAL HORSE ARTILLERY.

EDMUND GEORGE OSBORNE, who was killed in action at Maiwand on the 27th July, 1880, was the fourth son of Robert Osborne, Esq., of Laurence Weston, Henbury, Gloucestershire, and Emily Theresa, eldest daughter of Admiral Charles Warde, K.H., of Squerryes Court, Westerham, Kent. He was born on the 10th December, 1853, and was educated at Sydney College, Bath. In the spring of 1872 he competed for admission into the Royal Military Academy at Woolwich, and succeeded, out of a large number of candidates, in taking second place. Passing out of the Academy at Midsummer, 1873, he was gazetted to a Lieutenancy in the Royal Artillery, and shortly afterwards proceeded to Bengal in one of the garrison batteries. A few weeks after arriving in India he exchanged into Field Battery F/4 Royal Artillery, then stationed at Saugor. He was subsequently appointed District Adjutant of Artillery at Jabalpur, and retained the post till the autumn of 1878.

On the concentration of the troops on the frontier, in view of the impending invasion of Afghanistan, Osborne received the appointment of Adjutant of the Royal Artillery Kuram Valley Field Force, and subsequently served in his new capacity through the whole of the first campaign. For his conduct in the assault and capture of the Peiwar Kotal he was honourably mentioned in General Roberts' despatch of the 2nd December, 1878; and Colonel Lindsay, commanding the artillery of the force, reported that he had "received valuable assistance from Lieutenant E. G. Osborne, R.A., his Adjutant, and that this officer was most useful, in aiding the officers of No. 1 Mountain Battery, especially after Captain Kelso was killed." He subsequently took part in the Khost Valley expedition, and in nearly all the minor affairs in which the force was engaged.

On the conclusion of the first Afghan campaign, Lieutenant Osborne returned to England on leave. In less than a week after his arrival at home, however, the news of the Kabul massacre and of the renewal of hostilities reached him, and he at once hurried out with all speed to India. On arriving in Bombay, he was ordered to rejoin his battery at Saugor, but very shortly afterwards was again sent to the front for service with Sir Frederick Roberts' Division. On his way up country, the intelligence reached him of his transfer to Battery E/B, Royal Horse Artillery, then on its march to the front to form part of the South Afghanistan Field Force. Joining the battery *en route*, he accompanied it to Kandahar. He subsequently took part in the advance of Burrows' Brigade, in the first week in July, 1880, to the Halmand, and did excellent service with his guns in the encounter with the Wali's mutinied troops in the neighbourhood of Girishk. In the disastrous battle of Maiwand, on the 27th of the month, he remained unhurt till he was ordered to limber up his guns and retire. Few of his men were left at this time to carry out the order; and at once dismounting, he went to their assistance. It was in the performance of this act that he was shot dead, rendering up his life at his post with a heroism which has contributed in securing the verdict that on that ill-fated day " the conduct of the Artillery was beyond praise."

" I would bear testimony," writes Major A. H. Murray, R.A., " to his (Lieutenant Osborne's) high spirit and love of his profession. I am also aware that the late Major Blackwood had the highest opinion of him as an energetic and reliable young officer. Whenever there was tough work to do, young Osborne was to the front, and doing it well. He was a keen sportsman and brilliant polo player—altogether as fine a specimen of the British subaltern as I have met in twenty-four years' service."

LIEUT. W. C. OWEN, STAFF CORPS,

3RD BOMBAY CAVALRY (QUEEN'S OWN).

WILLIAM CHARLES OWEN was the only son of William Louis Owen, Esq., of the Bengal Police; was grandson of the late Major Arthur Owen, of the 26th Bengal Native Infantry, Honourable East India Company's Service; and great-nephew of the late General Sir John Hearsay. He was born the 11th of June, 1848, and received his education under Mr. Berridge, at the Collegiate School, St. John's Wood, and under Mr. Ogle, at St. Clere, Sevenoaks. From the school last named he passed into Sandhurst in February, 1871; and obtaining while at the college the first prize for drawing, and a prize for gymnastics, passed out in the first class.

In December, 1871, he was gazetted to a sub-lieutenancy in the 3rd King's Own Hussars, and joined that regiment at Ahmadnagar in November, 1872. While serving with the head-quarters at Mhow, he went through a course of garrison instruction. In May, 1878, he was appointed a probationer for the Bombay Staff Corps, and subsequently passed the final examination for that branch of the service—his papers being pronounced "first-rate."

Posted to the 3rd Queen's Own Bombay Light Cavalry, Owen did duty with it at various stations in the Presidency till February, 1880, when it was ordered up from Disa for service in the Afghan War. Accompanying it to Kandahar, he subsequently took part with it, in the first days of July, in the advance of Burrows' Brigade to the Halmand, and in the successful encounter, on the 14th, with the Wali's mutinied troops in the neighbourhood of Girishk. In the disastrous battle of Maiwand on the 27th, after being kept standing, with the rest of the regiment, under a murderous fire for four hours without a vestige of cover, he is said to have been shot while charging through the horde of Ghazis who were swarming on the rear of the then retreating Infantry.

This promising young officer met his death in the courageous discharge of his duty; and his name will not soon be forgotten in his regiment. "A more genuine and honest fellow"—to quote the words of one of his brother officers, written after his death—"never breathed." He leaves a widow and an infant son.

LIEUT. EDMUND PALMER, STAFF CORPS,

BENGAL COMMISSARIAT DEPARTMENT.

THE subject of this memoir was the eldest son of Lieutenant-Colonel Edmund Palmer, R.A., and great-grandson of John Palmer, Esq., M.P. for the City of Bath, and Comptroller-General of the Post Office. He was born at St. Helena, on the 10th February, 1851, and after receiving a private education, was prepared by Mr. Thompson, of St. Heliers, Jersey, for Sandhurst. He entered the Royal Military College in 1868, and passing out after the usual course, obtained a commission, by purchase, in November 1870, in the 1st Battalion the Buffs, which regiment he joined a few months afterwards at Sitapur. During his service in Bengal he acted for a short period as Interpreter to the Battalion, and only relinquished the post in order to enter the Staff Corps. Of his proficiency as a regimental officer, the late Colonel Cox, of the Buffs, on more than one occasion, expressed his appreciation.

In January, 1875, Lieutenant Palmer succeeded in passing the Higher Standard examination; and subsequently served as Wing Subaltern with the 41st Bengal Native Infantry, until he was appointed, in 1877, to the Commissariat Department of the Indian Staff Corps. After doing duty for a time at various stations in Bengal, he was selected, in February, 1879, to serve on the Commissariat Staff of the Khyber Field Force, and remained actively employed on the line of communications till the day of his death. During this period the zeal and intelligence with which he performed the harassing duties which fell to his lot, earned for him the character of a "hard-working man;" and his genial and cheerful disposition endeared him to his comrades, and helped to relieve the tedium of duty in the isolated forts on the line of communication. He was mortally wounded, on the evening of the 14th April, 1880, in the Hissarak expedition, while acting as galloper to Colonel Ball-Acton, commanding the force, and died on the morning of the 15th. On the following day he was buried with military honours at Pezwan.

Lieutenant Palmer leaves a widow (daughter of Dr. S. C. Amesbury, of the Bengal Army, Surgeon-Major Bengal Sappers and Miners, and Station Staff-Surgeon and Civil-Surgeon, Rurki) and an infant daughter.

LIEUTENANT EDMUND PALMER, STAFF CORPS.

The deceased officer was sprung from a family which has rendered the country good service. His grandfather, Captain Edmund Palmer, of H.M.S. " Hebrus," obtained a Companionship of the Bath and the gold medal for the capture of the French frigate, " L'Etoile," the last tricolour hauled down in the old war; his grandmother was niece of the great Earl of St. Vincent; and his maternal grandfather, Lieutenant-Colonel Ross, was dangerously wounded at the battle of Vittoria.

CAPTAIN E. W. PERRY,

40TH (2ND SOMERSETSHIRE) REGIMENT.

ERNEST WENMAN PERRY, who died of cholera at Quetta, Baluchistan, on the 19th of June, 1879, was the fourth son of James Bracey Perry, Esq., of Ley Hall, Handsworth, Staffordshire, and Marianne, his wife, daughter of William Wenman, Esq., of Gosbrooke, Staffordshire. He was born on the 2nd August, 1846, and was educated at Leamington. In May, 1870, he was gazetted to an Ensigncy in the 2nd West India Regiment, and in June, 1871, purchased his Lieutenancy. Exchanging shortly afterwards into the 40th Foot, he accompanied that regiment, in October, 1872, to India, and served with it for a period of six years at various stations in Bengal.

On the outbreak of hostilities with Afghanistan in the autumn of 1878, Captain Perry volunteered for active service in any capacity, and after some delay was sent to the front on Transport Service. Detailed for duty to General Stewart's Division of the Army of Invasion, he served through the whole of the first campaign on the Kandahar line of communication and at the base, sharing the arduous and important work which fell to the lot of the department to which he was attached, and approving himself an officer of energy and resource in overcoming the innumerable difficulties incident to his appointment. The exposure and hardship which he underwent in the course of the operations eventually proved, however, too much for him, and within a few weeks of the signing of the treaty of Gandamak, he fell a victim to the disease to whose ravages so many of his fellow-countrymen subsequently succumbed.

OFFICIATING DEP. SURG.-GEN. J. H. PORTER,

ARMY MEDICAL DEPARTMENT.

JOSHUA HENRY PORTER, who died in the Sherpur cantonment near Kabul, on the 9th of January, 1880, while serving as Principal Medical Officer of the Force under the command of General Sir F. Roberts, was the eldest son of the late Joshua Porter, Esq., High Sheriff of Dublin, and was born on the 24th May, 1831. He received his early education under the tuition of the Rev. Thomas Flynn, of Dublin, and went afterwards to the Diocesan School of Elphin, on Mr. Flynn becoming head master of that institution. His bright, happy disposition as a boy made him a general favourite with his masters and schoolfellows. At an early age he exhibited a special taste for mechanical pursuits, and in after life his aptness in this direction proved to be of much service to him in his surgical practice. He expressed a desire to become a surgeon while still very young, and when, on leaving school, he was apprenticed to his uncle, the late W. H. Porter—then the eminent Professor of Surgery in the Royal College of Surgeons of Ireland—he devoted himself to the study of Surgery and Medicine with the same steadiness of purpose and zeal that distinguished him subsequently throughout his professional career. The records of the Meath Hospital and County of Dublin Infirmary show that while a student there he gained the junior Surgical prize in the session of 1849-50, the prize in Clinical Surgery in 1850, and the senior Surgical prize in the session of 1850-51. Dr. Samuel Gordon, President of the College of Physicians, and Vice-President of the British Medical Association in Ireland, when commenting publicly in Dublin on the death of Mr. Porter, referred to this part of his life in the following terms:—" To some of us he was known in his student days as the most intelligent and painstaking clinical clerk of his time, and at the same time the most genial companion. His watchful care over the patients entrusted to his charge, and the sense of responsibility which he felt, augured well for the further development of industry, observation, and conscientiousness, when he came to be a qualified surgeon; and these three qualities he combined in a higher degree than perhaps is often met with."

In 1852 Mr. Porter became a Licentiate of the Royal College of Surgeons of

Ireland, and in June, 1853, he was gazetted Assistant-Surgeon in the 97th Regiment. In May, 1854, this regiment embarked for foreign service, and towards the end of the following month landed in the Piræus. Shortly afterwards, in July, the regiment was visited by an appalling outbreak of cholera, which taxed the energies of the regimental medical staff to the utmost. The conscientious and unselfish attention which Mr. Porter devoted to the discharge of his trying duties on this occasion, established his reputation among all ranks in the corps as a thoroughly good and reliable surgeon. In November of the same year, the 97th Regiment left Greece and proceeded to the Crimea, where it remained actively engaged in the siege operations until the fall of Sebastopol. In 1857 Mr. Porter proceeded with his regiment to India, and took part in numerous engagements with the Sepoy mutineers, including the siege and capture of Lucknow, and the storming of the Kaisèr Bagh. He was also engaged in the subsequent military operations in Bundlecund in 1859. The value of the services rendered by him during the nineteen years he passed in the 97th Regiment, and the feelings of esteem and affectionate regard which existed towards him in the minds of his comrades of all grades, cannot be better shown than by quoting from a farewell letter written to him by Major Annesley, the officer commanding the 97th, at the time he was leaving the regiment to take up another appointment:—

"As you will soon be leaving us," says the writer, "I hope you will allow me to bear testimony not only to your very high character as an officer and a gentleman, but to the invaluable services you have rendered the 97th Regiment as medical officer during the nineteen years you have served in it. I saw you join, and I now see you leave; and the very great regret I feel at losing you as a companion and medical adviser is shared by every officer and soldier in the regiment.

"I have had opportunities of witnessing and admiring the skill, energy, and unremitting attention you have always shown in the performance of your duties, and at times under very trying circumstances. During the fearful epidemic of cholera in the Piræus, where we lost so many men, during the terrible winter of 1854, in the Crimea, and later, when the 97th formed the assaulting and ladder party at the storming of the Redan, and you were in sole charge of the many wounded on that occasion; again in India during the Mutiny, when the regiment suffered from cholera, small-pox, and sunstroke;—on all these occasions your services were deserving of the highest praise. Under fire you have proved yourself a gallant soldier; in the hospital, a most careful, kind-hearted, and eminently skilful surgeon and physician.

"During your stay in the 97th Regiment you succeeded in gaining the confidence, respect, and esteem of every man in it."

It would not be easy to conceive a tribute to meritorious service of which an army medical officer might be more justly proud than of this.

The appointment which Mr. Porter entered upon after leaving the 97th Regiment, and for which he was selected solely from the professional reputation and high character he had already won in the service, was the Assistant Professorship of Military Surgery in the Army Medical School at Netley. In this new position he displayed all the superior qualities which had been anticipated. As an operating surgeon he proved himself to possess judgment, resolution, and skill. In his province of supervising and instructing the young surgeons who were about to enter the public service, while maintaining regularity and strict discipline, he was never wanting in kind consideration and tact. His industry and professional zeal formed a good example to all with whom he was associated. During the time he was holding the appointment, notwithstanding the numerous demands on his time, he found opportunities of publishing several surgical essays and reports of much practical value, more particularly a work which is now in its second edition, the "Surgeon's Pocket-book," specially adapted for the use of medical officers in the military medical service. This work had originally gained one of the prizes offered by the Empress of Germany, on the occasion of the Vienna World-Exhibition, for the "best handbook on surgical appliances and operations for the battlefield." During the same period, too, in April, 1876, the Alexander Memorial prize of £50 and a gold medal were awarded to Mr. Porter for the best essay on a particular surgical subject. This prize had been open to competition by all the executive medical officers of the Army. Mr. Porter also, during this period, took an active interest in the ambulance work of the Society of St. John of Jerusalem, in England, of which he was an Honorary Associate.

In January, 1879, Surgeon-Major Porter left England for active service in India, and was shortly afterwards posted to the charge of one of the field hospitals of Sir Sam. Browne's Division of the Army operating in Afghanistan. He accompanied the Division to Jalalabad, and afterwards moved to the front at Gandamak. When the troops were about to quit the last-named position, he was selected to accompany an officer of the Quartermaster-General's Department, and join in organizing the camping and hospital arrangements for the return of the troops through the Khyber Passes to India. He received great praise for the energy and judgment with which he accomplished this important duty under the trying circumstances of the intense heat and many difficult conditions which prevailed at the time. His Excellency Sir Frederick Haines, the Commander-in-Chief, by General Order, dated, Simla, 14th October, 1879, announced that "while grateful to all for the zeal and devotion displayed in the discharge of most trying duties, the Commander-in-Chief is more especially so to Surgeons-Major J. H. Porter and J. A. Hanbury, of the British Medical Service, for their able and efficient arrangements;" and in a subsequent paragraph conveyed the special thanks of the Viceroy and Governor-General in Council to these two medical officers. Surgeon-Major Porter remained a short time at Peshawar, where he superintended the hospital arrangements for the reception and treatment of the officers and men who had fallen sick during the return march to India, and was then appointed to officiate as Deputy Surgeon-General of the Allahabad Division.

On the resumption of hostilities which followed the massacre of the Staff of the British Embassy at Kabul, Mr. Porter was suddenly ordered to leave Allahabad and join the head-quarters of General Roberts at Ali Khel. On reaching his destination he was ordered to take charge of the Divisional Field Hospital, but on the first march of the force, on September the 27th, an attack was made upon it near Jaji Thana by some of the hill-tribes, and in this encounter Dr. Townsend, the Principal Medical Officer of the Division, was wounded in the face and compelled to retire from the field. This casualty left Surgeon-Major Porter senior medical officer, and from that date until his fatal illness, including the time when the Division fought its way over the Shutargardan Pass to the city of Kabul, up to the last assault of the enemy on the Sherpur cantonments, he discharged the duties of his new office. Here, again, although the period of his service with the Division was relatively brief, Surgeon-Major Porter acquired the confidence and regard of officers and men of all ranks in the force. The Divisional Order which was issued by Sir Frederick Roberts at the time of his decease runs as follows :—" The Lieutenant-General announces with deep regret the death of Officiating Deputy Surgeon-General J. H. Porter, Principal Medical Officer of the Division. Dr. Porter served in the Crimea, Indian Mutiny, and the late Afghan campaigns with distinction, and had gained experience from them which has been invaluable in the important office he has lately held. By his death Her Majesty's Service is deprived of an officer of great merit. The Lieutenant-General in company with the officers and men of the force, loses a friend whose professional skill was always at the service of the sick and suffering, and whose kindness of disposition had endeared him to all." And the then Minister for War, Colonel Stanley, in moving the Army Estimates for the year 1880 in the House of Commons, paid a striking tribute to his memory. " The medical service, and the medical world in general," he said, " have suffered a great loss by the death of Deputy Surgeon-General Porter at Sherpur. He died in the discharge of his duty as truly as if he had laid down his life on the field of battle. He leaves behind him a reputation to which his friends will look with satisfaction and a memory dear to all those who knew him.' " The illness to which Mr. Porter succumbed was a severe attack of pneumonia, a malady which was prevalent at the time in the cantonment.

Surgeon-Major Porter occupied a position in the estimation and regard of his professional brethren no less distinguished than that which he held among his military companions and friends of the combatant ranks. Professor Maclean of Netley, who was intimately acquainted with his personal character as well as with his work as a surgeon, thus publicly spoke of him : " I have in my life known few men more worthy of being loved and respected. As a surgeon he was cautious, patient, painstaking ; he laid surgical hands rashly on no man ; but, when his mind was made up to act, his hand executed with rare skill what his mind had conceived. He was eminently a successful surgeon. No woman had a more tender heart : he was a loyal colleague, and a much trusted friend."

This memoir cannot perhaps be more fitly closed than by quoting the words uttered by one on the first occasion which offered itself of publicly testifying to the admirable qualities which had distinguished his friend—of one who was ably assisted by Surgeon-Major Porter for five years in discharging the duties of the chair of Military Surgery at the Army Medical School at Netley, namely, Surgeon-General Thomas Longmore, C.B., to whom the editor of this work is indebted for the particulars already given. " The soundness of his judgment in surgical diagnosis," observed the professor in reference to his late colleague, " the dexterity he had acquired as an operator, his zeal for the professional reputation of his department, his indefatigable industry and devotion to duty, his warm-hearted and amiable disposition, formed a combination of qualities which made not only myself, but others who were well acquainted with him, look forward to his filling the highest posts in his department with distinguished credit ; and though all too brief, his career in Afghanistan, particularly that part of it when he was directing the medical affairs of the Kabul Field Force, as testified by the honourable tribute paid to it by the General Commanding and by the regrets of his comrades, sufficiently proved that these anticipations had been well grounded. The death of Surgeon-Major Porter was an irreparable calamity to his personal friends, and a grievous loss to the branch of the profession of which he had already become a conspicuous ornament."

Surgeon-Major Porter held the Crimean medal with clasp for Sebastopol, the fifth class of the Medjidié, and Turkish medal; and the Indian Mutiny medal with clasp for Lucknow. He also received the German steel war medal and the bronze cross of the French National Aid Society for service with the British ambulance during the Franco-German War of 1871.

The grave of Surgeon-Major Porter in the British cemetery near Sherpur has been protected by a massive stone, which bears not only an inscription in English, but also an appropriate one in Persian. The latter was added by his thoughtful and loving comrades in the hope of insuring to the ground hallowed by so many affectionate memories due respect in the future, after it had passed from their guardianship into the hands of others, strangers in race and religion. His brother-officers and friends have also placed a handsome marble monument to his memory in the chapel of the Royal Victoria Hospital at Netley. This monument bears upon it a medallion-portrait in profile of the deceased officer.

LIEUTENANT BROWNLOW POULTER,

ROYAL ENGINEERS.

THE subject of this notice, who died at Peshawar on the 22nd June, 1879, from the effects of illness contracted in the field, was the eldest son of Brownlow Poulter, Esq., of Lee Park, Blackheath, and Charlotte Laura, his wife, daughter of the Rev. John Drake, Rector of Stourton, Wilts. He was born on the 18th July, 1852, and received his education at Winchester College. Having entered the Royal Military Academy, Woolwich, in the autumn of 1869, he passed out after the usual course, and in February, 1872, obtained his commission in the Royal Engineers.

For some eighteen months he did duty at Chatham, at the expiration of which period (October, 1874) he was ordered out to India. After serving for two years at Bangalore he was sent to Tanjore, being selected for special duty in connection with the water supply of that place. There he remained, employed on Public Works, till December, 1878, when he was called upon for service with the Field Force in Afghanistan.

Accompanying the K Company Queen's Own Sappers and Miners to Jamrud, and from thence on to Landi Kotal, the subject of this notice did not spare himself —as is shown in the sad sequel—in the fresh sphere of activity which now presented itself.

In the month of March, 1879, the Company was transferred from the 1st to the 2nd Division of the Peshawar Valley Field Force, and moved forward to Jalalabad. During General Gough's action at Futtehabad, it was left in camp in reserve; but on the 4th April it formed part of the force taken out by the General towards Lakhi, and performed important service in blowing up the villages of the Khans who had not given in their submission. It was subsequently moved on to Gandamak, where it remained till the signing of the treaty of peace. During this period Lieutenant Poulter was detached in command of a party to reconstruct Fort Rosabad—a duty he performed with marked ability. A short time after he rejoined divisional headquarters, he took part in the return march of the troops to India. The heavy nature of his recent duties, however, carried out in a pestiferous climate, now began to tell upon him, and he reached Peshawar only to die. On the 22nd June, 1879, in the twenty-seventh year of his age, he fell a victim to enteric fever, honoured by his men and loved by his comrades, to whom he set a bright example by the courage and endurance with which he had met the hardships of the march, and by the resignation with which he eventually succumbed to them.

CAPTAIN C. F. POWELL, STAFF CORPS,

5TH GOORKHA REGIMENT.

CHARLES FOLLIETT POWELL was the youngest son of the late Captain Scott Powell, of the 23rd Royal Welsh Fusiliers, and nephew of Major Charles Powell, 49th Regiment, who was killed in the Crimea. He was born in the year 1844, and was educated at the Rev. W. Hodgson's school, at Streatham. After the death of his eldest brother, who had just been gazetted to the 19th Foot, he determined to enter the Army; and, having been prepared by private tuition, was eventually gazetted to the 96th Regiment, which he joined at Shorncliffe in March, 1864, shortly before it left England for the Cape. He served for four years in British Kaffraria; and after a year's leave home, rejoined his regiment in India, where it had, in the meantime, proceeded. While stationed at Dum Dum, he qualified for the Indian Service, and joined the Bengal Staff Corps. He was subsequently attached to the 1st and 2nd Regiments Punjab Infantry, and lastly, to the 5th Goorkhas, for which gallant corps he conceived a deep affection, and with which he served till the day of his death.

Captain Powell worked hard at the details of his profession, and was a thorough soldier. He was also a genial, and high-spirited lover of society, and entered with zeal into everything that might be going on. His short snatches of holiday were spent with the gun, and every autumn he would seek sport in Kashmir. Full of life and incident, were the letters he sent home, which did not omit to describe his failures in sport as graphically as his successes.

The only active service in which Captain Powell was engaged was the Afghan War. Taking part with his regiment, in the autumn of 1878, in the advance of the force under General Roberts into the enemy's country, he was present, on the 2nd December, in the assault and capture of the Peiwar Kotal, in which the 5th Goorkhas played so brilliant a part. Of this affair he sent an accurate account, not wanting in some humorous incidents, to his brother, Dr. Douglas Powell; but the letter was preceded, alas! by the intelligence of his own death.

In the return march of the brigade under General Roberts from Ali Khel to Fort Kuram, Captain Powell was with the baggage guard of the Goorkhas, which, for five hours, on the 13th December, 1878, repelled the attacks of the Mangal hordes in the Sapiri defile. He was there mortally wounded; and five days afterwards, on the 18th of the month, died.

"He was hit, poor fellow, in an unfortunate rear-guard affair, under my command, whilst discharging his duty most gallantly and well." The distinguished officer and dear friend of Captain Powell who wrote these words, Major Cook, V.C., did not long survive the subject of them. Similar testimony is given in the General's despatch, wherein allusion is made to Captain Powell as having been "most forward and gallant in the fight."

BREVET-MAJOR L. A. POWYS,

59TH (2ND NOTTINGHAMSHIRE) REGIMENT.

LITTLETON ALBERT POWYS, who died of cholera at Kandahar on the 6th August, 1879, was the eldest son of the Rev. Littleton Charles Powys, sometime Fellow of Corpus Christi, Cambridge, and for thirty years Rector of Stalbridge, Dorsetshire.

The subject of this notice was born on the 27th July, 1840, and was educated at the Sherborne Grammar School. In October, 1858, he was gazetted to an Ensigncy in the 83rd Foot, and proceeding shortly afterwards to Bombay, joined the head-quarters of the regiment in that presidency. He served with the 83rd at various stations in India, and subsequently in England and Ireland for a period of eight years, being promoted in the interval Lieutenant, in December, 1860, and Captain, in February, 1866.

On obtaining his company, Powys exchanged into the 59th Foot, then in Ireland. On the regiment completing its tour of home service, he embarked with it for Colombo, and did duty with it in Ceylon, and in India. An enthusiastic sportsman, he made many expeditions against the larger game of the country. While elephant hunting in the summer of 1868 in the neighbourhood of Trincomali, he narrowly escaped being killed, and with the last bullet in his pouch succeeded in saving the life of one of his brother officers.

In 1877 Captain Powys returned home on sick leave, but on the first rumour of the impending war with Afghanistan reaching him, he again hurried out to India. Rejoining his regiment at Dagshai, he accompanied it, in the autumn of 1878, in its forward movement to Multan, and proceeding with it at the close of the year through the Bolan, shared the arduous artillery-escort duties which fell to its lot in the Pass. He subsequently took part with the regiment, in Sir Donald Stewart's Division, in the advance on and capture of Kandahar.

During the occupation of Kandahar, Major Powys took an active part in making provision for the health and comfort, and forwarding the efficiency of his regiment, objects which he always had greatly at heart. From January to February, 1879, he commanded the Left half battalion, and in the last days of July he received the command of a cholera camp. The amount of labour which fell to his lot at this period was considerable. At the end of one long day spent in making arrangements for the comfort of his charges, he was himself stricken down with the disease with which he was attempting to cope. After the first seizure he rallied, but again losing strength, died on the 6th August.

A mural tablet in Stalbridge Church records the estimation in which Major Powys was held by his friends at home, and a monument in the cemetery at Kandahar, erected by the regiment, testifies to the regard entertained for him by his brethren in arms. "Genial, generous, gentle, and kind"—to quote the words of the little Journal published at Kandahar—"the heart and soul of his regiment, his loss will be felt not more by his brother officers than by the non-commissioned officers and men, whose welfare and happiness were equally his own."

CAPTAIN J. J. PRESTON,

4TH BATTALION, RIFLE BRIGADE.

JENICO JOHN PRESTON, who died at Safed Sung, Afghanistan, on the 1st May, 1879, was the eldest son of the Hon. Thomas Preston, of Silverstream, Co. Meath, Ireland, and of Margaret, his wife, daughter of John Hamilton, Esquire, of Sundrum, Ayr. He was born at Gormanston Castle, the residence of Viscount Gormanston, his grandfather, on the 11th February, 1846, and was educated at Dr. Newman's school at Edgbaston. Entering Sandhurst, he passed out from the college, after the usual course, first in the list at the final examination in December, 1865, and was gazetted, a month afterwards, to the 8th Foot. He did not, however, join that regiment, being transferred almost immediately to the 4th Battalion Rifle Brigade.

Proceeding to Canada, where the regiment was then stationed, he served with it in that country till its return home in September, 1867, and then continued to do duty with it in England and Ireland for the six years which elapsed before it was again ordered abroad. During that period he began to acquire—by devoting himself assiduously to the study of his profession, for which he had, from the first, conceived a strong affection—the high reputation for thoroughness for which he became pre-eminently distinguished. After taking a first-class certificate at Hythe, he officiated for two years as Musketry Instructor to his battalion, and subsequently, in 1870, received the appointment of Adjutant—a post he retained, and the duties of which he discharged with signal ability, till July, 1878, when he obtained his company.

In October, 1873, Preston proceeded with his regiment to India, and served with it at Umballa for two years. When, in 1875, General Ross took command of the force ordered to Perak, he was selected by that distinguished officer to serve as his Aide-de-Camp; and when, in the operations which ensued, Major Hawkins, Brigade-Major to the Force, was killed, Preston was appointed to take his place. The Perak expeditionary force was recalled in April, 1876; and he returned to his regiment at Umballa, decorated with the medal with clasp.

On obtaining his company in July, 1878, Captain Preston was posted to the Depôt at home, and was looking forward to some relaxation after his hard work. The outbreak of hostilities with Afghanistan, and the fact of his regiment being ordered to the front, caused him, however, instantly to abandon his intention of returning to England.

Accompanying the Battalion in its advance in Sir Sam. Browne's Division into the Khyber, he took part with it, on the 21st November, 1878, in the flank movement on Ali Musjid, in the subsequent advance to Jalalabad, in the Bazar Valley expedition under Brigadier-General Tytler in January, 1879, and in the pursuit of Azmatallah Khan in the month of April. In the expedition last named, an accident befell him which, in all probability, sowed the seeds of the illness to which he eventually succumbed. In fording the Surkab River at night, he was closely pressed upon by the man immediately following him; and losing his footing in the swift current, he was completely immersed. The baggage not being at hand, and no change of clothes procurable, he was nearly frozen in the extreme cold of the early morning, and was afterwards subjected to the violent alternation of excessive heat during the long and wearisome march which followed. The night of the 1st April he passed—still in the same clothes—in an open shed, and again on the following day took part in a trying march back to camp. From this time he was never quite himself, appearing to feel the heat very much—a most unusual thing for him, and a sure sign, with regard to one of his strong constitution and regular habits, that something was wrong. When on the 12th April the Brigade marched from Jalalabad, *en route* for Safed Sang, he was very unwell, though it is superfluous to say that while moving to the front no word of complaint passed his lips. On the 19th of the month matters became so bad, however, as to necessitate his being placed upon the sick list; and four or five days afterwards he was prostrated with a fever of malignant type. Dr. Wood, of the regiment, was unremitting in the care and attention he bestowed upon him, and he had the advantage of being nursed by his intimate friend Captain Howard, who was indefatigable in his devotion, and also by Captain Fitz-Herbert, another brother officer; indeed, all in camp vied in their endeavours to contribute any comfort or little luxury. His case, however, was hopeless. He died on the morning of the 1st May, and was buried next day in the corner of the cemetery at Safed Sang nearest to Kabul, where a monument surrounded by a wall of masonry, erected by his comrades to his memory, marks his grave.

Captain Preston was an officer who will not soon be forgotten in the regiment of whose honour he was as jealous as he was of his own good name; and to associate his memory in a fitting way with an object dear to him in life, his brother officers have subscribed to a fund to be invested in some institution devoted to the welfare of soldiers and their families. "It is needless to tell," wrote Colonel Newdigate, on the occasion of Captain Preston's death, "how universally he was loved in the Battalion, as it was impossible for anyone to know him without loving him and admiring his fine character. There was not a better soldier in the Army."

LIEUTENANT M. E. RAYNER,

66TH (BERKSHIRE) REGIMENT.

MAURICE EDWARD RAYNER, who was killed at Maiwand on the 27th July, 1880, was the second son of the late Lloyd Rayner, a Liverpool merchant. He was born at Liverpool on the 16th September, 1857, and was consequently in his twenty-third year at the time of his death. Educated at the Rev. O. C. Waterfield's school at East Sheen, Surrey, and subsequently at Harrow School, he left the latter at Christmas, 1874, to compete in the December open examination of that year for first Army appointments. He passed 65th in order of merit out of 329 candidates, of whom the first 152 were alone successful, and in 1875 received the offer of a direct commission in the 66th Regiment, then stationed at Belgaum, Bombay. Gazetted to a Sub-Lieutenancy on the 3rd February, 1875, he sailed from Southampton to join the Head-quarters of the 66th in the following March. In May, 1877, he obtained his Lieutenancy; and in the course of his Indian service he held for a time the post of Interpreter to the regiment, and subsequently that of Adjutant till the day of his death.

Lieutenant Rayner accompanied the regiment to Kandahar in February, 1880, and took part with it, in July, in the advance to the Halmand. At the battle of Maiwand, on the 27th of the month, he was last seen alive, but badly wounded, hard by the garden enclosure where the last desperate stand round the colours of the 66th was made. There his body was subsequently found, and was buried with those of his gallant comrades.

Lieutenant Rayner was a keen sportsman, and had shown considerable prowess in the cricket-field. A promising young officer, devoted to his profession, his example may serve to show that a military career may be auspiciously commenced without interest and without purchase.

CAPTAIN R. B. REED,

1st BATTALION, 12th (EAST SUFFOLK) REGIMENT.

OBERT BAYNES REED was the second son of Baynes Roach Reed, M.D., by his marriage with Emma, daughter of the late St. Paul Pane, Vicar of Tetbury, Gloucestershire. He was born on the 23rd November, 1837, and was educated at Cheltenham College, Gloucester Grammar School, and Marlborough College. After serving two trainings in the North Gloucester Militia, he entered the Army, being gazetted, in May, 1859, to an Ensigncy in the 2nd Battalion, 12th Foot. After doing duty in this country for a period of five years, and obtaining, in July, 1872, his Lieutenancy, he accompanied the regiment, in 1864, to India. In June, 1867, he received the appointment of Instructor of Musketry to the battalion, the duties of which post he discharged in a highly creditable manner till September, 1873, when he was selected to fill the office of Deputy Assistant Adjutant-General for Musketry, at Umballa. In the meantime (November, 1872), he had obtained his company.

Captain Reed continued to hold his staff appointment till 1879. Early in June of that year he effected an exchange from the 2nd into the 1st Battalion of the regiment, then on active service in Afghanistan, and obtaining permission to join head-quarters, hurried up with all speed to Landi Kotal, where they were at the time stationed, and reached that post on the 18th of the month. His term of active service, long eagerly looked forward to, was destined, alas! to be of short duration. The journey through the Khyber had been a trying one. Although in apparently good health on his arrival, he was shortly afterwards attacked with cholera, and in a few hours the gallant 12th had lost an officer and a friend who was loved and respected by every member of the regiment, even to the mothers and little children in barracks. In his last hours he was tended with all care by Dr. Wallace, the honoured surgeon of the battalion, who, succumbing a fortnight afterwards to the same fatal disease which carried off his patient, now rests in a grave by his side.

In a regimental after-order bearing date 24th June, 1879, the following words occur:—" Through his (Captain Reed's) death the Service has lost a most valuable officer. By those who have known him so well his many good qualities will be ever remembered.

"Lieut.-Colonel Walker feels that he speaks with the voice of the regiment in saying that its officers and men have lost in Captain Reed the kindest and most genial, warm-hearted friend."

LIEUT. T. J. O'D. RENNY, STAFF CORPS,

ADJUTANT, 4TH PUNJAB INFANTRY.

THOMAS JOHN O'DWYER RENNY, who died at Chinarak on the 15th December, 1879, from the effects of a wound received the day previous at the attack on Zawa, in the expedition under General Tytler against the Zaimusht tribe, was the third son of the late Colonel Robert Renny, C.B., Bengal Staff Corps, Adjutant-General Oudh Division, and of Caroline Franklin, his wife. He was born at Masuri, in the Himalayas, on the 15th August, 1846. After receiving the rudiments of his education at the Rev. Mr. Maddock's school at Masuri, and subsequently at the Manor House, another school in the same hill-station, he was sent home at the close of 1861, and was for some time at Merchiston Castle School, near Edinburgh. From Edinburgh he proceeded to Riga, and was for a time engaged in mercantile pursuits, but these proving distasteful to him, he studied for the Army, and succeeded in due course in passing the examination for direct commission. His appointment, however, was temporarily delayed in order to enable him to return to Bengal with Colonel Renny—at the time home on furlough—who had expressed a wish that his son might be posted to some regiment serving in India. Owing to the sad loss young Renny sustained in the death of his father within a few months of his arrival in India, the purchase of his commission devolved on his revered uncle, Mr. Thomas Renny, of Riga, and in April, 1868, he was appointed as Ensign to the 36th Foot. With that regiment he served for some four years, being promoted to his Lieutenancy in October, 1871.

Having devoted himself to the study of native languages, Lieutenant Renny succeeded in passing the test examination for the Bengal Staff Corps, and in January, 1872, was posted to the 4th Punjab Infantry. Taking part in the frontier affairs in which the regiment was from time to time engaged, he saw a good deal of active service, and was more than once mentioned in despatches. In November, 1877, he was appointed to the Adjutancy of his regiment, a post which he continued to hold till the day of his death.

Lieutenant Renny accompanied the 4th Punjab Infantry in its advance, in October, 1879, into Afghanistan, and subsequently took part with it in the punitory expedition under Brigadier-General Tytler, despatched against the Zaimusht tribes. It was while engaged with a large number of the enemy on the 8th December, in the forcing of the Zawa Pass, that he received his death-wound. Though he was at once carefully tended, he never recovered consciousness, and expired shortly afterwards. By the forethought of his brother officers his body was not suffered to remain in hostile territory, but was sent down to Kohat, and there buried.

In a letter received from the late Sir G. P. Colley, Private Secretary to the Viceroy, the following words occur :—" From my old connection with the Punjab Frontier Force, I know how highly Lieutenant Renny was valued in the force. The Viceroy was much distressed to hear of the loss of so valuable an officer." This tribute to the memory of the deceased is supplemented by the words of the Commandant of his regiment : " None," he writes, " was better or braver than this much-loved officer."

MAJOR WILLIAM REYNOLDS, STAFF CORPS,

3RD REGIMENT SIND HORSE.

HE subject of this notice, who was killed in action at Khushk-i-Nakhud, South Afghanistan, on the 26th February, 1879, was the eldest son of Major William Reynolds, of the Bombay Invalid Department, and grandson of William Reynolds, Esquire, of Milford House, Hants. He was born on the 31st October, 1841, and entered the Indian Army in January, 1859. The outset of his career was eventful. Gazetted to an Ensigncy in the 1st Bombay Grenadiers, he served with that regiment, a few months after joining it, in the expedition against the Waghirs in Okamandle and Kathiawar, and was present at the combined attack on their position on the Barda Hills on the 18th December, 1859. He was subsequently attached for a short time to the 19th Native Infantry, but in June, 1863, was transferred to the 3rd Sind Horse, with which regiment he served continuously till the day of his death.

After doing duty for some years on the frontier, he accompanied the regiment in 1867 to Abyssinia, and serving with it throughout the campaign, was present at the operations against Magdala, and received the medal. He subsequently returned with the regiment to India. In January, 1871, he was promoted to the rank of Captain, and in January, 1879, to that of Major.

On the breaking out of hostilities with Afghanistan in the autumn of 1878, the 3rd Sind Horse, which was stationed at Mustang and Dadar, was detailed to General Biddulph's Division of the Army of Invasion, and in December formed part of the garrison of Quetta. Taking part with the Division in the advance on and occupation of Kandahar, it participated, in the month of February, in the forward movement of the Brigade under General Biddulph to Girishk. On the withdrawal of the 2nd Division of the Column from that place on the 26th of the month, a small force composed of detachments of the 3rd Sind Horse and 29th Bombay Infantry, under Colonel Malcolmson, was detailed to act as a rear-guard. Reaching the village of Khushk-i-Nakhud about mid-day, the little force encamped, but was shortly afterwards threatened by a large body of the enemy. When the latter had advanced to within a few hundred yards, a heavy fire was opened by them, and

Major Reynolds, who was commanding the squadron of the Sind Horse, was struck with a bullet in the side. Colonel Malcolmson, unaware of what had happened, now ordered him to make a movement in preparation for charging the enemy, who were rapidly approaching ground favourable for the operations of cavalry; but being shortly afterwards informed of the wound he had received, directed him to give over the command of the squadron to another officer. This, however, Major Reynolds refrained from doing, and a few minutes afterwards took part in the effective charge which was delivered on the Afghan left centre. When, after ten minutes' fierce hand-to-hand fighting, the enemy broke, and the cavalry were ordered in pursuit, Major Reynolds, gallantly dashing forward with his squadron, sabred one of a group of Afghans who had gathered together and were making a last desperate stand. A moment afterwards his horse stumbled and threw him heavily; and before he could rise he was set upon and slain.

Major Reynolds's body was carried by his comrades to Kandahar, and buried in the Sirdar's garden. A headstone, erected to his memory by his family, marks his grave, and a mural tablet set up in Milford Church by his widow bears record of his heroic end; a mural tablet, too, has been erected to his memory in the Bombay Cathedral by Colonel Malcolmson and the officers of the 3rd Regiment Sind Horse. The regret which was universally felt for the loss of so highly esteemed and promising an officer, and the admiration for the manner in which he met his death, found expression—besides being testified to in many private letters—in the despatches both of Sir Donald Stewart and Colonel Malcolmson.

2ᴺᴰ LIEUTENANT W. P. RICARDO,

9TH (QUEEN'S ROYAL) LANCERS.

WILLIAM PERCY RICARDO, who fell in action in the neighbourhood of Kabul on the 11th December, 1879, was the only son of Frederick Ricardo, Esq., of Onslow Gardens, London. He was born on the 22nd April, 1857, and was educated at Edgbaston, under Dr., now Cardinal Newman. After three years' training in the Wilts Militia, he was gazetted, on the 13th March, 1878, to the 9th Lancers, and sailed for India in September of that year to join the Head-quarters of the regiment, then stationed at Sialkot, in the Punjab. By the time he reached Bengal, the 9th Lancers had been ordered up to Taru to form part of the Reserve Division of the Peshawar Valley Field Force, in view of the impending hostilities with Afghanistan. After serving for a few weeks with the Head-quarters, he proceeded with the detached squadron under Captain Apperley in January, 1879, to join the Kuram Valley Force, and subsequently took part with it, on the second outbreak of hostilities, in the advance on Kabul. He was present at the actions of Jaji Thana, Charasiab (in which he commanded, with marked ability, the main portion of the squadron), Kabul (8th and 9th October), and the operations outside cantonments in the second week in December. It was at the action of Killa Kazi on the 11th of that month, when gallantly charging the enemy with a troop of his regiment, that he lost his life.

Lieutenant Ricardo was buried on the evening of the same day in the little cemetery of Sherpur, where the remains of his brother officers Captain Butson and Lieutenant Hearsey have also found a last resting-place. Though cut short at its very outset, his career was yet not too brief to give evidence of his marked aptitude for the profession on which he had centred his affections and his hopes.

LIEUTENANT J. T. RICE,

ROYAL ENGINEERS.

JAMES THOMAS RICE was the youngest son of Colonel James George Allerton Rice, Honourable East India Company's Service, and was born at Calcutta in March, 1852. His educational career was a promising one. Early in 1865 he entered Cheltenham College, and gradually rose in the school till, at the age of sixteen years, he became prefect. Leaving Cheltenham in June, 1869, head of the Modern Department, and with the silver medal for Mathematics, he passed into Woolwich eighth in the list of successful candidates. On quitting the Academy he obtained the prize for Military History, and took sixth place in the list of cadets obtaining commissions in the Royal Engineers; and was gazetted to his Lieutenancy in December, 1871.

After passing through the usual course at Chatham, Lieutenant Rice embarked, in September, 1874, for India, and on arrival was posted to the Head-quarters Bengal Sappers and Miners at Rurki. Transferred in the course of a few months to the Public Works Department, and appointed to the 3rd Circle Military Works, Mirat Division, he became in a very short time Assistant Engineer, 1st Grade.

On the breaking out of the Afghan War in the autumn of 1878, Lieutenant Rice had the satisfaction of being selected to fill the important post of Assistant Field Engineer to the Khyber Line Force, and was at once ordered to the front. The ample promise of valuable service of which his brief career had given evidence was destined, however, never to be fulfilled. While journeying to Thal he caught a severe cold, and shortly after arriving at that post was prostrated with typhoid fever of so malignant a nature that from the first little hope was entertained of his recovery. He was removed as expeditiously as possible to Kohat, where, never rallying, he died at the house of his brother, Lieut.-Colonel Harry Rice, on the 23rd December, 1879.

LIEUTENANT S. W. T. ROBERTS,

PROBATIONER, BENGAL STAFF CORPS.

STEPHEN WILLIAM THORNHILL ROBERTS, who died from the effects of cholera on the 16th June, 1879, in the hospital at Landi Kotal, Afghanistan, was the fifth son of the late Arthur Austin Roberts, C.B., C.S.I., of the Bengal Civil Service, and of Elizabeth his wife, daughter of the late Colonel William Henville Wood, of the Honourable East India Company's Bengal Army.

He was born on the 25th August, 1854, at Naini Tal, India, and was educated at Harrow, subsequently receiving private tuition for the Army. In April, 1873, he was appointed Sub-Lieutenant in the Royal Lancashire Artillery Militia, in which he served two trainings. He was gazetted to a Lieutenancy in the 39th Foot, in February, 1875, and joining that regiment in Bengal, served with it for a period of two years. Being desirous to enter the Staff Corps, he was posted on probation, in June 1877, to the 4th Bengal Native Infantry, from which regiment he was transferred, in August of the same year, after passing the lower standard examination in Native Languages, to the 27th Punjab Infantry, then quartered at Naushahra. He subsequently served with that regiment throughout the Jowaki-Afridi campaign, approving himself, according to the testimony of his Colonel, a zealous and accomplished young officer.

On the return of the 27th Punjab Native Infantry to Naushahra, Lieutenant Roberts obtained leave to proceed to Rawal Pindi to pass in Garrison Drill; but hearing that a force was to be sent to Afghanistan, and that part of his regiment had been ordered up to the Khyber, he begged for permission to join it. After some delay and difficulty, his request was granted; but, to his disappointment, he did not arrive in the Pass till two days after the capture of Ali Musjid.

From this time to the day of his death he was actively employed. He took part in the memorable action of Futtehabad on the 2nd April, 1879, and in the expedition to the Bazar Valley, in which the troops suffered severely from cold and exposure. Colonel Hughes, who took over the command of the regiment shortly after the capture of Ali Musjid, expressing his appreciation of Lieutenant Roberts' services at this period, writes as follows: "He was a good officer, and never happier than when there was a chance of seeing service. He took great interest in the organization of the regimental transport, of which he took charge as Quartermaster, and he was of the greatest assistance to me in that capacity. His good temper and cheerfulness endeared him to all." General Tytler also commended the manner in which, when on detached service, he had performed his duty. It is some evidence, too, of his ability, that, during the excitement of the war, and in the midst of much engrossing work, he succeeded in passing one of the examinations requisite for entrance into the Staff Corps.

On the return march of the troops to India, Roberts suffered much from the effects of sunstroke and fever—consequences of exposure undergone during the great heat of the season. On reaching Daka, he was ordered to proceed by easy stages to Murree to recruit his strength; but on the way he was seized with cholera, which, acting on an enfeebled state of health, ended fatally the third day after his admission to the hospital at Landi Kotal. He was buried with military honours, and was followed to the grave by all at the station. His brother officers have expressed a desire to erect a monument to his memory; but owing to the uncertainty of retaining Landi Kotal as a military post, this has not yet been done.

Sir James Bourne, late Colonel of the Royal Artillery Militia, writing with reference to the subject of this notice, pays the following tribute to his memory: "We have lost a most earnest and accomplished young officer, and one who, had he been spared, would have continued an ornament to his profession. We were all glad to see him promoted to more active service, but have now to mourn that his career has been so suddenly brought to an end, even at the post of honour."

CAPTAIN WALTER ROBERTS,

66TH (BERKSHIRE) REGIMENT.

HE subject of this notice, was the third son of Major-General Howland Roberts, Honourable East India Company's Service. He was born at Haidarabad in the Deccan on the 9th March, 1846; was educated at Cheltenham College; and passed through the Royal Military College at Sandhurst. In February, 1865, he was gazetted to an Ensigncy without purchase in the 3rd West India Regiment, and obtained his Lieutenancy by purchase in December of the same year. He served on the West Coast of Africa till June, 1866, and in the West Indies till his regiment was disbanded in April, 1870. In September, 1871, he exchanged from half-pay into the 66th Regiment, then stationed at Karachi, Sind; and joining that corps two months afterwards, served with it for a period of three years. In September, 1874, he was appointed Staff Officer at Mount Abu Sanitarium, where he remained for his term of two years. On rejoining Head-quarters in November, 1876, he was appointed to act as Adjutant of the regiment—an appointment which he held until he obtained his company on the 14th November, 1879, and continued to hold subsequently during the march of the 66th to Kandahar in the spring of 1880.

At the engagement with the mutinous troops of the Wali Shere Ali Khan near Ghirish on the 14th July, 1880, Captain Roberts commanded his company on the right flank of the line. At the battle of Maiwand, on the 27th of the same month, he was mortally wounded while making a desperate stand with his men against overwhelming numbers. He was led out of the garden in which he had been hit, and taken to the rear, but shortly afterwards died from the effects of his wound and exhaustion from long exposure, without sustenance or relief, to the rays of a burning sun. His body was brought into Kandahar and buried on the night of the 28th in the palace garden.

Captain Roberts' memory will ever be held dear by those with whom he served. He was a thorough soldier, and a man beloved by all who knew him.

The deceased married, in July 1867, Julia Mary, daughter of the late Captain P. H. Delamere, of the 21st Fusiliers and 3rd West India Regiment.

LIEUTENANT H. R. ROSS,

ROYAL ARTILLERY.

UGH ROSE ROSS was the second son of George W. H. Ross, of Cromarty, N. B., Colonel of the Highland Rifle Militia, and Adelaide Lucy, his wife, third daughter of Duncan Davidson, of Tulloch, Lord Lieutenant of Ross-shire. He was born at Cromarty House on the 31st May, 1854, and was educated at the Rev. J. C. Jenkins' school at Brussels, aferwards studying with the Rev. Dr. Frost, LL.D., Kensington, and in 1872 passing into the Royal Military Academy, Woolwich. In October, 1873, he was gazetted to a Lieutenancy in the Royal Artillery, and did duty for a twelvemonth at Woolwich and Aldershot. In September, 1874, he was posted to Battery F/5, Field Artillery, which he joined, a month afterwards, at Sitapur, India.

For the next four years Lieutenant Ross served with the Battery in Bengal. That the manner in which he performed the duties allotted to him won the approbation of his Commanding Officer, is attested by the warm expressions of acknowledgment addressed to him by the latter on his being transferred to a new sphere of activity. "May you go on as well as you have done since I have had the pleasure of knowing you," is one amongst many kindly phrases used in a letter written to him on that occasion.

On the breaking out of hostilities with Afghanistan in the autumn of 1878, Ross volunteered for active service, and had the honour—of which he was justly proud—of being the first Artillery subaltern selected to fill a vacancy in one of the batteries ordered to the front. His promising career was destined, however, to be cut short at its very outset. When at Quetta on the march to Kandahar, he was attacked with dysentery, but refrained from reporting his illness, lest he might be left behind. Taking part in the further advance of the Battery, he continued to perform his duties with the utmost cheerfulness; at length, however, he became completely prostrated, and eventually died in camp in the Pishin Valley on the 12th January, 1879.

In a letter written by the Deputy Adjutant-General of Artillery in India, expressing his sorrow for the loss the regiment had sustained by the death of so promising an officer, the following passage occurs : " He was a good soldier, and a very fine young fellow. I took great interest in him." And an officer who was with him when he died, paying a well-merited tribute to his memory, writes : " He was universally loved, and will be very deeply regretted by us all."

CAPTAIN A. P. SAMUELLS,

32ND BENGAL N.I. (PUNJAB PIONEERS).

ALEXANDER PRINGLE SAMUELLS, the younger of two brothers who lost their lives in connection with the Afghan War, was the third son of the late Edward Alexander Samuells, Esq., C.B., of the Bengal Civil Service. He was born at Muzaffarpur, India, on the 8th August, 1843, and was educated at Loretto, Musselburgh, N.B., and Wimbledon. In 1860 he entered the Indian Army as an Ensign on the general list of Infantry, and was attached to the 7th Royal Fusiliers through the Umbeyla (N. W. Frontier) campaign of 1863-4, being present at all the operations in which that regiment took part. After hostilities were concluded, he was appointed to the 32nd Punjab Pioneers, with which corps he served continuously until his death. Alexander Samuells took part in the Bhutan campaign of 1864-65, and subsequently assisted in the construction of the Ranikhet road and in the Bengal Famine Relief Works of 1874. In 1877 he accompanied the 32nd to Quetta, Baluchistan, as Wing Commander, having been appointed successively Wing Officer, Quartermaster, and Adjutant; and took part in all the military works on which the regiment was engaged, both on the Quetta fortifications and in the Bolan Pass. He subsequently served with the regiment throughout the campaign in South Afghanistan, being present—during part of the time as second in command—in the advance over the Khojak Pass, the occupation of Kandahar, the reconnaissance to Girishk on the Halmand, and the expedition against the Kakur tribes in the Thal-Chotiali country. On the conclusion of hostilities he was appointed permanently second in command, in succession to Colonel Fellowes, who died on the return march.

Captain Samuells' health had suffered much during this campaign; and in the hot weather which succeeded, he became seriously ill with dysentery and fever. Notwithstanding his debilitated state, he accompanied the regiment to the Khyber Pass and Jalalabad Valley on the renewal of hostilities in the autumn of 1879, and remained with it—taking his share in all the trying work which fell to its lot in the second campaign—until July, 1880, when his health completely broke down. He was then invalided, but too late. The return through the Pass was more than he was equal to, and on arrival at Rawal Pindi he died of hospital abscess.

Captain Alexander Samuells had received the Indian war medal with clasps for Umbeyla and Bhutan, and was entitled to the Afghanistan medal. At a course of garrison instruction he had been specially mentioned for proficiency in Military Law; and he had successfully passed the examinations qualifying for service on the Staff. Throughout his career he bore the reputation of an officer possessing sound judgment and great *esprit de corps*. His loss was deeply felt by all ranks of the 32nd, both British and Native; for in life he had been distinguished for the sympathetic interest he took in all regimental matters and in every individual member of the corps, from his British comrades to the youngest Sepoy.

Captain Samuells married, in 1874, Georgina Margaret, eldest daughter of the late George Paterson, Esq., of Castle Huntly, Perthshire, N.B. A memorial has been erected over his tomb by the officers of his regiment and the Sepoys of his company.

CAPT. E. W. SAMUELLS, BENGAL STAFF CORPS,

DEPUTY SUPERINTENDENT OF REVENUE SURVEYS.

EDMUND WALKER SAMUELLS, was the second son of the late Edward Alexander Samuells, Esq., C.B., of the Bengal Civil Service. He had served in the Survey Department from the year 1863; and in the autumn of 1878, in view of the impending outbreak of war with Afghanistan, was ordered up from the Deccan to join Sir Sam. Browne's Division of the Army of Invasion. Taking part in the advance into the Khyber Pass, he was present, in his capacity as one of the Survey officers, at the attack and capture of Ali Musjid, on the 21st November, 1878, and subsequently proceeded as far as Basawal, with the view of procuring all the geographical information possible of the country traversed by our Army. The exertions he made to this end, however, brought on an attack of typhoid fever, which, acting on a constitution weakened by much exposure and hard work during several years previously, ended fatally. When the Force marched to Jalalabad, he was sent back on the 15th December, 1878, prostrated in health, from Basawal to the Base. The fatigue and hardships of the journey, however, caused a relapse; and arriving at Peshawar at 2 p.m. on the 20th of the month in a dying state, he expired in the 2nd Division Base Hospital at 10 p.m. on the same day, at the early age of thirty-six years. The surgeon (Ryan) who had charge of him on the journey down, writes: "He bore it all with the fortitude of a true soldier; and not a murmur ever escaped his lips."

The worth of this officer cannot be better attested than by a quotation from the official report of the services he rendered at the close of his career, made by his immediate superior on the spot: "At the taking of Ali Musjid," writes Major H. C. B. Tanner, "Captain Samuells was much exposed to the enemy's fire, but he carried on his plane-tabling under the cannon of the enemy as coolly as if he were in no danger. Unfortunately he has written no report of his proceedings, but he told me that one round shot actually passed beneath his plane-table, and that, in the Shaghai heights, he and his party had many narrow escapes. His plane-table section of the far-famed Khyber Pass will remain a record of Survey operations done in a most creditable manner under very adverse circumstances. Throughout the action he was under a hot artillery fire delivered frem twenty-four guns, and it is to be for ever regretted that he should only escape the dangers of that day to fall a victim to typhoid fever a few weeks later."

The following additional testimony to his worth and character will be found in the report submitted to the Indian Government by the Deputy Surveyor-General of India:—" During the course of Captain Samuells' service, he has been engaged in many varied and important duties, in all of which he so acquitted himself that he has acquired a high character for intelligence, energy, and perseverance. By the death of Captain Samuells the Revenue Branch of the Survey Department of India has lost one of its most valued officers."

CAPTAIN T. A'B. SARGENT,

78TH HIGHLANDERS (ROSS-SHIRE BUFFS).

HOMAS A'BECKET SARGENT, who died at Kandahar, of typhoid fever, on the 21st January, 1881, was the elder son of Thomas Sargent, Esq., of Porchester Terrace, Paddington, formerly Secretary to the Board of Inland Revenue, by his wife, Mary Jane, daughter of William Becket Turner, Esq., of Wantage, Berks, and of Penleigh House, near Westbury, Wilts. He was born at Paddington on the 30th October, 1845, and received his education chiefly at Eton, where he remained five years. His school career was a bright and happy one. Scarcely anyone could have been a more general favourite than he among his young contemporaries; and while quite a little library of presentation volumes received by him on quitting the college gives evidence of his popularity, numerous pieces of plate bear witness to a prowess on the river, and in athletic sports generally, for which he early became famed.

On leaving Eton at Christmas, 1864, at the age of nineteen years, he read with Mr. Arnold, of Surbiton, with a view to entering the Army; and passing the examination for direct commission shortly afterwards, was gazetted in November, 1865, to an Ensigncy in the 78th Highlanders. After doing duty for two years and a half at the Depôt at Stirling and Aberdeen, and purchasing, in the meantime, his Lieutenancy, he joined the head-quarters in Canada, and remained there till the regiment returned home in 1872—a period of three years and a half. He was subsequently detached, in April, 1873, and stationed at the Brigade Depôt at Fort George. In March, 1877, he obtained his company.

After serving at Fort George about two years, he obtained, on the recommendation of the Commandant, the Staff appointment of Aide-de-Camp to the General of the Northern District of England, a post which he held more than five years, resigning it only upon being ordered to rejoin his regiment in Afghanistan, in August, 1880. In the pestilential climate of Kandahar, he was cut off in the prime of his manhood, within the short space of five months from the date of his departure from England.

As in his school days, so also in after life, he made many friends. "He was a true and valued friend to me," wrote one of the Generals under whom he had served, on receiving the news of his death; and the other, in expressing his grief for the loss of so promising an officer, paid an equally warm tribute to his memory. The following words, written by an officer of the 78th Highlanders, are taken from one of the many letters testifying to his worth, received by his family after his death, and will serve to indicate the estimation in which he was held in his regiment. "He was a fine fellow," observes the writer, "every inch a soldier. It is sad to see anyone cut off so young, but doubly so, when he had such a career before him as he doubtless had. He will leave many in his profession to mourn him, for in his short, and as far as it went successful career, he made a host of friends. All ranks, from the highest to the lowest, who knew and appreciated his worth, will mourn his untimely end; and none more so than his old comrades of the 78th."

Captain Sargent's brother officers, in taken of their regard, have erected a monument over his grave; and one of the Generals to whom he acted as Aide-de-Camp, has also put up, in his own parish church, a cenotaph to his memory. It is some consolation to his family to learn how sincerely he was beloved by those with whom he was most intimately associated in his profession.

CAPTAIN E. D. SHAFTO,

ROYAL ARTILLERY.

EDWARD DUNCOMBE SHAFTO, who was killed on the 16th October, 1879, by the explosion of the magazine in the Bala Hissar, Kabul, was a member of an old County of Durham family, the Shaftos of Whitworth Park, being the eldest son of the Rev. A. Duncombe Shafto, Rector of Brancepeth, Durham, by his wife Dorothea Ann, second daughter of G. H. Wilkinson, Esq., of Haspeley Park, Durham. He was born at Houghton le Spring in the same county on the 14th June, 1843, and was educated, before entering Woolwich, at the Rev. E. Pound's school at Malton, and at Carshalton. In April, 1861, he was gazetted to the 9th Brigade Royal Artillery. After doing duty for a short time at Dover, he was appointed Aide-de-Camp to General Ormsby, Royal Artillery, and continued to hold the appointment until, in 1866, he was selected to fill the post of Aide-de-Camp to General Sir A. Borton, then commanding a brigade at the Curragh. In July, 1870, he quitted Ireland for India, accompanying Sir Arthur Barton to Bangalore, on the latter being ordered out to take up his appointment of General of the Mysore Army. On the expiration of his Chief's command in 1875, he returned to England, and in 1876 passed with such credit through the long course at Shoeburyness that he was offered the post of Instructor; on his declining this he was offered and accepted the Adjutancy of the 16th Brigade of Royal Artillery at the Mount, Madras; and on that brigade being absorbed into another in England, he was appointed District Adjutant.

On the outbreak of the Afghan War, volunteers were called for from the Artillery; and eagerly responding, Shafto was one of the first whose services were accepted. After doing duty in the Kuram Valley during the first campaign, he was appointed, on the renewal of hostilities, Ordnance Officer to the Force under General Roberts advancing on Kabul. It was on the fourth day after the Division reached its destination that the magazine explosion in which he met his untimely end occurred.

By the unassuming manliness of his ways and the sweetness of his temper, Captain Shafto had made many friends, and the news of his death caused deep sorrow to a wide circle. "His bright intelligent face won my heart the first time I saw him, and I never expect to replace him," wrote Sir Frederick Roberts; and Colonel Gloag, Royal Artillery, in a regimental order, refers to him as having been "an officer who was good, talented, and brave, and also a devoted servant of his Queen and Country,"—a verdict which will be concurred in by all to whom the deceased was known.

Captain Shafto's acquaintance with a soldier's work in all its details was thorough, and contributed largely to his high reputation. Besides being an ardent sportsman, and a deadly hand with gun or rifle, he was devotedly fond of travelling, and contrived during his annual privilege-leave to visit Japan, Java, and Kashmir. As master of the Bangalore foxhounds, no man could have given greater satisfaction or have been more popular.

BT. LIEUT.-COL. A. M. SHEWELL, STAFF CORPS,

OFFG. DEPY. COMMISSARY-GENERAL, 1st CLASS.

ARTHUR MARK SHEWELL was one of four brothers, sons of the late Edward Warner Shewell, of the Royal Crescent, Cheltenham, who joined the Honourable East India Company's Service between the years 1840 and 1856, and of whom three have since died in the service. The subject of this notice, the younger of the four, entered the army as ensign in December, 1856, and was posted to the 2nd Bombay European Light Infantry, now Her Majesty's 106th Regiment. He was promoted to a Lieutenancy in September, 1857; and in July, 1863, was appointed to the Staff Corps.

"One who knew him well," writing to the "Standard" newspaper after Shewell's death, records the following characteristic incident in his career at this period:—" In the year 1864 there was a fearful outbreak of cholera in B/18 Royal Artillery, at Baroda, where young Shewell was then Commissariat Officer. Not only did he voluntarily give his untiring aid day and night in nursing the sick, but every morning he was to be seen mounted on his pony with a large basket slung on his arm, which was filled with delicacies for the sick women and children who, being convalescents, were encamped two or three miles off. These delicacies were not provided by Government, but supplied by his own generosity and that of a few friends. Perhaps it needed more moral courage for a young officer thus burdened to ride through the camp than it would to face the enemy; but whenever a kindness or an unselfish action was to be done, Arthur Shewell was the man to do it."

On the war with Abyssinia being declared in 1867, Lieutenant Shewell volunteered for employment in his capacity of an officer of the Commissariat Department, which he had a short time before joined. His services were accepted, and were subsequently so highly appreciated by Lord Napier that, although only that of a subaltern, his name was specially mentioned in his Lordship's final despatch; and the same gazette which announced his promotion to the rank of Captain, contained an intimation of Her Majesty having conferred on him a brevet-majority.

On the breaking out of the Afghan War in 1878, Lieut.-Colonel Shewell (who had been, in the interim, again promoted) had important duties assigned to him, being placed in charge of the line of communications between Sukkur and Quetta—an appointment which entailed not only heavy responsibility, but excessive exposure in the most trying part of the year to the intense heat of the plains at the debouchure of the Bolan. Whilst he was employed on this duty, cholera broke out at Eri-Na-Dur. To the quiet steadfastness and self-abnegation with which he set himself to cope with this virulent disease, a letter written by his commanding officer to one of the daily journals bears ample witness. After quoting at length from a graphic record of his work which appeared in a paper entitled " A Transport Service for Asiatic Warfare," read at the United Service Institution in June, 1880, General Howard Vyse concludes his communication with these words :—" I saw Lieut.-Colonel Shewell after his return to Karachi during the summer of 1879, but with his innate modesty, he would say but little about his heroism. He did, however, admit that it was 'trying' when he had to bury seventeen poor natives during the twenty-four hours."

On the outbreak of the second campaign, Lieut.-Colonel Shewell, who was promoted Officiating Deputy Commissary-General for the occasion, was specially selected by Sir Richard Temple to assume entire charge of the commissariat arrangements of the Kandahar Field Force. That he performed the onerous duties incident to his appointment to the entire satisfaction of the whole Division, is evidenced by a most complimentary order on the subject issued by Sir Donald Stewart on his departure for Kabul.

The manner in which Arthur Shewell met his death is of a piece with the broad humanity of his life. On the morning of the 16th August, 1880, the day of the fatal sortie to Deh Khwaja, hearing that a wounded man was lying helpless outside the Kabul gate, he volunteered to take a dhoolie for him. In helping him into it, he himself received a wound from the effects of which he died a fortnight afterwards, on the 2nd September, 1880.

CAPTAIN H. F. SHOWERS, STAFF CORPS,

1st PUNJAB INFANTRY.

OWE FREDERICK SHOWERS, who was murdered by a body of Kakar Pathans on the 14th March, 1880, while riding on duty between Chapari and Quetta, was the bearer of a name, and a worthy descendant of ancestors well known in India for every soldierly quality, and whose services for four generations stand recorded in monumental tablets in the old Cathedral of Calcutta, and memorial tombs on some of India's most noted battle-fields. He was the eldest son of the late Major-General Sir George Showers, who commanded a brigade at the siege of Delhi, and nephew of Lieut.-General C. L. Showers. Educated at Wellington College, he proceeded to India in 1861, and was gazetted to the 104th Fusiliers, of which regiment he soon became Adjutant. On promotion to Captain, he entered the Staff Corps and was posted to the Central India Horse, and afterwards transferred, in 1872, to the 1st Punjab Infantry. In 1877 he was appointed Garrison Instructor in the Umballa Division, but threw up the post in order to join his regiment proceeding on service into Afghanistan on the breaking out of the war in 1878. He was present in the action fought by the Thal-Chotiali Column under Major Keen in forcing and opening that route, and was mentioned in the despatches. His conduct in the field and special acquirements brought him into notice. He was first appointed by Sir Donald Stewart to the Intelligence Department; and subsequently was employed by Sir Robert Sandeman, Governor-General's Agent in Baluchistan, in defining the boundaries of the Pishin district, and acquitted himself of his duties with signal ability and zeal. Attended by but a handful of men, Captain Showers was in the habit of traversing unknown routes in disturbed tracts, and returned with plans full of valuable information, on more than one occasion. He at length fell a victim through treachery, within a few weeks of his being appointed, in recognition of his services, to the command of the Baluch Corps of Guides.

"No more gallant officer fell during the war." The sentence occurs in a letter written with reference to Captain Showers by Sir R. Sandeman—who had many opportunities of observing the cool steadfastness with which his subordinate was wont to carry out the work to which he set his hand. It expresses nothing more than what might have been expected of one of the deceased officer's name and race.

The Editor of this work is indebted to the "Times" Kandahar correspondent for the greater portion of this notice.

BREVET MAJOR L. C. SINGLETON,

92ND (GORDON HIGHLANDERS).

THE subject of this memoir, though not one of those whose name is included in the death-roll of the Afghan War, was an officer who performed such distinguished service in the operations with which these volumes deal, and lost his life so soon after the close of the war, that some brief notes on his career will not be found out of place in this division of the work.

Loftus Corbet Singleton was the fourth son of Henry Corbet Singleton, Esq., J.P., D.L., of Aclare, Co. Meath, Ireland, and Jane Percival, his wife, daughter of Lieutenant-General William Loftus, and was one of five brothers who entered the Service within a short period of one another. He was born on the 2nd August, 1842, and after receiving his education at Cheltenham College, was gazetted, in March, 1861, to an Ensigncy in the 18th Royal Irish Regiment; he was shortly afterwards, however, transferred to the 92nd Highlanders, in which distinguished corps—serving in successive grades, and holding at intervals various appointments—he remained till the day of his death.

Joining the regiment in India, he returned with it, about three months afterwards, to England, and did duty with it in Great Britain till it was again ordered abroad. In the interval, (July, 1864), he purchased his Lieutenancy. In January, 1868, he embarked with the head-quarters for India, and served in Bengal for a period of three years. In September, 1869, he obtained his company by purchase, and during the term of his Indian service he held for a time the appointment of Musketry Instructor to the regiment.

Captain Singleton returned to England early in 1871, and shortly afterwards was selected to fill the important post of Adjutant of the Galloway Rifle Volunteers. During his tenure of this appointment—the duties of which he discharged with signal ability for a period of five years—he won a popularity such as it is accorded to few to earn, touching evidence of which is afforded in the letters of sympathy, addressed to his widow by each corps separately, on the occasion of his death.

In November, 1877, Singleton rejoined his regiment in India, and a twelve-month afterwards accompanied it in its advance to the frontier, in view of the recent outbreak of war with Afghanistan, subsequently proceeding with it to Ali Khel, where it joined the Advance Division of the Kuram Valley Field Force. Taking part with it, on the renewal of hostilities in the autumn of 1879, in the advance on Kabul, he served through the whole of the second campaign, leading the men of his company repeatedly into action, and receiving honourable mention on more than one occasion in report or despatch. He was present, on the 6th October, at the battle of Charasiab, in which the 92nd performed gallant service, and at the subsequent occupation of Kabul, and taking part in the train of important events with which the year closed, was present in General Baker's action on the 11th December, at the storming of the Takht-i-Shah on the 13th, and in the covering of the retirement from the Asmai Heights on the 14th idem. During the defence of Sherpur he was always to be seen at the head of his men, and at the action of Childukhtean, on the 25th April, 1880, the conspicuous gallantry he displayed in leading on the right of the fighting line obtained for him special commendation in despatches. Participating in the memorable march of Sir Frederick Roberts' force from Kabul to Kandahar, he was again present at the crowning defeat of the enemy on the 1st September, 1880. For his services during the operations he received the Brevet of Major.

Ordered to South Africa immediately after the outbreak of war with the Transvaal Boers, the 92nd Highlanders disembarked at Durban early in 1881. Accompanying the regiment to Mount Prospect, Major Singleton subsequently took part with it in Sir George Colley's ill-starred occupation of the Majuba Mountain on the night of the 26th February. It was at the moment when, shortly after dawn on the 27th, the enemy swept over the ridge of the mountain plateau in overwhelming numbers, and shot down or captured the few who were left to defend it, that he received his death-wound, being struck by rifle bullets twice during the engagement. He lingered on for two months, but rapidly sinking after undergoing amputation of a limb, eventually died on the 1st of May, and at the hands of his comrades received a soldier's sepulture.

"Most reliable in the field; possessed of excellent judgment." Such are the attributes of the deceased referred to in a private letter written by Sir Frederick Roberts, who, paying an earnest tribute to his memory, justly says that "by his death Her Majesty has lost a true and gallant soldier."

Major Singleton married, in 1872, Emmeline Theodora, only surviving daughter of Thomas de Moleyns, Esq., Q.C. He leaves a widow and two children, a son and daughter.

CAPTAIN H. F. SMITH, STAFF CORPS,

JACOB'S RIFLES.

HUGH FREDERICK SMITH, who was killed in action at Maiwand on the 27th July, 1880, was the younger son of Hugh W. Smith, Esq., M.A., of Westbourne Park, London, and of Julia Frances, his wife, and was a nephew of the late Captain C. F. Smith, 71st Highlanders, who was killed in action in the Umbeyla campaign of 1863.

The subject of this notice was born on the 28th June, 1846. Educated at Tonbridge School, where he early became a favourite with his young contemporaries, his devotion to all kinds of athletic exercises, in which he excelled, contributing not a little to his popularity, he proceeded to Sandhurst in February, 1865, and passing out of the college after the usual course, was gazetted, in June, 1866, to the 88th Foot. In the following year he joined that regiment in India, and remained with it until, in 1870, it returned to England, when he entered the Bombay Staff Corps. In the meantime (May, 1870) he had obtained his Lieutenancy. Posted now to Jacob's Rifles, he joined the Head-quarters at Jacobabad, and holding successively and with credit the various appointments tenable by a subaltern, continued in that regiment till the day of his death. In the course of his service he returned to England, in 1877, for a term of sick leave; and it is characteristic of him that during the brief period he remained at home, he undertook a four months' course of Engineering at Chatham, in addition to taking, after the usual course, an extra first-class Hythe certificate. Returning to India, he became Captain in June, 1878, and, notwithstanding his promotion, continued to retain to the last, in consequence of the dearth of junior officers of sufficient experience, the post of Adjutant of the regiment.

Taking part in the autumn of 1878 in the advance of the head-quarter wing of the regiment to Quetta in view of the impending hostilities with Afghanistan, Captain Smith shared with it throughout the first campaign the various garrison and escort duties which fell to its lot, holding for a brief period the post of Station Staff-Officer, and proceeding in the month of March, 1879, in charge of drafts for different corps to Kandahar. Accompanying the head-quarters and right wing of the regiment from Quetta in the advance into hostile territory in April, 1880, he proceeded a second time to Kandahar, and subsequently took part in the forward movement of Burrows' Brigade to the Halmand. In the disastrous encounter with the enemy at Maiwand on the 27th July, 1880, he fell early in the engagement, being killed by the bursting of a shell shortly after crossing the nullah with his regiment in support of the Horse Artillery.

Of the many sympathetic letters written with reference to the late Captain Hugh Smith to his family, one and all testify to his signal worth and to the high estimation in which he was held. By his death the Staff Corps lost an officer of great promise, and a blank was created in the regiment which will not soon be filled up.

MAJOR LIONEL SMITH, STAFF CORPS,

3RD GOORKHA REGIMENT.

THE subject of this memoir, who died at Kalat-i-Ghilzai on the 25th January, 1879, was the youngest son of E. J. Smith, Esq., of the Bengal Civil Service, and was born at Weymouth on the 5th May, 1838. After receiving his earlier education principally at private schools both abroad and at home, he entered the Army, being gazetted in July, 1856, to an Ensigncy in the 96th Foot. Within a few months of his obtaining his commission he elected to join the Honourable East India Company's Service, and was posted, in December, 1856, to the 36th Regiment Light Infantry. During the Indian Mutiny campaign he was engaged as a volunteer when the rebels were repulsed from the guns at Jalandhar on the night of the 7th June, 1857, and five days afterwards was promoted to the rank of Lieutenant. In October and November, 1858, he served with the Thamaon Battalion in Oudh. On the 30th July, 1862, he was appointed to Her Majesty's 104th Fusiliers, and in November, 1863, obtained his company in that regiment. He entered the Staff Corps in May, 1866; and again doing duty with the Thamaon Battalion in 1869, served in General Horsford's Brigade against the Mutineers on the Nipal frontier, and was present at the action of Sakla Ghât on the 9th February. In December, 1876, he was promoted to his Majority.

Major Lionel Smith was serving with the 3rd Goorkhas at the time of the breaking out of the Afghan War in the autumn of 1878. Sharing with the regiment the heavy duties which fell to its lot in the first campaign, he took part with it in Brigadier-General Hughes' Brigade of Sir Donald Stewart's Division, in the advance on and occupation of Kandahar, and in the subsequent advance on Kalat-i-Ghilzai. The unhealthy nature of the climate and the severity of recent work now began to tell upon him; he was taken ill with dysentery on the march, and eventually fell a victim to the complaint within a few hours of the column reaching its destination.

Major Lionel Smith had received during his service an extra certificate at the Royal Military College, a medal for the Indian Mutiny, and a first-class extra Hythe certificate.

SURGEON W. B. SMYTH, A.B., M.B., L.R.C.S.I.,

BENGAL MEDICAL DEPARTMENT,

ILLIAM BEATTY SMYTH, who was killed at Chapari, Afghanistan, on the 20th June, 1879, was the third son of William Smyth, banker, Strabane, Ireland. He received his early education at Raphoe Royal School and Dungannon Royal School, from whence, obtaining an exhibition, he proceeded to Trinity College, Dublin. During his University course he threw himself heart and soul into his work; and that he approved himself a scholar of no mean calibre, the many honours he reaped—including the silver medal *Hist. Scient., Polit., et Litt. Angl.*—bear ample witness.

Quitting the University in 1876, he underwent a short course of preparation for the Indian Medical Service; and passing the examination in January, 1877, entered the Army the same year. After spending a few months at Calcutta, during which he passed the examination in Native Languages, he was posted to the 8th Regiment Bengal Native Infantry, then serving at Agra.

On the breaking out of the Afghan War in the autumn of 1878, Dr. Smyth proceeded to the front in medical charge of No. 7 Company Bengal Sappers and Miners, which was detailed for service to General Roberts' Division of the Army of Invasion; and taking part in the advance into hostile territory, was present at the assault and capture of the Peiwar Kotal. In the course of his association with the Kuram Field Force, he was attached for duty to more than one of the regiments which formed part of the Division, and took a full share of the heavy work which fell to the lot of the Medical Department in the winter of 1878 and the spring of 1879. While at the Peiwar cantonments, he was ordered to Thal to take charge of a cholera camp; but on reaching his destination, he found that the camp had been broken up. Making his way back, he halted on the evening of the 25th June, 1879, at Chapari, pitching his tent away from the guard. During the night some thieves pulled down the loose stone wall of a surrounding enclosure without disturbing anyone; and one man entering the tent, seized and made off with the pillow on which Dr. Smyth was sleeping. Instantly starting in pursuit, but unhappily omitting to carry his revolver, Dr. Smyth came up with the thief, and threw him. In a moment he was surrounded and set upon by the whole band, and was so severely wounded that he died immediately. The crime was traced to the Watazai section of the Zaimusht race; but as the assassins could not be discovered, retributive justice was meted out by firing three large villages of the tribe to which they belonged.

Brave even to rashness, as the character of his tragic death gives evidence; carrying out, utterly regardless of consequences to himself, what he deemed to be his duty, Dr. Smyth was one of those officers of whom the profession has just occasion to feel proud. His nature was genial and kindly, and his death not only leaves a blank in his family that can never be filled, but is deeply mourned by all to whom he was known.

CAPTAIN N. J. SPENS,

72ND (DUKE OF ALBANY'S OWN HIGHLANDERS).

ATHANIEL JAMES SPENS, who was killed in action at Kabul on the 14th December, 1879, was the third and last surviving son of the late Nathaniel Spens, of Craigsanquhar, Fife, and of Janet Law Guild, his wife. He was born on the 3rd March, 1845, and was educated at Edinburgh and Woolwich. Entering the Army in June, 1864, he was gazetted to an Ensigncy in the 72nd Highlanders, then on its tour of home service, and at once joining his regiment, served with it at various stations in Great Britain and Ireland, obtaining his Lieutenancy by purchase in June, 1868.

In February, 1871, he accompanied the 72nd on its departure from Ireland for India, and continued serving with it in Bengal till, in November, 1878, it was ordered to the front in view of the impending hostilities with Afghanistan. In the meantime (March, 1878), he had been promoted Captain.

Captain Spens' company formed part of the left wing of the 72nd, which, under Lieut.-Colonel Clarke, remained in garrison at Kohat till the close of the year, and subsequently, in January, 1879, took part in General Roberts' occupation of the Khost district. In the action of Matun, on the 7th of the month, the 72nd defended the front and left flank of the camp, and subsequently, with the other units of Colonel Barry Drew's little force, carried the Mangal villages on the right and rear.

In April, 1879, the left wing, having joined the head-quarters, proceeded with the division to Ali Khel, and remained there till the massacre of the British Embassy necessitated an immediate advance on Kabul. At the battle of Charasiab, on the 6th October, the company commanded by Spens was one of the leading ones which took part in the attack on the Red Ridge, so obstinately held and so brilliantly carried; and which supported Chesney's company of the 23rd Pioneers in carrying the second ridge on which the enemy took up his position.

In the storming of the Asmai heights on the 14th December, in the operations round Kabul, Captain Spens was in command of the sixty-four men of the 72nd, who, with the Guides Infantry, under Lieut.-Colonel Clarke, successfully assaulted and for a time held the little conical hill to the right of the main attack. It was while endeavouring to prevent this position from being retaken, in a heroic personal attempt to stem the advance of the overwhelming numbers of the enemy, that he sacrificed his life. The incident is thus related by one of his brother officers. After telling how the Afghans, reassembled and reinforced, had rushed up the side of the hill, and that a charge was ordered to be made by the Sepoys, the writer continues as follows:—" Spens volunteered to lead, which he did in splendid style. Heading a good way in front, he dashed at the leading files of the enemy, cut down the front man, and was immediately cut down himself by the enemy as they surged forward." His body was recovered, and was buried by his brother officers in the cemetery at Sherpur, the pipers of the regiment striking up " Lochaber no more"— his favourite air—as it was lowered into the grave.

" Spens behaved most gallantly," wrote Sir Frederick Roberts, in a letter expressing a wish that it might have been possible to secure for the representatives of the deceased officer the Victoria Cross. The reflection that he was one who could not fail to acquit himself worthily when his opportunity might come, and that his death was therefore, under the circumstances, a necessity, is some poor consolation to his comrades in arms, by whom his memory will ever be held dear.

LIEUTENANT H. H. S. SPOOR,

1st BATTALION 25TH (KING'S OWN BORDERERS).

HE subject of this memoir, who died at Pezwan, Afghanistan, on the 1st of June, 1880, was a descendant of the Spoor family, of Trebartha, Cornwall, being the only son and heir, also last surviving child, of the late Nicholas Appleby Spoor, Esq., of Whitburn, Durham, and Warkworth, Northumberland, formerly a Captain in the 6th Royals, and latterly of the 25th King's Own Borderers, and of Dora Anna, his wife, second daughter of the late John Oliver, Esq., formerly of Newcastle-on-Tyne, and grand-daughter (maternally) of Henry Shadforth, Esq., of Over Dimsdale Hall, near Yarn, Yorkshire.

Herbert Henry Shadforth Spoor was born at Fulwood, Preston, Lancashire (where the depôt of the 25th was at the time of his birth stationed) on the 22nd of April, 1857, and was educated chiefly at the Proprietary School and the College, Cheltenham. Receiving a Queen's cadetship, he entered the Royal Military College at Sandhurst in February, 1877; and passing out after the usual course, was gazetted, in May, 1878, to the 8th (the King's) Regiment. Being anxious, however, to serve in his father's old corps, he was transferred to the "Borderers," and joined the 2nd Battalion at Plymouth on the 6th of July of the same year. In September, 1879, he embarked for India, and early in November joined the 1st Battalion of the regiment at Peshawar. Accompanying the head-quarters a month afterwards in the second advance into Afghanistan, he was sent in advance in command of the baggage-guard to Jalalabad. He subsequently took part with the regiment in the Lughman Valley expedition, and after returning to Jalalabad was sent in command of a company to assist in guarding the Daronta ford of the Kabul river. Finally he went on to Gandamak, Safed Sang, and Pezwan, where in April he was appointed General Transport Officer to the station. At this time he was suffering from tropical dysentery, brought on by exposure and fatigue. In May he was employed on a survey of the fortifications of Pezwan. Being in a weak state from his former illness, he was unable to withstand the effects of the intense heat, and was seized with an attack of enteric fever, to which he rapidly succumbed, having cheerfully and bravely performed the duties allotted to him to the last.

Herbert Spoor's remains rest in the little cemetery at Pezwan, where they were buried with military honours by his brother officers and the men of the regiment, by whom he was sincerely lamented.

LIEUT. F. C. STAYNER, STAFF CORPS,

19TH BOMBAY N.I.

FRANCIS CHARLES STAYNER, who fell in the disastrous sortie from Kandahar on the 16th August, 1880, was the second son of James Stayner, Esq., of Ilminster, Somerset. He was born on the 27th July, 1854; and after receiving tuition from the Rev. Edward Girdleston at Weston-super-Mare, passed on to Harrow, and from thence, in 1873, to Trinity College, Cambridge, with the intention of qualifying for the legal profession. During his academical course he evinced more than ordinary ability; and his amiable disposition rendered him a universal favourite amongst his schoolfellows and contemporaries at college.

In 1876 he relinquished his intention of embracing a legal career, and commenced, in London, a course of preparation for the Sandhurst examination. Succeeding in taking a place among the successful candidates, he entered the Royal Military College in February, 1876, and passing out after the usual course, was gazetted to a Sub-Lieutenancy in the 5th Fusiliers, then serving in Bengal. In February, 1877, he embarked for India to join the head-quarters; on arriving at Bombay, however, he was posted to the 15th Native Infantry as a probationer for the Staff Corps, and proceeded to join that regiment at Ahmadnagar.

After being attached for musketry instruction for a few months in the summer of 1878 to the 2nd Queen's, at Poona, Stayner was finally posted as Sub-Lieutenant to the 19th Bombay Native Infantry, then forming part of General Primrose's reserve force, and quartered at Karachi, at which station he arrived, in company with the General, in the month of December. During the year 1879 he took his share in the heavy work which fell to the lot of the regiment in its employment on the Public Works, in Baluchistan; and notwithstanding the exacting nature of his duties, succeeded in passing a highly creditable examination in the higher standard of Hindustani.

In March, 1880, Lieutenant Stayner took part with the regiment, as Adjutant, in its advance to Kandahar, and remained with the head-quarters in cantonments, and subsequently in the citadel, till the 16th August. In the attack upon the village of Deh Khwaja on that fatal day, he commanded the portion of his regiment which formed part of No. 3 Column under the command of Colonel Heathcote, and was ordered by him to assault the northern side of the position. Whilst gallantly performing this duty he was killed by a matchlock ball, death being instantaneous. His body was carried back to the citadel, and was interred the same evening with those of four other officers in separate graves in a corner of the new garden cemetery, the burial service being read by the Rev. A. Cane.

Colonel Heathcote, of the 19th Bombay Natal Infantry refers in the warmest terms to Lieutenant Stayner's zeal and bravery; while his brother officers have lost no opportunity of placing on record their deep appreciation of his noble, kindly and generous nature.

BREV. LIEUT.-COL. R. G. T. STEVENSON,

POONA HORSE.

RODERICK GEORGE THOMAS STEVENSON, who died at Quetta on the 24th April, 1880, was the fourth son of Brigadier-General Thomas Stevenson, who served for forty years in the Bombay Artillery. He was born at Poona on the 6th April, 1836, and was educated at Cheltenham College. Receiving a direct Bombay Cavalry cadetship, he was appointed Cornet in the 2nd Light Cavalry on arriving in India in August, 1855, and two years afterwards (November, 1857) obtained his Lieutenancy. During the six years succeeding the date of his arrival in India, he did duty with his regiment in Rujputana and Central India; and accompanying it on service in the Indian Mutiny, was present at the action of Nimbhaira, the siege of Nimach, the capture of Kotah, and with the force under Sir J. Michell, K.C.B., in Central India, receiving the Mutiny medal with clasps for Central India. In March, 1862, Stevenson proceeded on sick certificate to England, where he remained till March, 1865, obtaining promotion, in the interval, to the rank of Captain. On returning to India he was attached to the 3rd Bombay Light Cavalry, and did duty with a squadron at Kaladgi, where he also held the office of Station Staff Officer, until April, 1866, when he was appointed to command the 2nd Squadron of the regiment.

In February, 1867, Captain Stevenson exchanged into the Poona Horse, with which corps he served at Sirur, and on the frontier of Upper Sind, until June, 1871, when he was appointed to officiate as 2nd in command of the 3rd (Queen's Own) Light Cavalry, then serving at Nimach. He commanded that regiment for nine months, at the expiration of which (April, 1872) he took leave to England. Returning to India in April, 1874, after having, in the interval, obtained his Majority, he rejoined the Poona Horse at Sirur. In the following year he proceeded to command a detached squadron in Khandesh, where he remained until the withdrawal of the squadron in 1878. In 1876 he succeeded to the appointment of permanent second in command of the regiment.

Major Stevenson took part with the Poona Horse in January, 1880, in its forward movement into Baluchistan, *en route* for Kandahar. Proceeding in command of two squadrons to Quetta, he reached that station in the last days of March, and was looking forward eagerly to the stirring times which seemed imminent. His anticipations of further active service were, however, unhappily destined never to be fulfilled. A few days before the regiment quitted Quetta for Kandahar, he was attacked with pleuro-pneumonia, to which complaint, after a short illness, he succumbed on the 24th April, within ten days of his receiving his Brevet Lieutenant-Colonelcy.

Lieutenant-Colonel Stevenson was a thorough soldier, and was highly esteemed by both officers and men, European and Native, of the regiment, who sincerely regretted his death. He married, in 1865, Rosalie Maitland, daughter of Thomas Mackenzie, C.B., Indian Medical Department. His father, Lieutenant-Colonel Thomas Stevenson, died at Sukkur in Upper Sind, in the year 1849, while commanding the Horse Artillery Brigade, Sind Field Force.

CAPTAIN EDWARD STRATON,

2ND BATTALION, 22ND REGIMENT (THE CHESHIRE).

HE subject of this memoir, who was killed at the battle of Kandahar on the 1st September, 1880, was the fifth son of the late John Warde Straton. After passing the examination for direct commissions in the line, he was gazetted on the 25th June, 1861, to an Ensigncy in the 2nd Battalion, 22nd (Cheshire) Regiment, and soon afterwards joined that corps at Malta. He obtained a Lieutenancy, by purchase, on the 23rd June, 1863. In 1865, he embarked with the regiment at Malta for Mauritius, where it was stationed till 1867, when it returned to England.

Lieutenant Straton was appointed Adjutant of the Battalion on the 20th April, 1868, and held that appointment till the 23rd April, 1872. He obtained a second-class Musketry certificate on the 1st October, 1868. On the 14th May, 1872, he was gazetted a Captain without purchase, under the new regulations. In August of the same year he obtained a certificate of proficiency in Military Gymnastics, and was employed upon the Staff of the Northern Corps d'Armée in the autumn manœuvres.

In the autumn of 1873, Captain Straton accompanied his regiment to India, and was quartered at Hazarabagh. From thence the battalion was removed to Ranikhet, of which station Captain Straton was appointed Station Staff Officer on the 31st November, 1876, and held that appointment till the 31st December, 1877. He had previously acted as Staff Officer to Major-General Payn whilst at Hazarabagh, and subsequently to Major-General M. A. S. Biddulph, at Ranikhet.

During the time he was at Ranikhet, he studied heliography, and gained that knowledge of the work which proved so useful later on; and on the 22nd February, 1878, he obtained a certificate as a qualified Instructor in Army Signalling. In 1878 the regiment was ordered to Allahabad, and Captain Straton was appointed Transport Officer of that station 10th October, 1878.

On the outbreak of the Afghan War, Captain Straton applied to be employed in the Army Signalling Department, but was not ordered to the front till April, 1879, when he joined the Kuram Field Force as Superintendent of Army Signalling in succession to Captain Barstow, 72nd Highlanders. After the massacre of the Kabul Embassy, Captain Straton was attached to Sir F. Roberts' Field Force, and accompanying it throughout its advance, was present at Charasiab, and during the operations ending in the occupation of Kabul; also at the affair at Dulia on the 10th November, 1879; during the investment of Sherpur by the Afghans in December, 1879, and also at Ali Boghan, near Jalalabad, on 12th January, 1880.

In connection with the actions above referred to, Captain Straton was mentioned in the despatches both of Brigadier-General Baker and Sir Frederick Roberts. The former makes allusion to the signalling arrangements as having been " of great service during the day's operations; " and the latter writes as follows :—" I wish especially to bring to notice the valuable aid I have received from Captain E. Straton, 22nd Foot, Superintendent of Army Signalling. In a country like Afghanistan, signalling by heliograph and flags is of the greatest assistance; the able and intelligent manner in which Captain Straton has carried on his work has helped materially to the success of the operations." In submitting, too, an abridged list of those whose services had been more particularly marked and valuable, Sir F. Roberts a second time mentions Captain Straton's name, and again in his despatch of the 23rd January, 1880, writes :—" I cannot overrate the value of the work done by the Army Signallers with this force, and I consider that the success which has attended their efforts is mainly due to the energy and intelligence of Captain E. Straton, 22nd Regiment, Superintendent of Army Signalling."

Major A. Wynne, 51st Regiment, thus refers to the affair of Ali Boghan, on the 12th January, 1880, in a paper read at the United Service Institution on 13th March, 1880 :—

" But perhaps one of the most prominent services rendered as yet by the heliograph, was during Captain Straton's visit to Jalalabad in January last. On the 12th of that month, when at one of the signal stations of Ali Boghan, he found out that the Mohmands had crossed the Kabul river; this intelligence he at once flashed off to Jalalabad, and that night a brigade started to intercept the enemy. During the following day communication was successfully maintained between General Bright's Head-quarters at Jalalabad, the brigade sent out, and a detachment crowning the heights. At 1.15 p.m. on the 13th, Captain Straton saw about 1,500 men of the enemy retiring across the river at such a point that, if they had succeeded in crossing, the brigade would have been cut off from Jalalabad and the detachment from its main body. But intimation was at once signalled to all concerned, and by 3 p.m. a couple of guns sent out from Jalalabad were shelling the enemy with such good effect that they beat a hasty retreat."

Then followed the monotonous life in cantonments, broken only by short expeditions into the neighbouring country, until the end of July, when orders arrived for Sir F. Roberts to march to Kandahar. Captain Straton was attached to the Kabul-Kandahar Field Force, and again was successful in demonstrating the usefulness of the heliograph.

It was at the battle of Kandahar on 1st September, 1880, when the victory was almost won, and Captain Straton was on his way to the Baba Wali Kotal to announce the success to Sir F. Roberts by heliograph, that he met his death. The following are the words used by the General with reference to the event in his despatch describing the march and the battle :—

" Shortly before the final advance, Major-General Ross, wishing to inform me by heliograph that he had succeeded in turning the enemy's position, directed Captain Straton, 22nd Foot, Superintendent of Army Signalling, to proceed with a company of the 24th Punjab Native Infantry to the Baba Wali Kotal. This gallant officer had only gone a short distance when a Ghazi, springing out of a ravine close to him, shot him dead. In Captain Straton, Her Majesty's Service has lost a most accomplished, intelligent officer, under whose management Army Signalling, as applied to field service, reached a pitch of perfection probably never before attained. His energy knew no difficulties, and his enthusiasm was beyond praise. He had won the highest opinions from all with whom his duties had brought him in contact, and his death was very deeply felt throughout the whole force."

The value of the work done by the Army Signallers is thus referred to by Colonel Chapman, Chief of the Staff of the Kabul-Kandahar Field Force, in a paper read at the United Service Institution, 9th March, 1881:—

"It may here be noticed that the great perfection to which the practice of Army Signalling had been brought, made the heliograph a very important aid in the communication of intelligence. Under the direction of the late Captain Straton, Superintendent of Army Signalling at Kabul, the trained signallers of the force were constantly employed, and by the judicious use of the heliograph on many occasions, the troops, both cavalry and infantry, were spared fatigue, the several brigades being constantly in communication by signal. . . . . . . Later on, it will be seen how much depended on the working of the heliograph between Kandahar and the camp in the Tarnak Valley, on the 27th August; but the benefits conferred on the Kabul Field Force by its staff of army signallers under their gallant leader, cannot be forgotten."

The following extract, taken from the "Army and Navy Gazette" of the 11th September, 1880, may fitly close this notice:—". . . He (Captain Straton) fell in the performance of his duties almost in the moment of victory. His loss will be deeply deplored, not only by the officers and men of his regiment, but by a very large number of friends throughout the service. A man of indomitable courage and untiring energy, he was passionately fond of his profession, and singularly zealous in the performance of his duties. First in every manly exercise, kind-hearted, and courteous, he was a noble specimen of an officer and a gentleman."

CAPTAIN S. A. SWINLEY,

11TH (P.W.O.) BENGAL CAVALRY (LANCERS).

SILAS ADAIR SWINLEY, who died of typhoid fever at Safed Sang, Afghanistan, on the 24th May, 1879, was the second son of the late Major-General G. H. Swinley, Royal (late Bengal) Artillery. He was born at Agra, North West Provinces, India, on the 11th July, 1843. Obtaining a direct commission in April, 1861, he was placed on the General List of cavalry officers of the Bengal Establishment, and at once embarked for India.

Landing at Calcutta in May, 1861, Swinley proceeded to Mirat, and in June, 1861, was appointed to do duty with the 8th Hussars, with which regiment he remained till the 9th November, 1862; he was then posted to the 3rd Bengal Cavalry, and served with that corps in successive grades for a period of eight years. In the month of December, 1870, he met with an accident while on parade, falling from his horse and injuring himself so severely as to necessitate his taking furlough to England for two years on medical certificate. On his return to India in 1873, he received the appointment of Station Staff Officer at Nowgong, Bundelkhand; and officiating at intervals as cantonment Magistrate and first-class Political Agent at that station, retained that post till December, 1876. He was then despatched on special duty to Madras, and for several months did valuable and important work in connection with the famine which raged over that presidency in 1876 and 1877.

In November, 1877, Captain Swinley was appointed 3rd Squadron Commander to the 11th (Prince of Wales' Own) Bengal Lancers. On the outbreak of hostilities with Afghanistan in the autumn of 1878, he took part in the month of November, in the advance of Sir Sam. Browne's Division into the Khyber Pass, being present at the capture of Ali Musjid, and subsequently sharing with his regiment, during the succeeding winter and early spring, the heavy convoy and escort duties which fell to its lot. It was while he was on detached duty, commanding a post between Jalalabad and Gandamak, that he was attacked with the fever which subsequently proved fatal to him. It is characteristic of him that he sent no intimation of his illness to regimental head-quarters, but continued in a spirit of self-devotion to do duty for days after he should have applied to be relieved. When he rode into Gandamak with the daily escort, his health was completely broken; and a few days afterwards, on the 24th May, 1879, he died, deeply regretted by the many friends to whom his sterling qualities had endeared him.

Captain Swinley's commissions bear date as follows :—

Cornet, General List Cavalry	20th April, 1861.
Lieutenant	24th September, 1863.
Brevet-Captain	20th April, 1873.
Captain	4th September, 1873.

2ᴺᴰ LIEUTENANT B. S. THURLOW,

51ST (KING'S OWN LIGHT INFANTRY).

BENJAMIN SMITH THURLOW was a member of the Suffolk family of that name, being the third son of the late George John Thurlow, Esq. He was born on the 23rd July, 1858, and was educated at King Edward the Sixth's Grammar School, Birmingham, and Mr. Kippin's Military College, Woolwich. Competing at the examination for entrance into Sandhurst in December, 1877, he succeeded in taking a place among the successful candidates, and, passing out of the college with honours after the usual course, was gazetted, in May, 1878, to the 58th Foot. Being desirous, however, to join a regiment serving in India, he was transferred, almost immediately, to the 51st King's Own Light Infantry, and was attached for a few months to the 101st Light Infantry, then quartered in Guernsey, to await the trooping season in the autumn.

In November, 1878, Thurlow embarked for India, and on arriving, proceeded to join his regiment at Ali Musjid, in the Khyber Pass, where, at the time, it was stationed. Subsequently taking part with it in the forward movement to Jalalabad and Gandamak, he shared the convoy and escort duties upon which it was employed, and eventually returned with it, after the signing of the treaty of peace, to India.

Lieutenant Thurlow accompanied the regiment in its second advance into Afghanistan on the renewal of hostilities in the autumn of 1879, and, in the spring of 1880, was doing duty with a detachment in the neighbourhood of Jagdalak. On the afternoon of the 22nd March, he started with his brother-officer, Lieutenant Reid, to ride over to that post, which was about a couple of miles distant. After the two had proceeded a few hundred yards along the bottom of a gorge, Reid heard three or four musket-shots fired almost simultaneously from the hills on each side of the road. The horses started forward at a gallop, and Thurlow, who was a few yards in front, was seen by Reid to fall heavily to the ground. Directly the latter could rein in his horse, he turned, and perceived an Afghan running towards Thurlow's apparently inanimate body for the purpose of robbing it. Putting spurs to his horse, Reid dashed at full speed towards the thief, who raised his rifle and fired point blank at his heart. At this critical juncture the horse shied suddenly on one side, and by so doing almost miraculously saved the life of its rider, whose coat-sleeve—so near was he to the muzzle of the gun when the shot was fired—was burnt away above the elbow. Closing with the Afghan, Reid now succeeded in bringing his revolver to bear on him, and blew out his brains; but no sooner was this done than some thirty of the band rushed upon him. He succeeded, however, in escaping, and making his way to Jagdalak, from whence parties were subsequently despatched to the spot where the affray had taken place. There Lieutenant Thurlow's body was found, and was interred on the following day with military honours.

The untimely and tragical end of the subject of this notice called forth many expressions of sympathy from unexpected sources. Though the term of his service with the regiment was of short duration, it was nevertheless not too brief to admit of his winning the esteem and affection of his comrades.

MAJOR R. J. LE POER TRENCH,

19TH BOMBAY NATIVE INFANTRY.

RICHARD JOHN LE POER TRENCH, the youngest son of the late Rev. John le Poer Trench, of Temple Michael, in the parish of Longford, Ireland, was born at Temple Michael Glebe, his father's rectory, in the year 1843. He was educated at King William's College, Isle of Man, and Cheltenham, from whence he passed the examination for a direct appointment—given to him by Mr. Bailly, one of the then East India directors—in the Indian Army. Gazetted to an Ensigncy in the 24th Bombay Infantry in September, 1859, he served with that regiment for some three years, at the end of which he proceeded home on sick-leave. On his return to India he applied himself to the study of the native languages. Having passed the Higher Standard examination, he was appointed Quartermaster to the 19th Bombay Infantry, with which regiment he subsequently served continuously till the day of his death—a period of some thirteen years.

Major Trench was at home on leave in the summer of 1878, but returned to India in time to rejoin his regiment before it received orders, after the outbreak of hostilities with Afghanistan, to hold itself in readiness to form part of the Reserve Division, then in course of concentration on the frontier. During the last eventful year of his service, while employed with his regiment in the formidable work of constructing a military road through the hitherto almost impassable Bolan defile, he was "most conspicuous," to quote the words of General Creagh, "for the energy he displayed, and for his fertility of resource in overcoming difficulties in the work, never tiring, and always encouraging his men at their laborious and unaccustomed employment by his own ready and cheerful example."

In September, 1879, Trench was sent in command of an escort to Sir R. Sandeman into the Kakar Pathan and Marri country. This party remained in and about the assigned districts till January, 1880, accompanying Sir R. Temple in his tour made in the neighbourhood in November, 1879. Most of the marches performed were made through exceedingly difficult country; and Trench's name was more than once mentioned in the Bombay journals for the combination of skill and patience which he displayed in taking trains with camels over passes hitherto regarded as inaccessible to such beasts of burden.

Major Trench rejoined the Head-quarters of the 19th Bombay Infantry at Kandahar, having marched his escort party there on completion of its duty, and taken up detachments of infantry and of artillery *en route*. After sharing with the regiment during the siege the various duties which fell to its lot, he took part with it, on the 16th August, 1880, in the fatal sortie to Deh Khwaja, commanding the two companies which formed part of Colonel Daubeny's column. When they had advanced up to the village, Trench was ordered to take his men and some of the Fusiliers into an enclosed field on the right, and drive back the enemy, who were here showing in force and endeavouring to break through to help those inside. This work he performed—according to the testimony of eye-witnesses—splendidly, all who saw him being loud in their praise of the way in which he handled his men, and the very complete manner in which he drove back the enemy, giving them volley after volley until they turned and fled to cover. After this he was moved into the village. When the retreat was sounded, he was standing in a ditch with some eighty of his men, who were working terrible havoc amongst the enemy with their fire. He is reported to have leapt up with the exclamation, "Retreat? this is no time for retreat!"—his last words; for a few moments afterwards a bullet fired from a house-top struck him in the back of the head, killing him instantaneously. "Thus died," wrote Colonel Heathcote, in reference to his fall, "as gallant an officer as ever held Her Majesty's commission." His body was brought in by his men; and in the evening of the same day received at the hands of his comrades a soldier's sepulture.

It will perhaps not be out of place to conclude this brief notice with the following extract from a letter written with reference to Major Trench by Major-General William Creagh, one who was some time his commanding officer:—

"He was a perfect type of a fine open-hearted Irishman. As an officer he could not be surpassed in anything that constitutes a good soldier, full of zeal and devotion to his profession, as daring as a lion. His death was a severe loss, not only to his own regiment, but to the Army."

BRIGADIER-GENERAL J. A. TYTLER, C.B., V.C.,

BENGAL STAFF CORPS.

JOHN ADAM TYTLER, who died at Thal, Punjab, on the 14th February, 1880, was the third son of John Tytler, Surgeon, Honourable East India Company's Service, his mother being a daughter of W. Gillies, Esq., of London. He was born at Monghyr, Bengal, on the 29th October, 1825, and was sent home, when five years of age, to the care of his mother's sisters, under whose charge he remained until the arrival of his parents in England in 1835. The family resided for a year in London, and then proceeded to Jersey, where John Tytler attended a day school in the vicinity of St. Heliers, kept by a Mr. de Joux. In March, 1837, Mr. Tytler died; and in the autumn of 1838 his widow—having in view the education of her family, and desiring to be near her relations—took up her residence in Edinburgh. There John Tytler attended the Academy, and in course of time bore off several prizes. On attaining his seventeenth year, he was transferred to a school at Lisle, where, remaining for a twelvemonth, he completed his education. In 1843 he received an Infantry commission in the Company's Service from his father's old friend Sir Jeremiah Bryant, and in the autumn of that year proceeded to India. The various incidents of his subsequent career are so amply and ably set forth in an obituary notice which appeared in the columns of the "Times" newspaper on the 23rd February, 1880, that, with these brief premises, the Editor of this work takes the liberty of transcribing the memoir as it was given. After making allusion to the deceased officer as "one of the best and bravest of the rising Generals of the Army in India—the bearer of a name honoured alike in that country and in this," the writer continues as follows :—

"In December, 1844, John Adam Tytler entered the Indian Army, in the ranks of which several of his relations were then serving; he was posted to the 66th Native Infantry, and first saw active service on the Peshawar frontier, under Sir Colin Campbell, in 1851. In the Indian Mutiny he was unfortunate enough to be detained in the Kumaun hills, and so was present at none of the great sieges of that campaign; but in February, 1858, at the action of Churpura, his men, being somewhat staggered by the heavy fire of grape with which they were received on approaching the enemy's position, showed signs of wavering. Lieutenant Tytler, seeing that personal example was all that was necessary to rally them, put spurs to his horse, and, dashing on ahead, alone attacked the rebel gunners; for a few seconds he was personally engaged in a hand-to-hand fight, and before his men reached him had been dangerously wounded in three places. He recovered, however, sufficiently to take part in the closing scenes of the suppression of the Mutiny, and to receive the Victoria Cross for his indomitable valour at the action of Churpura. In the Umbeyla expedition of 1863 Captain Tytler, V.C., commanded his regiment, the 4th Goorkhas, with marked credit, and was prominently noticed in despatches. Four years later, in the Hazara expedition, under Sir Alfred Wilde, we find him again leading the same gallant regiment—one of the model corps in the Bengal Army—and once more his name is honourably mentioned in orders. In 1872 he served through the Lushai expedition, and for his eminent services was nominated a Companion of the Bath. On the outbreak of the Afghan War, it was inevitable that Colonel Tytler's services would secure for him a brigade command, and it was equally certain that his great experience in hill warfare would prove of equal value to himself and the Government he had served so well. After the fall of Ali Musjid, at which he commanded one of the flanking brigades, he was intrusted with the onerous task of maintaining communications between Sir Samuel Browne's force and Peshawar. Here he acted with rare skill and sagacity; twice he led his brigade into the Afridi hills in order to chastize certain sections of that turbulent clan who were harassing convoys in the neighbourhood of the Khyber. Later on he defeated the Shinwaris in a sharp engagement. After the Treaty of Gandamak General Tytler was placed in command of the troops between Landi Kotal and the old frontier; but ill-health compelled him to resign his brigade before the outbreak of last September. Immediately on learning of the massacre of the Embassy, though still suffering from the effects of the previous campaign, the gallant General placed his sword at the disposal of the Viceroy. He was a man who could not be permitted to rust in idleness when mountain warfare was on the *tapis*, and the Commander-in-Chief evinced a wise determination when he nominated General Tytler to the command of the troops destined to act against the hostile Zaimushts. These operations were conducted with consummate skill. A resolute stand was made by the enemy, and in the frontal attack we lost a brave young officer in Lieutenant and Adjutant Renney. The General's plans were not to be denied, and while the main body held the enemy in check in front, a strong force under the personal guidance of the Brigadier swept the Zaimushts from their rocky fastnesses, which they hitherto had deemed impregnable. Never physically a strong man, the exposure and hardship of the two winter campaigns must naturally have told on a frame enfeebled by dangerous wounds; and just as he was about to reap the rewards of a distinguished career, pneumonia—that fell disease on the Punjab Frontier—has claimed him as its last and most valued victim. Modest and unassuming, as all brave men are, few who did not know General Tytler would recognize in him a man who had won the Victoria Cross for an act which onlookers deemed a ride to certain death; still less would they consider him one capable of converting raw Goorkha levies into one of the smartest regiments in the Indian Army. A long record of hard service has been closed by a death no less honourable than if won on the battle-field. He will be mourned, not merely by the few who knew and loved him well, but by the many who admired his daring gallantry, his earnest perseverance, and the patience with which he bore what most men would have deemed official neglect; for though General Tytler commanded his regiment on three separate campaigns and earned the warmest praises of all the Generals under whom he served, he never received Brevet promotion for his distinguished services in the field. Even his brilliant conduct in the late Afghan War was unrewarded by riband or professional advancement. His death deprives the Queen of the services of one of the best and bravest men who have ever worn her Cross, and the Indian Army of a General whose place it will not be easy to fill. He was an officer of the old school, and one of its best and most valued representatives."

LIEUTENANT E. P. VENTRIS,

3RD REGIMENT (THE BUFFS.)

EDWARD PEYTON VENTRIS, who died at Bagh, Baluchistan, on the 14th April, 1879, was the eldest son of the Rev. Edward Favell Ventris, Rector of Church Aston, Shropshire, by his marriage with Rose, daughter of Mr. Thomas Fisher, of St. Osyth, Essex. He was born at Colchester on the 28th July, 1856, and was educated at Newport Salop Grammar School, under the Rev. Dr. Charles Waring Saxton and Mr. Thomas Collins, and subsequently at Spring Grove, under Mr. Wyatt. After passing a creditable examination for direct appointments, he obtained a commission in the Buffs, and was gazetted 2nd Lieutenant in February, 1874.

Leaving England for India in the following September, Ventris joined his regiment at Calcutta. Here he remained till the 27th September, 1875, when he proceeded to Lucknow for garrison instruction. Before he had completed his course, however, an order came for all officers to rejoin Head-quarters, in view of the departure of the Buffs, in the then impending expedition to Perak; and embarking with the regiment in November, 1865, he served with it in the Malay Peninsula throughout the operations of the force. The expedition terminating in the middle of March in the following year, he landed at Calcutta on the 27th of that month, and at once proceeded with his regiment to Cawnpore. Having contracted a slight fever after his return to India, he was compelled to have recourse to the hills for a few months, at the expiration of which, his health being recruited by the colder climate, he returned to complete his garrison course at Lucknow, from which he had been so unexpectedly called away. The regiment eventually removed from Cawnpore to Meerut.

On the outbreak of hostilities with Afghanistan, Lieutenant Ventris, eager to make his way to the theatre of war, volunteered for active service " in any capacity," and being a very good and promising officer, was appointed, on the recommendation of Colonel Morley, to the Transport Service of the South Afghanistan Field Force. Proceeding on the 1st February, 1879, to Lahore, he received orders to go on to Sukkur, and became finally located at Haji-ka-Shehar, where he became the assistant of Lieutenant-Colonel Cherry in the Transport Train. Here his arduous duties, carried out in a trying climate, and with only bad water to be had, brought on an illness from which he died.

Colonel Cherry, in writing of the subject of this brief notice, says:—"Ventris was always the same—amiable and gentlemanly, and ever anxious to do his duty;" and General Phayre, in recording his death, speaks of the energy and perseverance with which he performed the difficult duties assigned to him.

A tomb, surrounded by an iron railing, erected by the officers of the Transport Train and Staff, marks the spot where Lieutenant Ventris was buried.

SURGEON-MAJOR JOHN WALLACE,
M.A., M.D., M.R.C.S.,

ARMY MEDICAL DEPARTMENT.

THE subject of this memoir was the fourth son of Mr. Wallace, Chapel of Leggat, Auchterless, Aberdeenshire. He received his education in Scotland, and was a distinguished student both at the Universities of Aberdeen and Edinburgh. At the former he obtained the degree of M.A. in 1859; and at the latter that of M.D. in 1862, in which year he also became a member of the Royal College of Surgeons, England. Taking first place among the candidates for commissions for the Army Medical School in March, 1864, he left Netley at the close of the session, and did duty for a brief period on the Staff. He was then appointed to the 12th Regiment, and proceeded almost immediately afterwards to New Zealand. Serving with the regiment in the Maori War of 1864-1866, for which he obtained the medal, he was present at the attack and capture of the fortified pass of Otapawa, and several minor affairs. After three years spent in New Zealand, he returned with the regiment to England, and continued with it throughout the period of its home service.

His unostentatious self-devotion to duty, his wide sympathies, and his unfailing patience, had early brought him into cordial relationship alike with the officers and men of the regiment—relationship which his after association with the corps only served still further to strengthen and augment. In the autumn of 1875, when the battalion was stationed at Kinsale, typhoid fever of a most virulent type broke out in the ranks; and Dr. Wallace, who was at the time away on leave of absence, was at once telegraphed for. In reference to the services which he then rendered, a letter, couched in warm terms of admiration, was addressed by the Officer Commanding to the Assistant Adjutant-General of the District: "During the long and anxious time which followed the outbreak," wrote Colonel Foster, "it may be said that Surgeon Wallace almost lived in the Hospital; day and night was he to be found in attendance on the sick, taking only a snatch of rest now and then, and that very frequently by the bedside of a sufferer; in fact, his indefatigable exertions and untiring devotion to the patients were truly laudable." His services upon that occasion were brought under the notice of H.R.H. the Commander-in-Chief, and received his highest approval.

Dr. Wallace accompanied the regiment to India on the expiration of its term of home service, and was doing duty with it, when, on the outbreak of hostilities with Afghanistan, it marched from Naushahra, and joined the Peshawar Valley Field Force. In the previous autumn he had been much weakened by fever, then prevalent; and he now entered on the harassing duties of the campaign before his health was fully re-established. In the pestiferous climate of the country through which the Northern Division of the Army pursued its route, work soon fell to his hand which severely taxed even his unflagging energy. Worn out while in charge of the Field Hospital at Landi Kotal with the ceaseless exertion and anxiety entailed by his endeavours to cope with the fearful amount of sickness which was decimating the ranks at that post during the evacuation of the Northern line, he fell a victim on the 16th July, 1879, at the early age of thirty-nine years, to the terrible disease—cholera—which he had done so much to alleviate in others.

We may aptly conclude this brief notice of one who fittingly closed his useful life at the post of duty, by quoting at length from the official Orders issued on the occasion of his death. In a Regimental Order bearing date 16th July, 1879, the following tribute is paid to his memory; "In a period of thirteen years and upward that Dr. Wallace served with the regiment, he endeared himself to everyone, by the care and kind attention he bestowed so willingly on all. Lieut.-Colonel Walker, the officers, non-commissioned officers, men, women, and children, have by Dr. Wallace's death lost a most true, valued, and kind-hearted friend; and the Commanding Officer is well aware he cannot do sufficient justice to the many good and sterling qualities of the deceased: he can truly say, a less selfish man never lived, and he firmly believes that Dr. Wallace's deep sense of duty and devotion to the sick men of the battalion have been the cause of his most lamented death." And in a Brigade Order of the 17th idem, the last chapter of the deceased officer's career is thus epitomized:—" In charge of the Field Hospital at Landi Kotal, during a most trying and arduous time, he devoted himself to his duties with an energy which was ceaseless and untiring, and with a skill and kindness which will be remembered with gratitude by many a British soldier in this garrison. Thinking always of others, he took no heed of himself, but working on through sickness, as he had done in health, he laid himself open to the attacks of the disease which has stricken him down, and has robbed his profession and his regiment of an honour to both."

SURGEON J. E. WALSH, M.D.,

BENGAL MEDICAL DEPARTMENT.

JOHN EDWARD WALSH, who died of cholera at Kandahar on the 24th July, 1879, was the eldest son of J. R. Walsh, Esq., of Martinstown House, Co. Limerick. He was born on the 2nd of May, 1855, and received the rudiments of his education at home. When sufficiently prepared, he was sent to the Abbey Grammar School, Tipperary, one of Erasmus Smith's foundations, where he studied under the head-mastership of the late Mr. T. Matthews, M.A., of St. John's, Cambridge. Entering the Queen's College, Cork, in October, 1873, he took a first literary scholarship on Matriculation, and shortly afterwards a first prize in English composition. His career at Cork was one of high promise: in addition to bearing off numerous prizes, he obtained a Medical scholarship and several exhibitions. He took his degrees in Medicine and Surgery at the Queen's University, Dublin, in October, 1877; and in the following February was a successful candidate in London for an appointment in the Indian Medical Service.

In October, 1878, Walsh was ordered out to India. After being stationed for a time at Mirat he was sent to Mian Mir, where he was attached to one of the native regiments. His next move was to Multan. There he passed the lower standard examination in Hindustani; and there, too, he was subsequently appointed to take medical charge of the relieving force under the command of Colonel Bedford, Royal Engineers, then *en route* for Quetta and Kandahar. In view of the rough and difficult nature of the country, subsequently traversed by the troops after crossing the Indus, the fact that only one man was lost out of the 700 of which, including camp followers, the force was composed, speaks of itself for the efficiency of the medical care bestowed on it during the march. In recognition of the Surgeon's successful and zealous attention, the officer commanding made allusion to him, in the handsomest and most complimentary terms, in his report to the General.

Dr. Walsh had been barely two months in Kandahar, when, cholera breaking out among the camp followers, he was placed in charge of one of the wards of the hospital for patients suffering from that fatal disease. An enthusiast in his profession, he laboured with unceasing and devoted zeal, never sparing himself in his efforts to alleviate pain or soothe the last moments of a sufferer. For a time he continued cheerfully to cope with the ever-increasing work; but at length, utterly worn out, he fell at his post, a victim to the disease whose ravages he had been for weeks successfully combating. He died like a true soldier, in the performance of his duties, passing away after a few hours of great suffering, in his twenty-fourth year, in the springtime of his life, full of hope, of future promise, of intellectual and physical energy. His naturally spontaneous and affectionate disposition had endeared him to the whole garrison, and his death was mourned with a depth of feeling which, in view of the brief term of his service, was as remarkable as it was affecting.

It is some consolation to Dr. Walsh's family to know that he was watched over during his last hours by some of his comrades with a chivalrous devotion which no brother's care could exceed. His remains repose in the burial-ground outside Kandahar, where those of hundreds of his countrymen found a last resting-place forty years previously. A marble slab, erected by his brother medical officers to his memory, marks his grave.

2ND LIEUTENANT E. H. WATSON,

1ST BATTALION, 17TH (LEICESTERSHIRE) REGIMENT.

EDWARD HERBERT WATSON, who died on the 4th July, 1879, at Murree, Punjab, from illness contracted while on field service in Afghanistan, was the eldest son of Lieutenant-General E. D. Watson, of the Bengal Infantry, by his marriage with Adelaide, daughter of the late Venerable Archdeacon Barnes, Rector of Sowton, Devonshire.

The subject of this notice was born on the 13th December, 1858, and was educated at Haileybury, from whence, shortly after attaining his eighteenth year, he passed direct into the Royal Military College, Sandhurst. He there received a certificate of merit for Military Law, and honourable mention for exemplary conduct.

Gazetted, in May, 1878, to the 17th Foot, young Watson did duty for a few months at the Depôt, and at the close of the year embarked for India to join the 1st Battalion of the regiment, then on active service in Afghanistan. On the 25th January, 1879, he reached Basawal, where the Head-quarters were at the time stationed, and from that date till the signing of the treaty of peace, shared with the regiment, in the neighbourhood of that post, the various escort and other duties which fell to its lot. From the 18th to the 21st March he was present with the Head-quarters at Maidanak, subsequently proceeding with the battalion to Jalalabad and Safed Sang, and accompanying it, on its retracing its steps, to Landi Kotal. The trying nature of the march, the intense heat, and the pestiferous climate of the country traversed now began to tell upon him, and while at the post last named, he was seized with the deadly malarial fever to which so many of his countrymen fell victims. In the hope that a more bracing atmosphere might restore him to health, he was moved down, by easy stages, to Murree ; but the change came too late, and he died shortly after reaching his destination.

Though no opportunity presented itself to the subject of this notice, during the short term of his service, for distinguishing himself in action, his career was not too brief to admit of his winning the esteem and affection of his comrades. He had endeared himself—according to the testimony of his Commanding Officer—to all around him, and his early death was deeply lamented in the regiment.

SURGEON GEORGE WATSON, M.B.,

BENGAL MEDICAL DEPARTMENT.

THE subject of this notice was the eldest son of Mr. Edward Watson, farmer, Crawfordjohn Farm, Lanarkshire, Scotland. He was born on the 4th September, 1844, and received his earlier education at the Crawfordjohn Parish School, under the late Mr. Robb. At the age of fifteen he entered the University of Edinburgh to study Medicine; and passing in the greater number of his subjects with honours before obtaining his majority, took the degree of M.B. in the year 1866, at the age of twenty-one years. Shortly afterwards he received the appointment of House Surgeon to the Dumfries and Galloway Royal Infirmary, which responsible position he held for seventeen months, availing himself during its tenure of the daily opportunities which presented themselves for improving his professional attainments and acquiring a practical knowledge of the surgical art. Taking, in the year 1868, the degree of L.R.C.S., Edinburgh, he continued to practise in various parts until 1872, when he passed for the Indian Medical Service, his name appearing ninth in the list of successful candidates. He received his commission in March, 1872; and after passing through the usual course at Netley, embarked in the autumn for India.

On arriving at his destination, Watson did duty for a month at the General Hospital, and was subsequently posted successively to the 33rd Bengal Native Infantry, the 8th Bengal Cavalry, and the 14th Bengal Lancers. In January, 1876, he was permanently appointed to the 13th Bengal Lancers.

In the autumn of 1878 Dr. Watson volunteered for active service in Afghanistan, and was attached for duty to the Artillery of Sir Sam. Browne's Division of the Army of Invasion. Accompanying the Division into the Khyber, he was present, on the 21st November, at the attack and capture of Ali Musjid. In January, 1879, he took part with a detachment of his own regiment, which he had in the meantime rejoined, in the Bazar Afridi expedition under Sir F. Maude; and continuing with the regiment, subsequently did duty with it on the Northern Line at various posts extending to Jalalabad, eventually participating with it in the trying return march to India in June, 1879.

On the renewal of hostilities in the autumn, Watson proceeded with the 13th Bengal Lancers by forced marches to the Kuram Valley; and in the month of December, accompanied the portion of his regiment which took part in the expedi- against the Zaimushts, returning eventually to Kuram. In the course of his sub- sequent duties, which were performed in the unhealthy climate of the valley, he suffered repeatedly from attacks of fever, till at length, in July, 1880, a move to higher ground was deemed necessary for the re-establishment of his health, and he left for the Peiwar Kotal. The change came, however, too late: a few days after he arrived at his destination his fever took an enteric form, and on the 25th of the month he expired.

In addition to performing his regimental duties, Dr. Watson had been for some time in medical charge of the Head-quarter Staff. During the brief term of his service he had become universally beloved and esteemed.

The deceased officer was buried, with military honours, in the cemetery at Fort Kuram.

MAJOR S. J. WAUDBY, STAFF CORPS,

19TH BOMBAY NATIVE INFANTRY.

SIDNEY JAMES WAUDBY, who was killed at Dubrai, Southern Afghanistan, on the 16th of April, 1880, was the son of the Rev. W. R. P. Waudby, Rector of Stoke Albany, Market Harborough. He was born in 1840 at Kentish Town; and was educated at Marlborough College and Rossall. In 1858, having obtained a commission in the Company's Service, he proceeded to India, and was attached at first for a few months to the 72nd Highlanders, then stationed at Mhow. He was afterwards gazetted as Ensign to the 19th Bombay Infantry, with which corps he served uninterruptedly until the day of his death—a period of over twenty-one years.

In 1860 Waudby accompanied a field force sent to coerce some turbulent Bhils who had risen in rebellion near the Narbada, and contracted, when on that service, a very dangerous illness, from the pestilential nature of the jungles of the country in which the force was operating. In 1866 he was appointed to the Adjutancy of the regiment, a position he continued to hold until he was promoted to the rank of Major in 1878. The next eighteen years of his life, with the exception of two intervals in which he visited England, were passed in the uneventful duties of an Indian cantonment, varied, however, year by year, by expeditions against the large game of the country—tigers, bison, and bears, of which a great number fell to his rifle. Besides being a keen sportsman, he was a most daring rider, and almost always succeeded—no matter how large the field was—in taking the first spear in all the hunts he attended.

In November, 1878, Major Waudby accompanied his regiment as second in command on field service to Southern Afghanistan; but being in the Reserve Brigade, did not, during the first part of the war, get beyond the head of the Bolan Pass. For several months he was actively and continuously employed with his regiment on escort and other duties, but more especially in assisting in the construction of the military road, 165 miles in length, from Jacobabad to within a short distance of Quetta, the existence of which is mainly due to the exertions of the 19th Bombay Infantry. For his services on this work he was mentioned in the highest terms in General Orders by General Phayre, and Sir Richard Temple, Governor of Bombay.

In December, 1879, Major Waudby succeeded to the temporary command of the regiment, and marched with it to Kandahar. On a permanent commanding officer being appointed, in April, 1880, he—not caring for the quiet life of a peaceful cantonment, as Kandahar then was—applied for, and at once obtained the post of Road Commandant between Kandahar and Quetta, just then become vacant: a position of much responsibility in that wild, lawless country, and one that required constant moving about, together with great tact and vigilance. He at once started on his first inspection of the line; and on his return reached Dubrai—a small commissariat post about fifty miles distant from Kandahar—on the 16th April. On his arrival here, he was informed that an attack was to be made on the post that night by a large body of Kakur Pathans—a very formidable race. He had no one with him on whom he could rely except his small escort, consisting of two privates of his own regiment and three men of the Sind Horse—the guard belonging to the post being composed of some local Pathans lately engaged for the purpose, but who could not be trusted on an emergency, and who were, in consequence, more a source of danger than of help.

Major Waudby immediately proceeded to make the post—which consisted of a small enclosure surrounded by a wall some four feet high—as defensible as possible by means of grain bags and whatever material was near at hand, blocking up the one gateless entrance. At about 11 p.m. the enemy, over 300 in number, suddenly came on and commenced the attack. The native local guard all fled on their first appearance, one man, however, being cut down by a Sind Horseman just as he was in the act of joining them. After a time the assailants by mere force of numbers drove the defenders out of the large area of the courtyard into their redoubt, the top of the Commissariat buildings, which consisted of a single line of low sheds flanking the enclosure on the south side. These were built after the Afghan fashion, with domed roofs. Six of these small domes rose above the level of the façade; and from behind these Major Waudby's party held their attackers at bay for two or three hours. At length the numbers of the gallant little band grew smaller, and the enemy, having succeeded in effecting a lodgment upon the roof, drove them down again to the enclosure. Here they now took refuge inside one of the buildings, and here the last desperate struggle took place. Time after time the enemy charged the narrow gateway of the stronghold, but without success; for barring the approach stood Major Waudby, armed with his shot gun, and making terrible havoc with any who came near him. Eleven corpses were subsequently found at this spot lying close to one another, every one disfigured with shot-wounds—the charges at that close range flying almost like a bullet between the eyes. But at length the place became no longer tenable. The enemy had succeeded in breaking a hole through the roof, and a plunging fire upon the little party was now commenced. Major Waudby had been wounded in the foot already from above; the ammunition of his men was totally exhausted; and on both sides of them the buildings were blazing fiercely. The last rush was now made—not, alas! with any hope of escape on the part of the defenders, but with the fierce determination to sell their lives as dearly as possible. The struggle did not last long. What sword-cuts or bayonet-thrusts were interchanged can never be known; but just outside the little building which had been held so bravely was found the body of Major Waudby, and on each side of it, recognizable solely by the fragments of their uniform, lay those of the two brave soldiers of the 19th. In this gallant and memorable defence, the assaulting Afghans lost over thirty in killed and wounded, and were taught, not for the first time, that English officers and native soldiers know how to fight and how to die.

The following is an extract from a letter written to Major Waudby's father by General Brooke, commanding the Brigade of which the 19th Regiment formed a part, and who arrived at Dubrai the very morning after the occurrence above narrated took place:—"Before this time the telegraph has informed you of the death of your son, with an account of his splendid conduct; but being one of those who first visited the scene of his gallant fight, I cannot resist writing a few lines to assure you how deeply impressed I and every man both British and native in the force which I commanded, and indeed in the whole Army in Southern Afghanistan, have been by the grand example he has set us all—for no more noble instance of the sacrifice of self to the demands of duty has ever come to my knowledge than that displayed by your son, who accepted almost certain death rather than flinch from what he held to be his duty. Your son was warned early in the afternoon of the certainty and gravity of the impending attack, and asked by some of the native soldiers and servants who were with him to retire on the next post, which he could easily have done. I fully understand the fine spirit that induced him to refuse to listen to the suggestion, and, hopeless as he well knew the defence must be, to decide to lose his life rather than to throw even a shadow of discredit on the courage and spirit of Englishmen in the East. Had I, as a senior officer, been in the vicinity at the time, and learnt the exact situation, and the impossibility of reinforcing the garrison, I should have held myself bound to order the evacuation of the post; but this he—acting for himself—could not and would not do; and I honour him for his decision. He seems to have done all an educated and good soldier could have done to improve the defences, and to have made the best possible use of the means at his disposal; and appears to have held the overwhelming numbers at bay for a considerable time. It is clear that before he was overpowered and killed he and his two Sepoys had killed fifteen and wounded eighteen of the enemy. We actually found thirteen dead bodies of the attacking party on the ground; and the enemy acknowledged to having carried off two dead bodies and eighteen wounded. We have lost an admirable officer; but the sacrifice has not been in vain, as he has set an example which cannot be forgotten, and has by his gallantry stimulated the ardour of all our troops in a most remarkable manner. Major Trench (an officer of the 19th Bombay Infantry, who subsequently fell fighting in the sortie from Kandahar) will tell you of the real sorrow evinced by his regiment, and the anxiety of all, notably the natives, to commemorate his memory in a fitting manner. Nothing can compensate his family—his widow and his children—for their loss; but I trust their sorrow will be alleviated in some degree by learning how universally he was respected and liked in his life, and admired in his death."

Some months afterwards, the 19th Regiment, on their return march from Kandahar, had the melancholy satisfaction of performing the last sad rites of a soldier's funeral over the grave of their lamented comrade. It was then observed that other graves in the vicinity had been dug up and violated, even those of Muhamadans—co-religionists of the people of the country—not having escaped.

Major Waudby's alone was left uninjured and intact. On the villagers being asked the reason for such a distinction having been made, they replied, "An Afghan always respects the brave; and no braver man ever lived than the Englishman who lies buried there."

Major Waudby married, in 1875, Mary Alice, daughter of the late Edward Attwood, Esquire, and has left issue two sons.

CAPTAIN A. A. D. WEIGALL,

ARMY PAY DEPARTMENT.

THE subject of this notice was the youngest son of the late Rev. E. Weigall, Incumbent of Buxton, Derbyshire, and Rural Dean, and was a brother of the late Captain Stewart Weigall, of the 77th Regiment.

Arthur Archibald Denne Weigall was born in France on the 21st September, 1844, and received his early education at the Macclesfield Grammar School, whence he proceeded to Rossall School. From there he passed for direct commission in 1864, taking fifth place in the list of successful candidates. Gazetted in July, 1864, to an Ensigncy by purchase in the 76th Regiment, he did duty for a few months at the Depôt at Belfast, and then embarked, in 1865, for India, to join the Head-quarters in the Madras Presidency. In June, 1867, he purchased his Lieutenancy. In the course of his Indian service he passed the examination for the Staff Corps; but being reluctant to sever himself from his old regiment, abstained from availing himself of his success. After serving at various stations in the Madras Presidency, he proceeded with the regiment to Burmah. He had not been long in that country, however, before he became a martyr to so acute a form of rheumatism as to necessitate his being invalided home for eighteen months. On the expiration of his leave in 1869 he returned, restored to health, to his regiment in India, and remained with it till it came home in 1876. He at this time held—and for some time previously had held—the post of Adjutant.

On obtaining his company in October, 1876, and having passed the Hythe Musketry course with a first-class certificate, Captain Weigall exchanged into the 57th Foot, and proceeded to join the Head-quarters of the regiment in Ceylon. Thence he accompanied the 57th to Natal; and serving with the regiment in the Zulu War, was present at the relief of Ekowe and in all the subsequent operations, including the battle of Ginghilovo. At the engagement last named he was struck by a spent ball; but though his arm was contused he did not return his name in the list of wounded. He continued to serve with the regiment in South Africa till it was ordered home in 1879, when he accompanied it to Ireland.

A few months after returning from South Africa, Captain Weigall, seeing no prospect of promotion, joined the Army Pay Department, and was posted to the 2nd Battalion, 11th Regiment, then on active service in South Afghanistan. He at once embarked for India, and in due course made his way to Sibi. The effects of the African climate, from which—though he had never been off duty during the whole of the campaign in Zululand—he suffered when in Dublin, rendered the long and trying march through the Bolan Pass, to join the Head-quarters of the regiment, a task of exaggerated magnitude, and he arrived at Quetta completely exhausted. Though he became sufficiently restored to health to enable him to take part in the forward movement of the regiment into Afghanistan, he never completely recovered; and reaching Kandahar only to die, eventually succumbed on the 22nd December, 1880, in the thirty-seventh year of his age. He left behind him an enviable memory: to know him was to love him, as the universal sympathy manifested at his death fully testifies—officers and men feeling that a brave and thorough soldier and a true friend had passed away from them.

Captain Weigall married, in September, 1876, Alice Henrietta Leveson, second daughter of Surgeon-General Cowen, A.M.D. (retired). He leaves a widow and two children—the youngest, a boy born only five weeks before his death—to mourn his loss.

LIEUTENANT C. G. WHITBY,

PROBATIONER, BOMBAY STAFF CORPS.

CLEMENT GEORGE WHITBY was the eldest son of Dr. Whitby, of Leamington, and was born at Ottery St. Mary, in 1854. He was educated at Wellington College, where he obtained an open classical scholarship, and at Keble College, Oxford, from whence, after passing his moderations, he entered the Army on the 16th February, 1874, as a Sub-Lieutenant in H.M.'s 17th Foot, which his grandfather (one of the Whitbys of Creswell Hall, Staffordshire) had at one time commanded. He immediately proceeded to join his regiment at Peshawar, where it was then quartered. After serving with it for nearly two years, he became a Probationer for the Staff Corps, and joined the 4th Bombay Native Infantry, at Satara. When the Afghan war broke out, Whitby was at once attached to Jacob's Rifles, then quartered at Quetta, and with this regiment he served for some time, being for many months on detachment at Kalat. He was subsequently attached, during the constructing of the road through the Bolan Pass, to the 1st Grenadiers, and assisted in that undertaking till it was completed.

Lieutenant Whitby was well known throughout India by his many contributions to various journals, his chief writings being the "Jottings of a Subaltern," in the "Times of India." He was the originator of the "Kandahar News" (the little journal now so well known throughout both India and England), of which he continued editor until he marched with General Burrows' Force, for the disastrous enterprise in which he lost his life.

In the action near Girishk on the 14th July, 1880, he took no part, being left to guard the camp; but on the fatal 27th July, at Maiwand, he was given command of the baggage guard, which during the engagement twice repulsed the enemy's attack. His horse being still fresh when the retreat was ordered, he managed to struggle on as far as the last village, ten miles from Kandahar, where, within sight of the walls of the city, he was shot through the head by one of the villagers who came swarming out to attack the exhausted remnant of the brigade.

Lieutenant Whitby had passed in the Higher Standard examination in Hindustani, and the Final examination for the Staff Corps, to which he would have been gazetted in a short time, had he survived.

LIEUTENANT FRANK WHITTUCK, STAFF CORPS,

1st BOMBAY N.I. (GRENADIERS).

THE subject of this notice, who died at Kandahar on the 5th September, 1880, was the fifth son of Captain Whittuck, late of Her Majesty's 82nd Regiment, of Ellsbridge House, Keynsham, Somersetshire, by his marriage with Frances Matilda, eldest daughter of the late Lieut.-Colonel Slater, 82nd Regiment.

He was born on the 16th July, 1856, and was educated at the Hermitage, Lansdown, and Sydney College, Bath, eventually passing into the Royal Military College, Sandhurst. In January, 1876, he was gazetted to the 1st Battalion, 17th Regiment (Leicestershire), then in India; but as a probationer for the Staff Corps he at once joined the 12th Bombay Native Infantry at Dharwar. After doing duty for a period with this regiment, he was attached for a short time to the 20th Native Infantry at Baroda, from whence he was ordered to Mhow, to do duty for six months with Her Majesty's 17th Foot. He then rejoined the 12th Native Infantry at Rajkot, and was finally posted to the 1st Bombay Grenadiers, then employed in constructing the military road through the Bolan Pass. After a long and toilsome journey undertaken in the coldest season of the year, he came up with his regiment, and afterwards proceeded with it to Kandahar.

Taking part with the Grenadiers, in the first days of July, 1880, in the advance of Burrows' Brigade to the Halmand, and in the return march to Khushk-i-Nakhud, Lieutenant Whittuck was present with them at the battle of Maiwand, on the 27th of the month, being one of the three officers of the regiment who escaped untouched on that disastrous day. The trials and privations endured through the terrible retreat in which for thirty hours the troops were without food or water, and the subsequent very heavy duties which devolved upon the garrison (at the time sadly reduced in numbers), during the siege, must have been too much for this young officer's strength. Towards the end of August he was attacked with dysentery whilst on duty on the ramparts, from the effects of which—owing to his constitution being much weakened by previous attacks of fever—he never recovered. The last letter his family received from him was penned just one week before the battle of the 27th July; its writer was full of hope and spirits, and apparently without the least idea of the enemy's proximity in such formidable strength.

Lieutenant Whittuck was an officer devoted to his profession. During the short period of his service he was an earnest student of native languages, several examinations in which he passed very creditably. He was also much attached to sport of every kind, and being a good rider and a light weight, he not infrequently rode successfully at race meetings. Of an essentially honourable nature, he endeared himself to all who knew him by his pleasing manners and amiable, unselfish disposition.

LIEUTENANT H. V. WILLIS,

ROYAL ARTILLERY.

HERBERT VALIANT WILLIS, who was assassinated at Kandahar on the 10th January, 1879, was the eldest son of William Valiant Willis, and Eliza Frances, his wife. Born at Waterloo, in the County of Lancashire, on January 18th, 1856, he passed his early days at Arley, in Staffordshire. He was educated at St. Nicholas College, Lancing, Sussex, till he attained the age of seventeen years, when he was placed under the care of Dr. Frost, of Kensington Square, London, to be prepared for the Royal Military Academy, into which he passed, after nine months' study, in February, 1875. Whilst at Woolwich, he distinguished himself in drawing and horsemanship, and ultimately passed out from the Academy tenth in priority for the Artillery. After attending the gunnery course at Shoeburyness, he was gazetted to E/4 Royal Artillery, then in India, and proceeding out in the "Malabar" troopship in October, 1877, joined his battery at Allahabad, where it had halted on its march to Multan. During the following hot season he was sent in charge of invalids to Dalhousie, where he remained until war was declared with Afghanistan.

Lieutenant Willis was enthusiastically fond of his profession, and from the first earnestly studied it. On the outbreak of war he immediately applied for, and obtained permission to rejoin his battery, which had been ordered to the front, and overtook it on the banks of the Indus. From the time of his leaving Dalhousie until the day after the entry of the troops into Kandahar (being the day before he received his death-wound) he kept a most interesting record of the arduous march of the battery through the Bolan Pass, in the form of a diary, contriving to send it home with great regularity. The chief part of this account, which was published in a local newspaper, was eagerly looked for and read, and created much interest in the neighbourhood of the writer's home. He possessed a singularly humane and gentle disposition, and was beloved by all with whom he associated. In his letters written during the campaign, he repeatedly mentions with pain the sufferings of the camp-followers and of the animals. On one occasion, having been sent back during the night to bring up some waggons which had stuck in an almost impassable part of the route, he came upon about a dozen natives, who had dropped behind, unable to walk farther. On his return he picked them all up, putting them, where there was room, on the waggons and horses, giving them restoratives, and bringing them all safely into camp. But for his timely aid they would all have perished during the night. To his subordinates he endeared himself by his consideration for them, and his cheerfulness in sharing their hard work; and he would frequently dismount and walk in order that some tired man might rest.

The day after the entry of the troops into Kandahar, Willis obtained leave to go into the city, attended by an escort of men and accompanied by Lieutenant Williams, R.A., of the same battery. With his usual thought for those under him, he gave the men leave to go about the town to make purchases, telling them to be careful, and not to separate. He and Lieutenant Williams then dismounted, holding their horses, and taking the precaution to stand back to back. Whilst they were watching some shoemakers at work in one of the bazaars, a fanatic, creeping stealthily up, suddenly pushed between them, and stabbed Lieutenant Willis in the chest. A short struggle ensued, but the fanatic escaped, and after slightly wounding several other victims, was cut down by a non-commissioned officer of the 2nd Punjab Cavalry, aided by Captain Harvey of the 1st Punjab Cavalry, who was himself wounded in the hand. Lieutenant Willis fell down fainting, the knife having penetrated some way into the right lung. Carried to the camp, he received unremitting attention, and for a time hopes were entertained of his recovery; during the third night, however, the wound broke out afresh, and then all hope was over. He was tenderly cared for and watched by his brother officers, the battery doctor, and the chaplain to the forces, the Rev. G. M. Gordon, who, in a letter announcing his death to his mother, stated that he felt it a privilege to have been with him in his last hours, and added that his manly simplicity, and his cheerful endurance of the hardships of the recent trying march, had endeared him to all around him. The major of his battery, Major T. C. Martelli, wrote in the same tone of affectionate regard towards him, as also did many other of his brother officers. He was buried in a quiet and shaded spot in the midst of the Fort garden, within the walls of Kandahar, chosen by General Biddulph, who, with his Staff and the greater part of the troops, attended his funeral. His early death under such melancholy circumstances cast a gloom over the camp, and called forth an expression of deep commiseration and sympathy with his bereaved family, which was most touching, and will always be remembered by them with great gratitude.

Lieutenant Willis died on the 15th January, 1879, within three days of his twenty-third birthday.

CAPTAIN F. H. WINTERBOTHAM,

MADRAS INFANTRY.

FRANCIS HESKINS WINTERBOTHAM, a member of the old Gloucestershire family of that name, was the fifth son of the late John B. Winterbotham, solicitor, of Cheltenham, by his marriage with Mary Prowse, daughter of Mr. James Batten, of Plymouth, and was a cousin of the late Mr. Henry Winterbotham, M.P. for Stroud, whose premature death soon after his appointment as Under Secretary of State for the Home Department was the cause of much regret.

The subject of this memoir was born on the 19th November, 1838, and was educated at Cheltenham College, where he had the advantage of studying under the head-mastership of the late Rev. William Dobson. He continued as a pupil at the College till 1857, and subsequently matriculated at the London University.

Obtaining a commission in the then East India Company's Army, Winterbotham was sent out, in the spring of 1859, to the Madras Presidency; on arrival he was posted to the 40th Native Infantry, and subsequently did duty with that regiment at Bangalore, at Singapore, and at Cannanor in Malabar. In 1867 he was granted two years' sick-leave to England, and paid this country what proved to be his first and last visit during a term of twenty years' foreign service.

He returned to India in 1869, and having passed with credit the requisite Examinations in Surveying and Military Engineering, was permanently posted to the Queen's Own Sappers and Miners.

On the outbreak of the Indian famine of 1876-77, Captain Winterbotham proceeded on special duty—waiving his claim to the well-earned furlough to which he was entitled—to Bellary, and was employed in the relief camps for a period of several months, rendering valuable and important service.

While engaged on detachment with a portion of his company in a series of experiments in night signalling, shortly after returning to Bangalore on the conclusion of the famine campaign, he received the message, "Sappers ordered on foreign service. Destination unknown. Return immediately." It proved to be a summons for departure on the expedition to Malta, of which so much was afterwards heard.

The opportunity of seeing active service seemed at last to have arrived; but, much to Captain Winterbotham's disappointment, his company was not one of those which were ultimately sent to the Mediterranean. The prospect of war, however, kept him in India; and in December, 1878, he had the satisfaction of receiving orders to proceed in command of his company to join Sir Sam. Browne's Division of the Army of Invasion in Afghanistan. He accomplished more than 2,000 miles of the journey from Bangalore most satisfactorily, and wrote home from Jhelum in good health and spirits; but during the forward march from that station the cold and exposure he underwent brought on a violent attack of pneumonia, and on arriving at Peshawar in the first week of January, 1879, he had at once to go into hospital. There, under the watchful care of Dr. Molloy, A.M.D., aided by the kind attentions of Major and Mrs. Pearson, he was slowly recovering, when dysentery supervened, and he died on the 14th February.

Captain Winterbotham had considerable skill as a draftsman, as the plans and charts prepared by him on various occasions show; his power of organization, too, was great, as also was the faculty he possessed of attaching to himself the men under his command, and few deaths have been more keenly felt at Bangalore than his. An eye-witness relates that many swarthy faces were moist with tears when the announcement that he had fallen a victim to the rigours of the war was made to the men on parade. His career, like those of many of his gallant brethren in arms, was cut short just when the long-awaited chance of earning distinction seemed at hand. The "Madras Mail," in concluding a notice of his death, truly says:—"In the deceased the Madras Army has lost a man of the highest integrity, and a thoroughly efficient and painstaking officer"—a verdict which has had the unanimous concurrence of all those amongst whom he worked, and by whom he was known.

The portrait is from a photograph of the deceased taken before he left England, no recent likeness having been sent by him from India.

LIEUTENANT N. C. WISEMAN,

1ST BATTALION, 17TH (LEICESTERSHIRE) REGIMENT.

NO accurate account of the antecedents of this young officer has, up to the present, been obtained. The Army Lists show that he purchased an Ensigncy in the 17th Regiment in June, 1868, became Lieutenant in October, 1871, and was holding the appointment of Interpreter at the time of his death.

Lieutenant Wiseman accompanied his regiment into Afghanistan on the outbreak of war in the autumn of 1878, and served in the flank march over the Rhotas heights in reverse of Ali Musjid from the 20th to the 22nd November; was present at the affairs at Chinar on the 9th and 10th December; took part in both the first and the second Bazar Valley expeditions; and was also present at the affairs at Maidanak (18th to 21st March, 1879), and Deh Sarak (24th March, 1879), and at the action of Futtehabad on the 2nd April, 1879, in which he was killed while capturing one of the enemy's standards in a most gallant and determined manner.

The deceased, had he lived, would have been entitled to the medal with clasp.

2ᴺᴰ LIEUTENANT F. P. F. WOOD,

7TH (ROYAL FUSILIERS).

FREDERIC PHILIP FORSTER WOOD was the elder son of the Rev. Frederic Wood, M.A., Rector of Erwarton with Woolverstone, Suffolk, by his marriage with Emily, second daughter of the late John Pratt, Esq., J.P., of Adderstone, Northumberland. He was born on the 13th March, 1857, and was educated at Rossall, and Bury St. Edmund's Grammar School, from whence he proceeded to the Royal Military College, Sandhurst. Passing out after the usual course, he was gazetted, in January, 1878, to a second-lieutenancy in the 33rd Foot, but was temporarily attached to the 76th Regiment at Aldershot. In September, 1878, he exchanged into the 2nd Battalion, 7th Royal Fusiliers, and sailed for Bombay on the 13th December of that year to join the regiment at Kolaba.

In February, 1880, Wood embarked with his battalion in H.M.S. *Crocodile*, for Karashi, on its being ordered to the front, and subsequently took part in its march from Sibi to Kandahar through the deep hot sands and the Bolan and Khojack Passes. His diary, written with the utmost regularity up to the night before he fell, is full of very interesting details of the advance, the daily routine in Kandahar, and the preparations for the defence of the city against the advance of Ayoub Khan's army. He appears to have thrown himself heart and soul into fulfilling the new duties which devolved upon him, and to have early won the love and esteem of all with whom he came in contact.

On the morning of the 16th August, in the disastrous sortie to Deh Khwaja, Lieutenant Wood commanded the support of the leading party (the company under Captain Chard, brother of Major Chard, V.C., R.E., of Rorke's Drift fame) in the attack. To the conspicuous gallantry with which he bore himself on this occasion, the united testimony of his Colonel, his brother officers, and his men, bears vivid witness. Colonel Daubeny, in a letter to Wood's father, relates how his son " was shot when leaving an enclosure that he had stormed and cleared at the point of the bayonet;" Major Keyser, of how " he won the admiration of every man under his command," a statement corroborated by one of the men of his company in simple language noted down by Captain Chard : " Mr. Wood, he did lead us well, Sir!"

When he had received no less than five gunshot wounds, and his life-blood was ebbing fast, his brother officer, Lieutenant Marsh, got him into a dhoolie, and in doing so rendered up his own life. The end was by this time near. "As I helped him into the litter," writes Surgeon-Major Byng Giraud, of the Medical Department, in a letter to the Rev. Mr. Wood, "he flung his arms round my neck, and said, 'God bless you, old fellow. Tell my father that I have done my duty.' I sent him off the field in charge of a soldier who was wounded in the arm, but by the time he reached the Kabul gate, he had only strength to point to a ring on his finger, to Dr. Kelsall, but was unable to say what he wanted done with it. He died immediately after this."

A transcript of the following particulars penned by the writer last named in the letter already quoted from, may fitly close this brief notice :—" A Fusilier who was with him told me that just before he was wounded, your son and a party of some ten of the Fusiliers had stormed into a walled enclosure full of Afghans, and that he had slain five or six with his own sword, and when I came up it was still wet with their blood. Your son fought and died as became an English soldier."

LIEUTENANT I. D. WRIGHT,

ROYAL ARTILLERY.

HE subject of this memoir, who was killed in action at Jagdalak on the 29th December, 1879, was the eldest son of C. Ichabod Wright, Esq. (Lieutenant-Colonel, late commanding the Robin Hood Rifle Volunteers, and M.P. for Nottingham in 1868-69), of Mapperley, and Stapleford Hall, Notts, and Watcombe Park, Torquay, was a grandson of the late I. C. Wright, Esq., the translater of Homer and Dante, and a great-grandson of the first Lord Denman.

Ichabod Denman Wright was born on the 4th April, 1853, and received his education at the Rev. E. Burney's Academy, Gosport. Entering the Royal Military Academy at Woolwich in July, 1871, he passed out after the usual course, and was gazetted, in April, 1873, to the Royal Artillery. For some two years he was quartered at Aden, at the expiration of which period he proceeded to India, and served there until the end of 1878, when he was sent home on sick-leave. In September, 1879, he was offered a transfer into a battery stationed in England; but preferring to return to India, he was allowed to do so, and was sent out in command of drafts on the 30th of that month. After taking these to Peshawar, he was to have rejoined his own battery at Mhow; but being most anxious to see active service, he obtained permission to take the next detachment towards the front.

Lieutenant Wright was shortly afterwards attached to Battery 11/9 Royal Artillery, which he joined at Gandamak on the 26th December, 1879, his Christmas-day having been spent in a twenty-one mile march, through heavy sand, in pouring rain, and without food. The Battery, under the command of Major J. M. Douglas, R.A., was at the time *en route* from Landi Kotal to Jagdalak. On the 29th of the month, about 4 p.m., whilst on the last march (from Pezwan), a rapid firing was heard in advance, and the enemy was found in force on a mountain to the right of the road, engaged with a party sent out to reconnoitre from Jagdalak. The battery wheeled to the right, proceeding a short distance up a nullah, and then ascended a hill to the left. Just as the summit was reached, Lieutenant Wright, who was standing at the side of Major Douglas taking directions as to the disposition of the guns, was struck by a musket-shot, the ball passing through his body and lodging in the base of his spine. He fell back with the exclamation, "I have got it"; and instantly losing consciousness, expired a few minutes afterwards. His body was conveyed by his comrades into Jagdalak, and was buried, just outside the ramparts, the same evening, the Officer Commanding the Battery officiating by the light of a lantern at the impressive ceremony over the grave.

Of a singularly bright and happy disposition, accustomed to treat the little worries and discomforts of life with a whimsical gaiety which rarely failed to communicate itself to those about him, Lieutenant Wright was one whose company was always welcome. "I liked him very much," wrote his Commanding Officer after a three days' acquaintance with him, "he was so cheerful and zealous;" a view of his character which is supported by Surgeon-Major Oughton of the Battery, in a letter in which occurs this passage:—" He had a singular faculty of ingratiating himself with his comrades in a very short time. On the night of the 27th December, with the snow lying a foot deep outside, he contributed not a little to the general joviality of the season by playing songs and fantasias on the violin, on which instrument he was an accomplished performer."

Lieutenant Wright possessed, in addition, more sterling qualities; and his death has been justly described by Major Douglas as "a loss to the Battery and to the regiment at large."

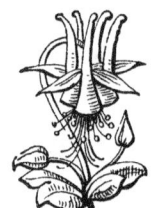

SURGEON-MAJOR J. H. WRIGHT, M.R.C.S. AND L.S.A. LOND.,

ARMY MEDICAL DEPARTMENT.

JOHN HARRINGTON WRIGHT, who died at Attock, British India, on the 21st June, 1879, was the only son of the late John Wright, M.D., of Story's Gate, Westminster; was stepson of the late William Edmunds, Esq., M.R.C.S., J.P., Surgeon Superintendent of Robben Island, Cape of Good Hope; and was a grandson of the late Thomas Wright, M.A., formerly Rector of Whitechapel, his maternal grandfather being the late J. Harrington, Esquire, who served on the Army Hospital Staff through the whole of the Peninsular campaigns.

The subject of this memoir was born at Story's Gate on the 31st May 1841, and subsequently accompanied his mother and stepfather to the Cape Colony, where he spent his earlier years, receiving his education at the Grahamstown College. Passing through the medical curriculum at King's College Hospital, London, he became a Member of the Royal College of Surgeons in April, 1865, and a Licentiate of the Society of Apothecaries in December of the same year. In March, 1866, he entered the Army as a Staff Assistant Surgeon, was promoted Surgeon in March, 1873, and in March, 1878, attained the rank of Surgeon-Major.

Almost the whole of his life in the Service was spent abroad. After quitting Netley, he was first attached, in October, 1866, to the Royal Engineers, at Aldershot. In July, 1867, he sailed for the Cape of Good Hope; and from the time of his arrival until he again returned to England in May, 1871, was constantly on the move, visiting in the interim St. Helena, Mauritius, Singapore, Hong Kong, and Japan, and being in medical charge successively, of no less than ten different corps or regiments. For a short time after his return home he was attached to the 19th Hussars. In August, 1871, he was transferred for duty to the 17th Brigade Royal Artillery, and remained with it until the autumn of 1873. In October of that year he embarked for India, attached to the 4th Battalion Rifle Brigade, with which distinguished corps he continued, with the exception of a brief interval in 1879, until the day of his death.

Mr. Wright took part with the regiment in the Jowaki expedition of 1877-1878, and for his services therein was recommended for the Medal and Clasp.

After five years' service in the hottest parts of India, he was under sailing orders to return to England in November, 1878; but the Afghan War having been determined upon, the exigencies of the Service necessitated his abandoning his intention. Taking part with his regiment in its advance, in Sir Sam. Browne's Division, into the enemy's country, he was present with it at the capture of Ali Musjid on the 21st November, 1878, in the subsequent operations in the Khyber, and in the march to Jalalabad. In January, 1879, he was detached from the Rifle Brigade and placed in medical charge of the Field Hospital of the 2nd Division Peshawar Valley Field Force, the duties in connection with which were harassing and incessant.

The heavy work of the campaign, following on his five years' previous service in India, now began to tell heavily upon him, and frequent breaks of continuity in his diary of 1879, together with casual remarks which occur in it, indicate that although he was bravely doing his work, he was quite unfit for it, and only managed to struggle on from a high sense of duty. His condition gradually became worse and worse, till at length, utterly worn out, he succumbed at Attock to an attack of heat apoplexy, which his enfeebled constitution was unable to throw off.

In a letter written from Peshawar in the month of August, 1879, Dr. A. C. Keith—a promising young officer of the Medical Department who himself subsequently fell a victim to the rigours of the war—gives the following characteristic details of the closing chapter of the late Surgeon-Major Wright's career:—" I urged him," he writes, after describing how he found him at Attock utterly prostrated in strength, but still continuing to discharge his duty, "to leave the tent in which he was staying (the weather being very hot and close at that time), and stay with me at my bungalow till the regiment crossed the river; but his well-known and excessive zeal prevented his doing what was absolutely necessary for his own health, and to all my propositions he replied that the regiment was too sick to leave in the hands of a junior officer," and that " by crossing the river he would be too far from the regiment to carry on his work.

" In the Medical Department his loss is sincerely regretted by all. In the regiment to which he belonged the men have lost their best friend, and the officers a brother of whom all were proud."

The verdict contained in the last paragraph is concurred in by all who had the privilege of being on terms of intimacy with the deceased officer, and has been expressed in equally warm terms by another writer—Colonel Newdigate, late Commanding the Battalion.

LIEUTENANT G. M. YALDWYN,

2ND BATTALION 6TH (ROYAL 1ST WARWICKSHIRE) REGIMENT.

ILBERT MOORCROFT YALDWYN was the youngest son of the late General Yaldwyn, H.M.'s Indian Army, of Blackdown, Sussex. He was born at Bellary, in India, on the 31st of May, 1854, and was educated at Wellington College. Entering the Army in October, 1873 he was gazetted to a Lieutenancy in the 2nd Battalion 6th Foot, and did duty with the regiment in this country till the conclusion of its term of home service. During this period he went through the course at the School of Musketry at Hythe, and obtained a double first certificate.

In October, 1878, he sailed with his regiment for India, and shortly after arriving there volunteered for active service in Afghanistan, into which country he was subsequently sent on transport duty.

Stationed at various posts on the Khyber line, he shared throughout the first campaign in the heavy and important duties which fell to the lot of the branch of the Service to which he had been detailed, meeting the incessant calls made upon him, and the innumerable difficulties with which he was beset, with a readiness of resource remarkable in one so young. The wear and tear of the work, coupled with constant exposure under violent alternations of temperature, at length, however, proved—as it did to so many of his gallant comrades—too much for him, and while stationed at Gandamak he was attacked with typhoid fever. After some weeks' illness, he became convalescent, and had reached Peshawar on his way to the hills for change of air, when he was seized with cholera, to which fatal disease he succumbed in a few hours, on the 12th June, 1879.

A handsome brass tablet has been erected in Lurgashall Church, Sussex, to Lieutenant Yaldwyn's memory, by his brother officers, as a token of the affection and esteem in which they held him.

THE VICTORIA CROSS.

GAZETTED PARTICULARS OF THE ACTS OF VALOUR FOR WHICH THE
RECIPIENTS OF THE VICTORIA CROSS WERE RECOMMENDED,
WITH OTHER RECORDS OF SERVICE.

THE REV. J. W. ADAMS,* BENGAL ECCLESIASTICAL ESTABLISHMENT, LATE CHAPLAIN TO THE KABUL FIELD FORCE.—*London Gazette, 26th August,* 1881 :—" During the action of Killa Kazi, on the 11th December, 1879, some men of the 9th Lancers having fallen, with their horses, into a wide and deep 'nullah' or ditch, and the enemy being close upon them, the Rev. J. W. Adams rushed into the water (which filled the ditch), dragged the horses from off the men upon whom they were lying, and extricated them, he being at the time under a heavy fire, and up to his waist in water.

" At this time the Afghans were pressing on very rapidly, the leading men getting within a few yards of Mr. Adams, who, having let go his horse in order to render more effectual assistance, had eventually to escape on foot."

Mr. Adams, V.C., was ordained in 1863 by the Bishop of Winchester, and proceeded to India in 1868, being appointed Military Chaplain at Peshawar. He subsequently served in the same capacity at Lord Napier's Camp of Exercise at Hassan Abdal, in the Punjab, where he also had charge of the General Hospital for Europeans—at Kashmir, at Mirat, and at the Army Head-quarters Camp formed at Delhi in 1875, when the Prince of Wales visited India. In 1878 he accompanied the Kuram Valley Field Force into Afghanistan, and served under General Roberts' command throughout the war. He has been repeatedly mentioned in despatches, and several times thanked for the brave and noble work done by him during the cholera epidemics at Peshawar and elsewhere.

LIEUTENANT WILLIAM ST. LUCIEN CHASE, BOMBAY STAFF CORPS, AND PRIVATE JAMES ASHFORD,* THE ROYAL FUSILIERS.—*London Gazette, 7th October,* 1881 :—" For conspicuous gallantry on the occasion of the sortie from Kandahar, on the 16th August, 1880, against the village of Deh Khwaja, in having rescued, and carried for a distance of over 200 yards, under the fire of the enemy, a wounded soldier, Private Massey, of the Royal Fusiliers, who had taken shelter in a block-house. Several times they were compelled to rest, but they persevered in bringing him into a place of safety.

"Private Ashford rendered Lieutenant Chase every assistance, and remained with him throughout."

Lieutenant W. St. L. Chase, V.C., entered the Army in 1875, being gazetted, in the month of September of that year, to Her Majesty's 15th Foot. After doing duty with the Head-quarters of his regiment in India for a period of two years, and passing, with distinction, the necessary examinations, he was admitted to the Bombay Staff Corps, and did duty, successively, at Poona, Ahmadabad, Baroda, and Surat. Serving with the 28th Bombay Native Infantry in the Afghan War, he accompanied the Head-quarters of the regiment—a constituent of the Kandahar Field Force—in January, 1880, to Chaman, from whence he was subsequently detached, after the massacre of Major Waudby and his party at Dubrai, in May, 1880, to the command of the post of Gatai. He was present with the 28th Native Infantry throughout the defence of Kandahar, taking part with the four companies in the ill-starred sortie to Deh Khwaja, in reference to which the appalling casualty-roll of the regiment included Lieut.-Colonel Newport and thirty rank and file killed, and Lieut.-Colonel Nimmo (commanding) and twenty rank and file wounded. "Many gallant deeds," wrote the late Lieut.-Colonel A. G. Daubeny, 7th Fusiliers, in giving a vivid account of the affair in a private letter, "were done on that day. Thus, while holding our ground to cover the retreat of stragglers or wounded, an officer (Lieutenant Chase) was suddenly seen coming towards us from the block-house with a wounded soldier on his back, and attended by a Fusilier. The enemy had also seen him, and turned their fire on him. A few yards, and he is down, and all thought he was done for. Not so; he only wanted breath; and, jumping up, he brought his man in amid a shower of bullets, and the cheers of our men." The Rev. A. G. Cane, late Chaplain to the Force, writing on the same event, observes: "I soon had my attention directed to a man leaving one of the Ziarets with another on his back. He was then, I suppose, about 400 yards off, and running as fast as possible towards the walls. There was a fearfully heavy fire directed on him from the villages (Kairabad and Deh Khwaja) on both sides. After running for about a hundred yards I saw both fall and lie flat on the ground, the bullets all the time striking the ground, and raising the dust where they struck all round them. I, of course, was under the impression that they had been hit. Soon, however, I noticed Mr. Chase get up again, and again take the man on his back for another stage of about the same distance, and again lie down for rest. Again he got up and carried his burden for a third stage, and again lay down. By this time he had got close to the walls. Only those who saw the terrific fire that was brought to bear on those two coming in can realize how marvellous was their escape untouched. At the time they came in they were almost the only object on which the enemy were directing their fire, as the rest of the fugitives had already reached shelter." For this feat, the subject of these allusions was subsequently decorated with the Victoria Cross.

After the regiment left Kandahar, Lieutenant Chase was given the command of the Killa Abdulla Post, and continued in the tenure of the appointment until relieved in the month of November. In January, 1881, he was again sent to command the post of Jatai on the line of communications, and remained there until all the troops of the Kandahar Evacuating Force had passed through it en route to India.

GUNNER JAMES COLLIS,* ROYAL HORSE ARTILLERY.—*London Gazette, 17th May,* 1881:—"For conspicuous bravery during the retreat from Maiwand to Kandahar, on the 28th July, 1880, when the officer commanding the battery was endeavouring to bring on a limber, with wounded men, under a cross fire, in running forward and drawing the enemy's fire on himself, thus taking off their attention from the limber."

BREVET-MAJOR O'MOORE CREAGH, BOMBAY STAFF CORPS.—*London Gazette, 18th November,* 1879:—"On the 21st April, Captain Creagh was detached from Daka with two companies of his battalion to protect the village of Kam Daka on the Kabul River against a threatened incursion of the Mohmands, and reached that place the same night. On the following morning the detachment, 150 men, was attacked by the Mohmands in overwhelming numbers, about 1,500; and the inhabitants of Kam Daka, having themselves taken part with the enemy, Captain Creagh found himself under the necessity of retiring from the village. He took up a position in a cemetery not far off, which he made as defensible as circumstances would admit of, and this position he held against all the efforts of the enemy, repeatedly repulsing them with the bayonet until three o'clock in the afternoon, when he was relieved by a detachment sent for the purpose from Daka. The enemy were then finally repulsed, and being charged by a troop of the 10th Bengal Lancers, under the command of Captain D. M. Strong, were routed and broken, and great numbers of them driven into the river.

"The Commander-in-Chief in India has expressed his opinion that but for the coolness, determination, and gallantry of the highest order, and the admirable conduct which Captain Creagh displayed on this occasion, the detachment under his command would, in all probability, have been cut off and destroyed."

Major Creagh, V.C., was gazetted to an Ensigncy in the 95th Regiment on the 2nd October, 1866, and after serving at the Depôt at Pembroke Dock till January, 1869, embarked for India, and joined the service companies of his regiment at Mhow. In June, 1870, he entered the Bombay Staff Corps, and was promoted Lieutenant. After serving for a few weeks with the Marine Battalion and 25th Bombay Light Infantry, he was appointed Officiating Adjutant of the Deoli Irregular Force, and Station Staff Officer at Deoli. In June, 1871, he was selected to fill the post of Adjutant of the Mhaiwara Battalion, then being reorganized on its transfer from the Civil to the Military establishment. Of this corps he was appointed, in 1878, while still holding the post of Adjutant, Officiating Commandant; and in the month of October in the same year he was promoted Captain in the Bombay Staff Corps.

When the Mhairwara Battalion volunteered for service in Afghanistan on the outbreak of hostilities, Major—then Lieutenant—Creagh, was the only European officer present with it, and commanded it throughout its subsequent march from Ajmir, Rajputana, to Hassan Abdal, Punjab. Prior to this occasion the corps had not, since its establishment in 1822, moved more than thirty miles from its head-quarters.

As second in command, Major Creagh took part in the subsequent operations of the battalion in Afghanistan, serving in the Peshawar Valley Force, at Ali Musjid till March, 1879, when the regiment was ordered to garrison Daka Fort. During this interval Major Creagh surveyed the route through Bourg to the Bazar Valley, and took part in the first expedition into that district. On the 20th April he was sent with a detachment of his regiment to Kam Daka, and for the services he there rendered, as already described, the Victoria Cross has been conferred upon him by his Sovereign. "I consider the cool determination of Captain Creagh to do his duty," wrote Lieutenant-General Mande with reference to this affair, "his self-possession, and the gallant example he set to his little band, were most conspicuous;" and in the report of Major Barnes, Commanding at Daka Fort, the following words occur: "In this miserable position, fully commanded by the surrounding hills, he (Captain Creagh) made a noble defence, and deserves the greatest praise I can afford him." On the signing of the peace of Gandamak the subject of these allusions returned with the Mhairwara Battalion to Ajmir. For his services in the campaign he was awarded, in addition to the Victoria Cross, a Brevet-Majority.

On the renewal of hostilities in the autumn of 1879, Major Creagh volunteered for service, and was ordered to Ali Khel with Brigadier-General Gordon. After arriving there, he was appointed Deputy Assistant Quartermaster-General to the Kuram Force, and subsequently Quartermaster-General. He served in Kuram from September, 1879, to November, 1880, and was senior officer of his department with the force. He was present at the repulse of the attack on Ali Khel on the 14th October, and served in the Zaimusht expedition. On peace being concluded, he rejoined the Mhairwara Battalion.

CAPTAIN WILLIAM HENRY DICK CUNYNGHAM, THE GORDON HIGHLANDERS.—*London Gazette, 18th October,* 1881:—"For the conspicuous gallantry and coolness displayed by him on the 13th December, 1879, at the attack on the Sherpur pass, in Afghanistan, in having exposed himself to the full fire of the enemy, and by his example and encouragement rallied the men who, having been beaten back, were, at the moment, wavering at the top of the hill."

Captain W. H. Dick Cunyngham, V.C., is the youngest son of the late Sir William Hamner Dick Cunyngham, Baronet, of Prestonfield, and Lambrughton, N.B. He was born on the 16th June, 1851, and was educated at Trinity College, Glenalmond, N.B., and the Royal Military College, Sandhurst. Gazetted to an Ensigncy in the 92nd Highlanders in February, 1872, he was successively promoted Lieutenant, in February, 1873, and Captain, in October, 1881. His services with the 92nd include a term of eight years (January, 1873, to January, 1881) spent in India, during which period he held the appointment of Adjutant of a wing of the regiment from January, 1877, to April, 1878. Eventually, in October, 1880, he was selected to fill the regimental Adjutancy—a post he continues to hold at the present time.

Captain Dick Cunyngham served over a wide extent of territory and in various capacities, through the whole of the Afghan War. Detailed, in the first instance, to the Transport Department of the Quetta Field Force, he took part in the advance of Sir Donald Stewart's Division on Kandahar. In the subsequent forward movement on Kalat-i-Ghilzai he was attached to the Head-quarters Staff; and on the return of General Biddulph's Column by the Thal-Chotiali route to India, he accompanied it in the capacity of Transport Officer. Rejoining his regiment, which had, in the meantime, been sent to the front on the Kuram line, he served with it in nearly the whole of its diverse operations in the second campaign, from the renewal to the cessation of hostilities. Besides taking part in numerous minor affairs, he was present at the action with the hill tribes at Ali Khel on the 14th October, 1879, in the expedition to Maidan in November, and in the operations in the neighbourhood of Kabul from the 8th to the 23rd December, including the assault of the Takht-i-Shah (for the valour he displayed on which occasion the Victoria Cross was subsequently conferred on him), and the action of the 23rd of the month. "After the fall of the officer and colour-sergeant," writes Sir Frederick Roberts with reference to the deaths of Lieutenant

St. John Forbes and Colour-Sergeant James Drummond, in describing in his despatch, bearing date 23rd January, 1880, the brilliant manner in which the commanding position held by the enemy on the 13th December was carried by the 92nd Highlanders, "there was a momentary waver, when Lieutenant W. H. Dick Cunyngham rushed forward and gallantly exposing himself to the full fire poured upon this point, rallied the men by his example and cheering words, and calling upon those near to follow him, charged into the middle of the enemy." As Adjutant of a wing of the 92nd, the subject of this allusion was present, on the 25th April, 1880, at the action at Childukhtean (for his services on which occasion he was mentioned in despatches); and after participating with the regiment in the memorable march of General Roberts' column to the relief of Kandahar, he took part in the reconnaissance of the 31st August, and the final crushing defeat of the enemy on the 1st September, for his services on which occasion he was again mentioned in despatches.

On the conclusion of the Afghan War, Captain Dick Cunyngham accompanied the 92nd to South Africa, and served with it in the Transvaal campaign of 1881. In addition to the Victoria Cross, he has received the Afghan medal with two clasps, and the Kabul-Kandahar bronze star.

MAJOR ARTHUR GEORGE HAMMOND, BENGAL STAFF CORPS.— *London Gazette*, 18th October, 1881 :—" For conspicuous coolness and gallantry at the action on the Asmai Heights, near Kabul, on the 14th December, 1879, in defending the top of the hill with a rifle and fixed bayonet, against large numbers of the enemy, whilst the 72nd Highlanders and Guides were retiring ; and again, on the retreat down the hill, in stopping to assist in carrying away a wounded Sepoy, the enemy being not sixty yards off, firing heavily all the time."

Major A. G. Hammond, V.C., entered Addiscombe College in February, 1861, and on the 7th June of the same year obtained his commission, gaining second place in the examination, and taking four prizes. He landed at Calcutta on the 31st December, 1861, and was attached to Her Majesty's 82nd Regiment, then quartered at Delhi. On the 17th October, 1862, he joined the 12th (Kalat-i-Ghilzai) Native Infantry, and having passed the P. H. examination in Hindustani, was posted, in September, 1863, to the Corps of Guides, which regiment he joined on the 17th of that month at Mardan. The Guides formed part of the army which was then being assembled for the Umbeyla campaign; and Lieutenant Hammond was placed in command of the detachment of the corps which was left to hold the fort at Mardan. In May, 1864, he was appointed Quartermaster of the Regiment; in November, 1865, Wing Commander; in June, 1867, he was admitted to the Bengal Staff Corps; and in April, 1875, he passed in Military Surveying and Field Engineering at the Rurki College by " the Higher Standard, with great credit."

Major—then Captain—Hammond served with his regiment as Wing Commander through the whole of the Jowaki campaign of 1877-78, including the capture of Payah and Jammu, and the forcing of the Naru-Kula Pass, receiving the medal and clasp. For the "gallant actions" he performed, and for the "zeal and energy" he displayed in the campaign, he was twice mentioned in Brigadier-General Keyes' despatch of the 15th August, 1878. He was with his regiment, too, in the operations against the Ranizai village of Skhakat on the 14th March, 1878, and also in the attack on the Utman Khel villages on the 21st idem.

Major Hammond served with the Guide Infantry through the whole of the

Afghan War. Besides taking part in numerous minor affairs, he was present at the capture of Ali Musjid, the operations round Kabul in December, 1879, including the storming of the Takht-i-Shah on the 13th, and the Asmai Heights on the 14th of the month, the march into Koh-i-Daman, and the second action at Charasiab on the 25th April, 1880. With reference to his conduct on the 14th December, 1879, for which Her Majesty the Queen conferred on him the Victoria Cross, Sir Frederick Roberts, describing the events of that day in his despatch bearing date 23rd January, 1880, uses the following words:—"*Another officer who greatly distinguished himself on this occasion was Captain A. G. Hammond, Queen's Own Corps of Guides. He had been very forward during the storming of the Asmai Heights, and now, when the enemy were crowding up the western slopes, he remained with a few men on the ridge until the Afghans were within thirty yards of them. During the retirement, one of the men of the Guides was shot. Captain Hammond stopped and assisted in carrying him away, though the enemy were at the time close by, and firing heavily.*"

Major Hammond's commissions are dated as follows:—Ensign, 7th June, 1861; Lieutenant, 14th May, 1862; Captain, 7th June, 1873; Major, 7th June, 1881.

CAPTAIN REGINALD CLARE HART, ROYAL ENGINEERS. *London Gazette*, 10*th June*, 1879:—"For his gallant conduct in risking his own life to save the life of a private soldier.

"The Lieutenant-General commanding the 2nd Division Peshawar Field Force, reports that when on convoy duty with that force on the 31st January, 1879, Lieutenant Hart, of the Royal Engineers, took the initiative in running some 1,200 yards to the rescue of a wounded Sowar of the 13th Bengal Lancers in a river-bed exposed to the fire of the enemy, of unknown strength, from both flanks, and also from a party in the river-bed.

"Lieutenant Hart reached the wounded Sowar, drove off the enemy, and brought him under cover with the aid of some soldiers who accompanied him on the way."

Captain R. C. Hart, V.C., is the second surviving son of the late Lieutenant-General H. G. Hart, and was born on the 11th June, 1848, at Drewsborough, Co. Clare. He was educated at Marlborough and Cheltenham Colleges; passed into the Royal Military Academy in June, 1866; and was commissioned Lieutenant in the Royal Engineers on the 13th January, 1869. After doing duty for three years in England, he embarked, in October, 1872, for India, and was posted to the Bengal Sappers and Miners. From September, 1874, to March, 1878, he filled the office of Assistant Garrison Instructor at Umballa, subsequently returning to England on sick leave.

In January, 1879, Captain—then Lieutenant—Hart proceeded a second time to India, and serving with the Khyber Field Force in the Afghan War, was at first attached as a regimental officer to the 24th Punjab Infantry, a unit of the 2nd Division. In this capacity he took part in the 2nd Bazar Valley expedition against the Zaka Khel Afridis; and for his distinguished conduct on the 31st January, while on convoy duty, was awarded the Victoria Cross. He afterwards served in the 1st Division of the Force, and was several times employed by the Quartermaster-General's Department in making reconnaissances.

In February, 1881, it was reported that the Ashantis had declared war and invaded the Gold Coast Colony. Lieutenant Hart, receiving his orders only a few hours before starting, accompanied Sir Samuel Rowe, the Governor and Commander-

in-Chief, to the West Coast of Africa, and served on the Special Service Staff of that officer from February to June. In the succeeding month he received his promotion.

Captain Hart was present at the siege of Paris during the Commune war of 1871. He has been awarded the Silver Medal of the Royal Humane Society; a Medallion from the Mayor, in the name of the City of Boulogne, and a Medal of Honour of the First Class, presented by the President of the French Republic, for saving the life of a Frenchman who was drowning in the harbour of Boulogne-sur-Mer, on the 27th July, 1869. In accomplishing this feat, Captain Hart received several severe wounds on the head and face, from striking, in leaping from the pier, some sunken piles or rocks. He is also the holder of a 1st Class Extra Hythe Musketry certificate, and has passed the final examination at the Staff College. At the present time he is employed on special duty at the Intelligence Department, Horse Guards.

BREVET LIEUT.-COLONEL EDWARD PEMBERTON LEACH, ROYAL ENGINEERS.—*London Gazette*, 9th December, 1879 :—" For having, in action with the Shinwarris, near Maidanah, Afghanistan, on the 17th March, 1879, when covering the retirement of the Survey Escort who were carrying Lieutenant Barclay, 45th Sikhs, mortally wounded, behaved with the utmost gallantry in charging, with some men of the 45th Sikhs, a very much larger number of the enemy.

" In this encounter Captain Leach killed two or three of the enemy himself, and he received a severe wound from an Afghan knife in the left arm. Captain Leach's determination and gallantry in this affair, in attacking and driving back the enemy from their last position, saved the whole party from annihilation."

Lieut.-Colonel E. P. Leach, V.C., is a son of Colonel Leach, late Royal Engineers. He entered the Army on the 17th April, 1866, served at Chatham till October, 1868, and proceeded to India in the following December. From March, 1869, till February, 1870, he commanded a detachment of the Bengal Sappers and Miners at Rawal Pindi. In the succeeding month he entered the Public Works Department as Assistant Engineer, proceeding to Morar, Central India. Appointed, in October, 1871, to the Indian Survey, he did duty, in his new capacity, with the Lushai Expeditionary Field Force, receiving at the close of the campaign the thanks of the Secretary of State and the medal with clasp. In November, 1877, he returned to England on furlough, and in October of the following year accompanied Mr. Caird, C.B., one of the Indian Famine Commissioners, to India as Private Secretary.

Serving in the Peshawar Valley Field Force in the Afghan Campaign of 1878-1879, Lieut.-Colonel—then Captain—Leach accompanied the expeditions into the Bazar and Lughman valleys. Whilst employed upon a survey reconnaissance of the Shinwari country with detachments of the Guide Cavalry and the 45th Sikhs, he was attacked by the enemy on the 17th March, 1879, and severely wounded. For his distinguished conduct on this occasion he received a Brevet Majority, and subsequently the Victoria Cross.

Major Leach was invalided to England at the close of the year 1879, but returned to India in the following March. Joining, in charge of the Survey operations, the Kandahar Field Force under Major-General Primrose, he accompanied, in July, 1880, the brigade under Brigadier-General Burrows in its advance to the Halmand. He was present at the battle of Maiwand—during which his horse was wounded—and the subsequent siege of Kandahar, and for his conduct was three times mentioned in *despatches. Again on the 1st September, 1880, he was present at the crowning defeat of the enemy by Sir Frederick Roberts. At the close of the campaign a Brevet Lieutenant-Colonelcy was conferred upon him, and the medal with clasp.*

SERGEANT PATRICK MULLANE,* ROYAL HORSE ARTILLERY.—*London Gazette*, 17th May, 1879:—"For conspicuous bravery during the action at Maiwand, on the 27th July, 1880, in endeavouring to save the life of Driver Pickwell Istead.

"This non-commissioned officer, when the battery to which he belonged was on the point of retiring, and the enemy were within ten or fifteen yards, unhesitatingly ran back about two yards, and picking up Driver Istead, placed him on the limber, where, unfortunately, he died almost immediately.

"Again, during the retreat, Sergeant Mullane volunteered to procure water for the wounded, and succeeded in doing so by going into one of the villages in which so many men lost their lives."

MAJOR EUSTON HENRY SARTORIUS, THE EAST LANCASHIRE REGIMENT.—*London Gazette*, 17th May, 1881:—"For conspicuous bravery during the action at Shah-jui, on the 24th October, 1879, in leading a party of five or six men of the 59th Regiment against a body of the enemy, of unknown strength, occupying an almost inaccessible position on the top of a precipitous hill.

"The nature of the ground made any sort of regular formation impossible, and Captain Sartorius had to bear the first brunt of the attack from the whole body of the enemy, who fell upon him and his men as they gained the top of the precipitous pathway; but the gallant and determined bearing of this officer, emulated as it was by his men, led to the most perfect success, and the surviving occupants of the hill-top, seven in number, were all killed.

"In this encounter Captain Sartorius was wounded with sword-cuts in both hands, and one of his men was killed."

Major E. H. Sartorius, V.C., entered the Army in July, 1862, being gazetted—after passing out first in order of merit from the Royal Military College, Sandhurst—to an Ensigncy in the 59th Foot. Continuing in that distinguished regiment up to the present time, he became Lieutenant in July, 1865, obtained his company in September, 1874, received a Brevet Majority in March, 1881, and was promoted to a Regimental Majority in July of the same year. In December, 1870, he passed the examination at the Staff College, and subsequently, for a period of four years, served as Instructor in Military Surveying at the Royal Military College, Sandhurst. Proceeding to India to join his regiment, he travelled for a year, en route, in Persia, adding largely to his experiences, and obtaining a great variety of valuable information.

In the Afghan War, Major Sartorius commanded the company of the 59th which escorted the guns of Battery D/2 Royal Artillery, from Quetta to Kandahar, and afterwards served with the regiment in the advance to, and capture of Kalat-i-Ghilzai, in January, 1879. Acting as Assistant Field Engineer, he was present at the subsequent occupation of that place in October, 1879, and was in command of the company which took part in the advance of Brigadier-General Hughes' force to Tazi. At the action of Shah-jui on the 24th October, 1879, he commanded the detachment of his regiment which was present, and for the distinguished service he then performed obtained the Victoria Cross and his Brevet Majority. In addition to being twice mentioned in despatches, his "*excellent work and gallant conduct*" *in connection with the Survey Department received special commendation in the Report of the Proceedings of the Government of India in the Home Revenue and Agricultural Department, bearing date 17th May,* 1880.

Major Sartorius has been decorated with—besides the Victoria Cross—the Royal Humane Society's medal for saving, on the 29th June, 1869, the lives of three young ladies at Broadstairs. From the wounds he received at the action of Shah-jui, he has partly lost the use of his left hand.

LANCE-CORPORAL GEORGE SELLAR,* SEAFORTH HIGHLANDERS (ROSS-SHIRE BUFFS).—*London Gazette, 18th October,* 1881 :—" For conspicuous gallantry displayed by him at the assault on the Asmai Heights, round Kabul, on the 14th December, 1879, in having in a marked manner led the attack, under a heavy fire, and, dashing on in front of the enemy up the slope, engaged in a desperate conflict with an Afghan, who sprang out to meet him. In this encounter Lance-Corporal Sellar was severely wounded."

BREVET MAJOR WILLIAM JOHN VOUSDEN,* BENGAL STAFF CORPS.—*London Gazette, 18th October,* 1881 :—" For the exceptional gallantry displayed by him on the 14th December, 1879, on the Koh Asmai Heights, near Kabul, in charging, with a small party, into the centre of the line of the retreating Kohistani force, by whom they were greatly outnumbered, and who did their utmost to close round them. After rapidly charging through and through the enemy, backwards and forwards, several times, they swept off round the opposite side of the village and joined the rest of the troop."

Major W. J. Vousden, V.C., is the only son of the late Captain Vousden, of the 51st (N. B.) Fusiliers. He was educated at Dr. Hill's establishment at Sandwich, and the Grammar School, Canterbury. Entering the Army in 1864, he was gazetted, in the month of January of that year, to an Ensigncy in the 35th Regiment. In October, 1867, he obtained his Lieutenancy, and in due course was admitted to the Bengal Staff Corps. His commission as Captain bears date 8th January, 1876. In both phases of the Afghan War, he participated with his regiment—the 5th Punjab Cavalry—in the heavy and important work which fell to its lot. Besides being employed in numerous minor operations, he served in the Khost Valley expedition, in January, 1879, including the action at Matun on the 7th of the month; took part, in the second campaign, in the advance of the Division under Sir Frederick Roberts on the capital; was present, on the 27th September, 1879, at the skirmish at Karatiga, in which his charger was shot; at the action at Charasiab, on the 6th October, the capture of Kabul on the 8th, and the cavalry pursuit of the enemy on the 9th idem; was with General Baker's brigade in the flank march on the 9th to the 12th December; was present in the actions in the neighbourhood of Kabul on the two succeeding days, earning, by his distinguished gallantry on the 14th, the Victoria Cross; formed one of the beleaguered force in Sherpur from the 15th to the 23rd December, and was present at the action of the 23rd, and in the succeeding cavalry pursuit.

In the cavalry affair on the 14th December, in which Captain Vousden earned his Victoria Cross, the squadron of the 5th Punjab Cavalry, under Captain Carr, with which he was employed, was acting as escort to Battery G/3, R.A. At midday,

Captain Vousden, with about a dozen men, came across on the Bala Hissar road, and in open and level country, a body of Kohistanis, numbering from three to four hundred, making for the bridge over the Kabul River. It is a significant fact, and one which speaks of itself for the gallantry displayed in encountering such stupendous odds, and of the undaunted spirit with which the encounter was sustained, that, in the charge which ensued, six men of Captain Vousden's little band of twelve were wounded, of whom three subsequently died, and that when the enemy dispersed they left no fewer than thirty of their number on the ground, all killed by the sword—of whom Captain Vousden had himself cut down five.

For the services he rendered in the war, Captain Vousden has been twice mentioned in despatches, and has received, besides the Victoria Cross, a Brevet Majority, and the Afghan medal with two clasps.

LIEUT.-COLONEL GEORGE STEWART WHITE,* C.B., THE GORDON HIGHLANDERS.—*London Gazette, 3rd June,* 1881 :—" For conspicuous bravery during the engagement at Charasiab on the 6th October, 1879, when, finding that the artillery and rifle fire failed to dislodge the enemy from a fortified hill which it was necessary to capture, Major White led an attack upon it in person.

"Advancing with two companies of his regiment, and climbing from one steep ledge to another, he came upon a body of the enemy, strongly posted, and outnumbering his force by about eight to one. His men being much exhausted, and immediate action being necessary, Major White took a rifle, and, *going on by himself,* shot the leader of the enemy. This act so intimidated the rest that they fled round the side of the hill, and the position was won.

"Again, on the 1st September, 1880, at the battle of Kandahar, Major White, in leading the final charge, under a heavy fire from the enemy, who held a strong position and were supported by two guns, rode straight up to within a few yards of them, and seeing the guns, dashed forward and secured one, immediately after which the enemy retired."

Lieut.-Colonel G. S. White, V.C., entered the Army in November, 1853, *became Lieutenant in January,* 1855, *obtained his company in July,* 1863, *was promoted Major in December,* 1873, *Brevet Lieut.-Colonel in March,* 1881, *and Lieut.-Colonel in July of the same year. In the Indian Mutiny in* 1857-59, *he was actively employed with the 27th Regiment on the North-West Frontier, and after the conclusion of hostilities, received the medal. His brilliant services in the Afghan War have caused him to be repeatedly singled out for commendation in despatches. Taking part with his distinguished regiment, the 92nd Highlanders, in October,* 1879, *in the advance of the division under Sir Frederick Roberts on Kabul, he commanded the right attack at the action of Charasiab on the 6th of the month—for his gallantry on which occasion the Victoria Cross was subsequently conferred upon him; was present in the pursuit of the enemy on the 8th idem, and the occupation of the capital; commanded the regiment in the expedition to Maidan, under Brigadier-General Baker, in November; served in the operations around Kabul in December, commanding four companies of the 92nd in the brilliant assault and capture of the Takht-i-Shah, and being present at the action on the 23rd; again, at the action of Childukhtean on the 25th April,* 1880, *commanded a wing of the regiment; and after taking part in the memorable march of the relieving force from Kabul to Kandahar, was present at the recon-*

naissance on the 31st August, and the crowning defeat of the enemy on the 1st September.

Lieut.-Colonel White at the present time occupies the office of Military Secretary to the Viceroy of India. In addition to the Victoria Cross, a Companionship of the Order of the Bath and Brevet promotion were conferred upon him for his services in the Afghan War, and he has also received the medal with three clasps and the Kabul-Kandahar bronze star.

* *Portraits and additional particulars of the services of these officers, non-commissioned officers, and men, have not been received in time for insertion in the first edition of this work.*

INDEX TO BIOGRAPHICAL DIVISION.

PORTRAITS AND BIOGRAPHICAL NOTICES OF OFFICERS WHO LOST THEIR LIVES IN THE WAR.

		PLATE		PAGE
MAJOR A. D. ANDERSON, Staff Corps	*portrait*	I.	*notice*	1
LIEUTENANT P. E. ANDERSON, Staff Corps	,,	,,	,,	3
LIEUTENANT F. C. C. ANGELO	,,	,,	,,	4
SURGEON-MAJOR G. ATKINSON, M.B.	,,	,,	,,	5
LIEUTENANT F. M. BARCLAY, Staff Corps	,,	,,	,,	7
CAPTAIN W. B. BARKER	,,	,,	,,	8
2ND LIEUTENANT H. J. O. BARR	,,	,,	,,	10
MAJOR WIGRAM BATTYE, Staff Corps	,,	II.	,,	12
MAJOR H. G. BECHER, Staff Corps	,,	,,	,,	15
CAPTAIN JOHN BEEKE	,,	,,	,,	16
MAJOR H. H. BIRCH, Staff Corps	,,	,,	,,	17
LIEUTENANT W. H. BISHOP	,,	,,	,,	19
MAJOR G. F. BLACKWOOD	,,	,,	,,	20
SURGEON-MAJOR R. H. BOLTON	,,	,,	,,	23
BRIGADIER-GENERAL H. F. BROOKE	,,	III.	,,	24
LIEUT.-COLONEL F. BROWNLOW, C.B.	,,	,,	,,	27
LIEUTENANT A. BURLTON-BENNET, Staff Corps	,,	,,	,,	29
CAPTAIN S. G. BUTSON	,,	,,	,,	31
LIEUTENANT J. F. M. CAMPBELL, Staff Corps	,,	,,	,,	33
CAPTAIN C. A. CARTHEW, Staff Corps	,,	,,	,,	35
MAJOR SIR P. L. N. CAVAGNARI, K.C.B., C.S.I., Staff Corps	,,	,,	,,	37
CAPTAIN D. T. CHISHOLM	,,	IV.	,,	42
LIEUTENANT R. T. CHUTE	,,	,,	,,	43
BREVET LIEUT.-COLONEL W. H. J. CLARKE	,,	,,	,,	44
LIEUT.-COLONEL R. S. CLELAND	,,	,,	,,	46
LIEUTENANT DUNCAN COLE, Staff Corps	,,	,,	,,	48
LIEUT.-COLONEL J. J. COLLINS	,,	,,	,,	50
BREVET MAJOR JOHN COOK, V.C., Staff Corps	,,	,,	,,	52
SURGEON-MAJOR H. CORNISH, F.R.C.S.	,,	V.	,,	55
LIEUT.-COLONEL G. B. CRISPIN, Staff Corps	,,	,,	,,	57
CAPTAIN E. W. H. CROFTON	,,	,,	,,	59
CAPTAIN G. M. CRUICKSHANK	,,	,,	,,	61
CAPTAIN F. J. CULLEN	,,	,,	,,	63
LIEUTENANT R. E. L. DACRES	,,	,,	,,	65
LIEUT.-COLONEL A. G. DAUBENY	,,	,,	,,	66
LIEUTENANT G. G. DAWES, Staff Corps	,,	VI.	,,	68
LIEUTENANT A. E. DOBSON	,,	,,	,,	70
CAPTAIN J. DUNDAS, V.C.	,,	,,	,,	72

	PLATE	PAGE
LIEUT.-COLONEL H. FELLOWES, Staff Corps . . . . . *portrait*	VI.	*notice* 75
LIEUTENANT T. O. FITZGERALD, Staff Corps . . . . . ,,	,,	,, 77
LIEUTENANT ST. J. W. FORBES . . . . ,,	,,	,, 79
CAPTAIN ST. J. T. FROME . . . . ,,	,,	,, 81
LIEUTENANT C. H. GAISFORD . . . . ,,	VII.	,, 82
LIEUT.-COLONEL JAMES GALBRAITH . . . . . . ,,	,,	,, 84
CAPTAIN J. H. GAMBLE . . . . ,,	,,	,, 86
CAPTAIN E. S. GARRATT . . . . ,,	,,	,, 88
CAPTAIN F. T. GOAD, Staff Corps . . . . . . ,,	,,	,, 90
MAJOR J. GODSON, Staff Corps . . . . ,,	,,	,, 92
THE REV. G. M. GORDON, M.A. . . . . ,,	,,	,, 94
SURGEON H. A. C. GRAY, M.B., C.M. . . . . . ,,	VIII.	,, 96
LIEUTENANT W. R. P. HAMILTON, V.C., Staff Corps . . . ,,	,,	,, 98
LIEUTENANT EDWARD HARDY . . . . ,,	,,	,, 101
CAPTAIN G. J. HARE, Staff Corps . . . . . . ,,	,,	,, *
SUB-LIEUTENANT F. H. HARFORD . . . . . . ,,	,,	,, 103
LIEUTENANT C. J. R. HEARSEY . . . . ,,	,,	,, 105
CAPTAIN P. C. HEATH, Staff Corps . . . . . . ,,	,,	,, 106
LIEUTENANT T. RICE HENN . . . . ,,	IX.	,, 107
LIEUTENANT W. F. HENNELL, Staff Corps . . . . . ,,	,,	,, 110
2ND LIEUTENANT A. HONYWOOD . . . . ,,	,,	,, 111
W. JENKYNS, M.A., C.I.E., Staff Corps . . . . . ,,	,,	,, 112
LIEUTENANT W. N. JUSTICE . . . . ,,	,,	,, 115
SURGEON A. C. KEITH, M.B. . . . . ,,	†	,, 116
SURGEON A. H. KELLY . . . . ,,	,,	,, 117
SURGEON-MAJOR H. KELSALL . . . . ,,	,,	,, 119
CAPTAIN J. A. KELSO . . . . ,,	X.	,, 121
LIEUTENANT F. G. KINLOCH, Staff Corps . . . . . ,,	,,	,, 123
LIEUTENANT S. E. L. LENDRUM . . . . ,,	,,	,, 125
2ND LIEUTENANT E. D. LOS . . . . ,,	,,	,, 127
LIEUTENANT G. H. LUMSDEN . . . . ,,	,,	,, 129
LIEUTENANT H. MACLAINE . . . . ,,	,,	,, 131
CAPTAIN W. H. MCMATH . . . . ,,	,,	,, 135
2ND LIEUTENANT E. S. MARSH . . . . ,,	XI.	,, 138
LIEUTENANT C. A. MONTANARO . . . . ,,	,,	,, 139
CAPTAIN C. S. MORRISON . . . . ,,	,,	,, 141
LIEUTENANT A. R. MURRAY, Staff Corps . . . . . ,,	,,	,, 143
BREVET LIEUT.-COLONEL W. H. NEWPORT . . . . . ,,	,,	,, 144
LIEUT.-COLONEL G. NICHOLETTS, Staff Corps . . . . ,,	,,	,, 146
LIEUTENANT C. NUGENT . . . . ,,	,,	,, 148
COLONEL J. J. O'BRYEN, Staff Corps . . . . . . ,,	XII.	,, 150
MAJOR C. V. OLIVER . . . . ,,	,,	,, 152
2ND LIEUTENANT W. R. OLIVEY . . . . ,,	,,	,, 154
LIEUTENANT E. G. OSBORNE . . . . ,,	,,	,, 155
LIEUTENANT LORD OSSULTON . . . . ,,	,,	,, *
LIEUTENANT W. C. OWEN, Staff Corps . . . . . ,,	,,	,, 157
LIEUTENANT E. PALMER, Staff Corps . . . . . . ,,	†	,, 158
CAPTAIN E. W. PERRY . . . . ,,	,,	,, 160
OFFICIATING DEPUTY SURGEON-GENERAL J. H. PORTER . . ,,	XIII.	,, 161
LIEUTENANT BROWNLOW POULTER . . . . . . ,,	,,	,, 166
CAPTAIN C. F. POWELL, Staff Corps . . . . . . ,,	,,	,, 168
BREVET-MAJOR L. A. POWYS . . . . ,,	,,	,, 170
CAPTAIN J. J. PRESTON . . . . ,,	,,	,, 172
LIEUTENANT M. E. RAYNER . . . . ,,	,,	,, 174
CAPTAIN R. B. REED . . . . ,,	,,	,, 175
LIEUTENANT T. J. O'D. RENNY, Staff Corps . . . . ,,	XIV.	,, 177
MAJOR W. REYNOLDS, Staff Corps . . . . . . ,,	,,	,, 179

* *Materials for memoirs of these officers have not been received in time for insertion in the first edition of this work.*
† *A portrait of this officer has not been received in time for insertion in the first edition of this work.*

INDEX TO BIOGRAPHICAL DIVISION.

		PLATE	PAGE
2ND LIEUTENANT W. P. RICARDO	portrait	XIV.	notice 181
LIEUTENANT J. T. RICE	,,	,,	,, 182
LIEUTENANT S. W. T. ROBERTS	,,	,,	,, 183
CAPTAIN W. ROBERTS	,,	,,	,, 185
LIEUTENANT H. R. ROSS	,,	,,	,, 186
CAPTAIN A. P. SAMUELLS	,,	XV.	,, 188
CAPTAIN E. W. SAMUELLS, Staff Corps	,,	,,	,, 190
CAPTAIN T. A'B. SARGENT	,,	,,	,, 192
CAPTAIN E. D. SHAFTO	,,	,,	,, 194
BREVET LIEUT.-COLONEL A. M. SHEWELL, Staff Corps	,,	,,	,, 196
CAPTAIN H. F. SHOWERS, Staff Corps	,,	,,	,, 198
BREVET MAJOR L. C. SINGLETON	,,	,,	,, 200
CAPTAIN H. F. SMITH, Staff Corps	,,	XVI.	,, 202
MAJOR L. SMITH, Staff Corps	,,	,,	,, 204
SURGEON W. B. SMYTH, A.B., M.B., L.R.C.S.I.	,,	,,	,, 205
CAPTAIN N. J. SPENS	,,	,,	,, 207
LIEUTENANT H. H. S. SPOOR	,,	,,	,, 209
LIEUTENANT F. C. STAYNER, Staff Corps	,,	,,	,, 210
BREVET LIEUT.-COLONEL R. G. T. STEVENSON	,,	,,	,, 212
CAPTAIN E. STRATON	,,	XVII.	,, 214
CAPTAIN S. A. SWINLEY	,,	,,	,, 217
2ND LIEUTENANT B. S. THURLOW	,,	,,	,, 219
MAJOR R. J. LE POER TRENCH	,,	,,	,, 221
BRIGADIER-GENERAL J. A. TYTLER, C.B., V.C., Staff Corps	,,	,,	,, 223
LIEUTENANT E. P. VENTRIS	,,	,,	,, 226
SURGEON-MAJOR J. WALLACE, M.A., M.D., M.R.C.S.	,,	,,	,, 228
SURGEON J. E. WALSH, M.D.	,,	XVIII.	,, 230
2ND LIEUTENANT E. H. WATSON	,,	,,	,, 232
SURGEON G. WATSON, M.B.	,,	,,	,, 233
MAJOR S. J. WAUDBY, Staff Corps	,,	,,	,, 235
CAPTAIN A. A. D. WEIGALL	,,	,,	,, 239
LIEUTENANT C. G. WHITBY	,,	,,	,, 241
LIEUTENANT F. WHITTUCK, Staff Corps	,,	,,	,, 242
LIEUTENANT H. V. WILLIS	,,	XIX.	,, 244
CAPTAIN F. H. WINTERBOTHAM	,,	,,	,, 246
LIEUTENANT N. C. WISEMAN	,,	,,	,, 248
2ND LIEUTENANT F. P. F. WOOD	,,	,,	,, 249
LIEUTENANT I. D. WRIGHT	,,	,,	,, 251
SURGEON-MAJOR J. H. WRIGHT, M.R.C.S., and L.S.A. Lond.	,,	,,	,, 253
LIEUTENANT G. M. YALDWYN	,,	,,	,, 255

PORTRAITS AND RECORDS OF SERVICE OF RECIPIENTS OF THE VICTORIA CROSS.

		PLATE	PAGE
THE REV. J. W. ADAMS, V.C.	portrait	*	notice 259
PRIVATE J. ASHFORD, V.C.	,,	*	,, 259
LIEUTENANT W. ST. L. CHASE, V.C., Staff Corps	,,	XX.	,, 259
GUNNER J. COLLIS, V.C.	,,	*	,, 260
MAJOR J. COOK, V.C., Staff Corps	,,	IV.	,, 52
BREVET-MAJOR O'M. CREAGH, V.C., Staff Corps	,,	XX.	,, 261
CAPTAIN W. H. DICK CUNYNGHAM, V.C.	,,	,,	,, 262
MAJOR A. G. HAMMOND, V.C., Staff Corps	,,	,,	,, 263

* *Portraits and additional particulars of the services of these officers, non-commissioned officers, and men, have not been received in time for insertion in the first edition of this work.*

		PLATE		PAGE
LIEUTENANT W. P. R. HAMILTON, V.C., Staff Corps	portrait	VIII.	notice	98
CAPTAIN R. C. HART, V.C.	,,	XX.	,,	264
BREVET LIEUT.-COLONEL E. P. LEACH, V.C.	,,	,,	,,	265
SERGEANT P. MULLANE, V.C.	,,	*	,,	266
MAJOR E. H. SARTORIUS, V.C.	,,	XX.	,,	266
LANCE-CORPORAL G. SELLAR, V.C.	,,	*	,,	267
BREVET-MAJOR W. J. VOUSDEN, V.C., Staff Corps	,,	*	,,	267
LIEUT.-COLONEL G. S. WHITE, V.C., C.B.	,,	*	,,	268

* *Portraits and additional particulars of the services of these officers, non-commissioned officers, and men, have not been received in time for insertion in the first edition of this work.*

CHISWICK PRESS:—C. WHITTINGHAM AND CO., TOOKS COURT, CHANCERY LANE.

www.ingramcontent.com/pod-product-compliance
Lightning Source LLC
Chambersburg PA
CBHW082006220426
43670CB00014B/2559